Educational Reforms in India for the 21st Century

J.C. Aggarwal

SHIPRA

(4th Revised Ed. 2010, 1st Published 2000)

Rs 1500; US$ 50

ISBN: 978-93-86262-70-7

2025 Imp.

Educational Reforms in India for the 21st Century

Published by:
SHIPRA PUBLICATIONS
LG 18-19, Pankaj Central Market
I.P. Ext., Patparganj, Delhi 110092, India
91 11 47322068; 9650028065, 9810522367
info@shiprapublication.com
www.shiprapublication.com

Preface to the Revised Edition

The author is grateful to the readers for their response to this publication.

Besides updating the data on the expansion and expenditure on education in India, the following chapters are added:

- Major Recommendations of the High Level Committee to prepare a Report on the Social, economic and Educational Status of the Muslim Community in India (2005-06) – Sachar Committee Report
- Major Observations and Recommendations of the National Knowledge Commission (2006)
- Advice on Renovation and Rejuvenation of Higher Education Committee Report—2009

The author expresses his thanks to the publishers and authors whose publications he has made use of in the revision of this publication.

It is hoped that the data and contents of this book would suitably meet the needs of several sections engaged in the field of education and allied disciplines.

J.C. Aggarwal

Contents

1

Curriculum Defined

The following views of experts should enable us to have a comprehensive and enlightened perspective on the various dimensions of the curriculum.

1. Curriculum is the sum total of student activities which the school sponsors for the purpose of achieving its objectives.

Alberty A. and Alberty E. *Reorganising the High School Curriculum.* The Macmillan Company, New York, 1959.

2. Curriculum has been most commonly defined as all of the directed learning experiences of children and youth under the influence of the school.

American Association of School Administrators. *American School Curriculum,* 1953.

3. Curriculum is conceived as the whole of the interacting forces of the total environment provided for pupils by the school and the pupils experiences in that environment.

Anderson, V.E. *Principles and Procedures of Curriculum Improvement.*

4. Curriculum should be conceived as the design of a social group for the educational experiences of their children in school. This design should take into account all the demands upon a school programme.

Beauchamp, George, A. *Curriculum Theory.* Itasca, IPR, F.E. Peack, 1981.

5. Curriculum is the sum of the educational experiences that children have in school.

Beck, N. Robert; Cook, W. Walter and Kearney C. Nolan. *Curriculum in Modern Elementary School,* Bentice Hall inc., i960.

6. Curriculum is all the experience which a pupil has under the guidance of the School.

Blond's Encyclopaedia of Education. Blond Educational Ltd: London, 1969.

7. Curriculum is that series of things which children and youth must do and experience by way of developing abilities to do things well that make up the affairs of adult life; and to be in all respects what adults should do.

Bobbit F. *The Curriculum.* Houghtan Miffin: Boston, 1918.

8. Popularly the curriculum has been thought of as those compendiums of information and skills which the school has made available for study.... It consists of experiences the learner has under the direction of the school.

Bossing, L. Nelson, *Principles of Secondary Education.*

10. Curriculum is all the learning which is planned and guided by the school.

Brown, Army Francis, *Curriculum Development.* W.B. Saunders Company.

11. Curriculum is defined broadly enough to include any materials or activities that will affect the learning, development, attitudes or behaviour of the child.

Carleton Washburne, *Introduction to Thirty Eight Yearbook, National Society for the Study of Education.* NIE: Washington, 1939.

12. Curriculum is all of the experiences children have under the guidance of teachers.

Caswell, H. and Campbell, D., *Curriculum Development.* American Book Company: New York, 1935.

13. Experiences which children undergo under the guidance of the school.

Davis, Hurley Beatric, *Curriculum for Elementary School Children.*

14. Curriculum can refer to the total structure of ideas and activities developed by. an educational institution to meet the learning needs of students and to achieve desired educational aims.

Derek Rowntree, *A Dictionary of Education.* Harper and Row: London, 1981.

15. Curriculum embodies all the experiences which are offered to learners under the auspices or direction of the school.

Doll, R.C., *Curriculum Improvement: Decision Making and Process.* Allyn and Bacon: Boston, 1982.

16. A curriculum shows by what kind of educational activities the teacher will fulfill the requirements of the syllabus. The syllabus prescribes the content of the teaching to be given and the curriculum prescribes the methods to be used. It is made up of pedagogical directives intended to provide assistance, advice, suggestions and information to assist the teacher in carrying out his task successfully.

Dotterns Robert, *The Primary School Curriculum.* UNESCO, 1962.

17. Curriculum is the whole of the various courses of study and learning experience conducted by or under the auspices of the school.

Douglass, R. Harl, *The High School Curriculum.* Ronald Press Company, New York.

18. The curriculum is often defined today as the total learning experience which pupils have in and out of school under the guidance of the faculty.

Draper, E.M., *Curriculum Research 'Education Digest'.* September 19, 1950.

19. Curriculum can no longer be regarded as a fixed set of courses. It must be regarded, rather, as defined by a set of principles which constitute a means of structuring the association of the teacher and the student to the end of educating the student.

Dressell, Paul, *The Undergraduate Curriculum in Higher Education.* 1963.

20. Curriculum may refer to the composite array of learning experiences

provided by an institution or department or to a fixed course of study (programme) learning to a certificate or degree.

Dressel, P.L. (1980).

21. We conceive of the school curriculum as the totality of learning experience that the school provides for the pupils through all the manifold activities in the school or outside, that are carried on under its supervision. From this point of view, the distinction between curricular and extra-curricular work ceases to exist, and a school camp and games and reports are curricular or rather co-curricular activities.

Education Commission, 1964-66, 8. 101, p. 207

22. The school curriculum must therefore be democracy in action giving the learner many opportunities to use and test social and democratic principles.

F. Lorence B., *Guide to a Curriculum for Modern Living.*

23. A curriculum, then, as defined here is a set of intended learnings.

Goodlad, J.I. (1972).

24. Curriculum is a body of prescribed educative experiences under school supervision, designed to provide an individual with the best possible training and experience to fit him for the society of which he is a part or to qualify him for a trade or profession.

Goods Dictionary of Education.

25. All experiences, in and out of school, used by the school to attain educational objectives constitute the curriculum.

Goodrich, T.Y. and Folsons, A.E., *Frame of Reference for Curriculum Planning.* 'Elementary School Journal', Jan. 1944.

26. The curriculum is the means of attaining the aims or philosophy of education. Being means to the end, and not an end in itself, it usually follows and reflects educational trends and changes in philosophy.

Gwyan, J. Minor. *Curriculum Principles and Social Trends.* The Macmillan Company, New York, 1956.

27. Curriculum embodies all of the teaching-learning experiences guided and directed by the school.

Harnack, R., *The Teacher: Decision Maker and Curriculum Planner.* Scranton Pa: International Textbook, 1968.

28. The curriculum is all of the experiences that individual learners have in a programme of education whose purpose is to achieve broad goals and related specific objectives, which is planned in terms of a framework of theory and research or past and present professional practice.

Hass, G., *Curriculum Planning: A New Approach.* Boston: Allyn and Bacon, 1980.

29. ...A simple way of considering the curriculum is to see in terms of four facets: content, methods, purposes, evaluation.

Hills, P.J., *A Dictionary of Education* (1982).

30. The curriculum is all that goes on in the lives of the children, their parents and their teachers. The curriculum is made up of everything that surrounds the learner in all its working hours. In fact, the curriculum has been described as, "the environment in motion".

Hollis L. Caswell, *Curriculum Improvement in Public School.*

31. Correlation (curriculum) means the teaching and learning of essential parts of the content of subjects or broad fields which have observable relation to a common topic or them. It is a method of unifying subject matter, but it does not necessarily represent any change in the original requirements of the individual subjects.

Hopkins L. Thomas, *Encyclopaedia of Modern Education,* 1969.

32. Curriculum is the body of value—goal-oriented learning content, existing as a written document or in the minds of teachers, that, when energized by instruction, results in change in pupil behaviour.

Inlow, Gail M., *The Emergent in Curriculum.* Willy: New York, 1973.

33. All the learned experiences which are planned and sponsored by the school.

Jameson, M.C. and Hicks, W.V., *Elementary School Curriculum.* American Book Company, New York, 1960.

34. Curriculum is a structured series of intended learning outcomes. Curriculum prescribes (or at least anticipates) the result of instruction.

Johnson, M. Jr., *Definitions and Models in Curriculum Theory.* (1967).

35. All the experiences that a learner has under the guidance of the school.

Kearney and Cook, (1960).

36. Those experiences and activities which are devised by the school for the purpose of modifying the learner's behaviour.

Keilh Lowell, Blake Paul and Tiedt Sidney, *Contemporary Curriculum in the Elementary School.* Harper and Row. New York, 1968.

37. Curriculum manifests life in its reality.

Kailpatrick

38. The curriculum consists of the means of instruction used by the school to provide opportunities for student learning experience leading to desired learning outcomes.

In most present day discussion and writing, these means of instruction include the classroom studies, the guidance or counselling programme, school and community service projects, school-related work experience, school health services, school camps, the school library and those activities known as' extra curricular' or 'extra class'.

Krag, A. Edward, *Curriculum Planning.* Harper and Brothers New York, 1957.

39. School Curriculum a selection of the culture.

Lawton, D., *The Politics of School Curriculum* (1975).

40. Curriculum is an organised list existing in advance of any face to face relationship between pupil and teacher.

Lees Joseph, Frasure Kenneth; and Johnson Maurit, *The Teacher in Curriculum Making.* Harper and Brothers, New York.

41. The curriculum for each child is the sum total of all his experiences which are in any way affected by the school.

Lee, J. Murray and Lee, D.M., *The Child and His Curriculum,* Appleton-Century-Crofts, New York, 1950.

42. In our view, curriculum is the cultural environment which has been properly selected as a set of possibilities of facilitating educative transactions.

Macdonald, J., Wolfson and B. Zaret, E., *Reschooling Society*, 1973.

43. Curriculum is the environment in which the education takes place.

Mcnerney T. Chester, *The Curriculum*. McGraw-Hill Book Company, 1953.

44. All the activities of the school-play, games, classwork-activities of all those who have anything to do with the school.

Mead, A.R., *General Concepts Basic to the Curriculum*. Curriculum Journal, Feb., 1940.

45. If the fundamental task of the school is to prepare children for life, the curriculum must be as wide as life itself. It should be thought of as comprising all the activities and the experiences afforded by the community through the school whereby the children may be prepared to participate in the life of the community.

Michigan, *Department of Public Instruction*.

46. The curriculum is a general overall specification of organized learning activity that a school plans to offer its students.

National Association of Secondary Schools, *Principal*. Feb. 1956, Vol. 40, Number 217.

47. Curriculum is defined as all of the planned experiences provided by the school to assist pupils in attaining the designated learning outcomes to the best of their abilities.

Neagley, Ross L. and Evans V. Dean, *Handbook for Effective Curriculum Development*. Prentice Hall Inc., 1967.

48. All the educational experiences that a learner has under the guidance of the school.

Nolan, C. Kearney and Walter W. Cook., 'Curriculum' *Encyclopaedia of Educational Research* (Chester W. Harris ed.). The Macmillan Company, 1960.

49. The curriculum consists of all the experiences which the child has irrespective of their character or when or where they take place.

Norton, John K. and Norton, Margaret A., *Foundations of Curriculum Building*. Ginn & Co. Boston, 1936.

50. The curriculum should be viewed as various forms of activity that are grand expression of the human spirit and that are of the greatest and most permanent significance to the wide world.

Nunn, T.P.

51. Curriculum is a plan of programme for all experiences which the learner encounters under the direction of the school.

Oliva, A., *Curriculum Improvement*. New York, Harper and Row 1977.

52. 'Curriculum' is the educational programme of the school with attention to the elements of (1) programme studies, (2) programme of experience, (3) programme of service, and (4) hidden curriculum.

Oliver, A., *Curriculum Improvement*. New York, Harper & Row, 1977.

53. Curriculum comes into existence only in the experience of children. Teachers, administrators and children are always in a process of creating the curriculum.

Ragan, William B., *Modern Curriculum.* Holt, New York.

54. 'Curriculum' is a slippery word. Broadly defined, it means nothing less than the education process as a whole. Narrowly defined, as is usually done, the term is regarded as being more or less synonymous with 'the syllabus', 'scheme of work' or simply 'subjects'. According to one, no sharp distinction can be drawn between curricular, co-curricular and extra-curricular activities, all of which are held to play their part in the pupils' total experience; according to the latter, the line between formal instruction and informal learning needs to be drawn much more firmly. The difference between two positions corresponds to the difference between child-centred and discipline-centred.

Richamond, W. Kennet, *The Leisure of Education: A Critical Bibliography,* 1945-1970 (1972).

55. Curriculum includes the goals, objectives, content, processes, resources and means of evaluation of all the learning experiences planned for pupils both in and out of the school and community through classroom instruction and related programmes (for example, field trips, library programmes, work experience education, guidance and extra classroom activities).

Robinson, Agnes S. (1971)

56. Curriculum is the selection, organisation and administration of a body of subject matter designed to lead the pupils on some definite life objective.

Roswell, C. Puckett, *Making a High School Schedule of Recitations.* Longman Green and Company, New York, 1931.

57. Our attitude towards the curriculum has been influenced by a desire to assist children to acquire or develop the habits, skills, interests and sentiments which they will need both for their well-being and for that of the people among whom they will live.

Ross, James S., *Groundwork of Educational Theory.*

58. Curriculum includes total structure of ideas and activities developed by an educational institution to meet the learning needs of students and to achieve desired educational aims.

Rowntree, Derek, *Dictionary of Education* (1981).

59. The elementary school curriculum is essentially a process of living and learning within a democratic, problem-solving climate for children, each of whom has a unique development growth pattern. The curriculum process encompasses the total of all experiences children have under the guidance of the school. Since each child differs from every child in a host of ways and looks out upon the world from his unique behavioural field, the curriculum is different for each child.

Ruckner, Ray W., *Curriculum Development in the Elementary School.* Harper and Brothers, New York.

60. Curriculum in its broader sense, includes the complete school environment, involving all the courses, activities, readings and associations furnished to the pupils in the school.

Rudyard K. Bent and Henry H. Kronenberg.

61. The curriculum is really the entire programme of the school's work. It is the essential means of education. It is everything that the students and their teachers do.

Rugg, Harold, *American Life and the School Curriculum.* Boston, Gim and Company, 1936.

62. The curriculum should not be conceived as a collection of subjects. At the secondary stage, as at the primary stage, it should be a field of creative activities, with instruction as incidental or instrumental to the aims of these activities. If at the infant stage, these activities may be described as 'play' activities, and at the primary stage, as projects, then at secondary stage they merge into 'constructive' works.

Read, Herbart

63. The curriculum is primarily an aid in the process of adjusting the child to the environment in which he functions from day to day and in the wider environment in which he will have to organise his activities later.

64. The curriculum is the sum total of the school's efforts to influence learning whether in the classroom, on the playground, or out of school.

It (Curriculum) encompasses all learning opportunities provided by the school.

Saylor, T.G. and Alexander, W., *Curriculum Planning for Modern Schools.* New York: Holt, Rinehart and Winston, 1966.

65. Theoretically, and more and more in practice, the term "Curriculum" is used to mean the students' total learning activities or experiences that take place under the direction of the school.

Herbert, Schueler, *Encyclopedia of Modern Education,* Ed. Harry N. Rivlin (1969).

66. Curriculum is, in fact, the interaction of classroom commonplaces: teachers, learners, subject matter and milieu.

Schubert, W.H. (1973).

67. 'Curriculum' is derived from Latin roots that refer to the course of a chariot race; and ordinary educational discourse designates the common dictionary usage of "Course of Study". Although curricularists have long debated the meaning of the term, "Curriculum" can be treated as the essence and/or subject matter of educational experiences. Indeed, the etymological metaphor can be extended to designate not only a race course but also a journey, expedition, or even pilgrimage.

Schubert, William H., *Encyclopedia of Educational Research* 1982.

68. It must be clearly understood that, according to the best modern educational thought, curriculum in this context does not mean only the academic subjects traditionally taught in the school but it includes the totality of experiences that a pupil receives through the manifold activities that go on in the school...in the classroom, library, laboratory, workshop, play-grounds and in the numerous informal contacts between teachers and pupils. In this case, the whole life of the school becomes the curriculum which can touch the life of the students at all points and help in the evolution of balanced personality.

Secondary Education Commission, 1952-53.

69. The present view of the curriculum is that it consists of all the educative

experiences under the conscious guidance of the school. This conception differs from the older idea of the curriculum as a body of subject matter to be learned. Just as the assigned lesson was the basic unit in the older definition, so an experience is the unit of the new. In the overall, it means a rounded programme of living for every child as opposed to the curriculum as a series of lessons or a collection of courses. Finally in this modern view, the curriculum is not confined to the classroom but flows out into the life of the school and beyond the school itself.

Sharp, George, *Curriculum Development as Re-Education of the Teacher.* Teachers College Press, New York, 1951.

70. The elementary (or secondary) school curriculum consists of those experiences that the school consciously and purposefully provides for children (and youth) in the light of the accepted purposes of the school using these experiences, also, as the major source of data upon which to have the evaluation of individual and group progress towards these purposes.

Sowards, G. Welsely and Scobey M. Margaret, *The Changing Curriculum and the Elementary Teacher.*

71. Curriculum is a sequence of potential experiences set up in the school for the purpose of disciplining children and youth in group ways of thinking and acting.

Smith, B.B., Stanley W.D. and Shores, S.M. *Fundamentals of Curriculum Development.* World Book Co. 1957.

72. Curriculum in the strict sense is a statement of or programme of courses of teaching and instruction.

Spens Report (1938)

73. The curriculum is currently defined in three ways...the courses and class activities in which children and youth engage: the total range of in class and out of class experiences sponsored by the school; and the total life experiences of the learner.

Stratemeyer, Florence and others, *Developing a Curriculum for Modern Living.* Bureau of Publications, Teachers College, Columbia University, 1947.

74. A curriculum is a plan of learning.

Taba, H., *Curriculum Development: Theory and Practice.* Brace Govanovich, New York: 1962.

75. Curriculum is that construction of knowledge and experience systematically developed under the auspices of the school (or university), to enable the learner to increase his or her control of knowledge and experience.

Tanner, D., and Tanner, L, *Curriculum Development.* New York: Macmillan, 1980.

76. Curriculum means all the experiences which take place under the sponsorship of the school. The English course, the publication of the school paper, the football games are all a part of the high school curriculum. All aspects of the child's school life...classwork, play activities, special projects and group life are a part of the child's curriculum.

Tom, C. Venable, *Patterns in Secondary School Curriculum.*

77. Curriculum.

(i) The whole body of courses offered by an educational institution or one of its branches;
(ii) Any particular body of courses set for various majors (such as engineering);
(iii) All planned school activities including courses of study for organised play, athletics, dramatics, club, etc.;
(iv) (a) General education and breeding; and
(b) A work schedule.

Webster's Third New International Dictionary.

78. The formal curriculum consists of the units of credits that are offered, the courses that are made available to students, the syllabi for those courses, the bibliographies and materials used, and the evaluative devices that are selected. The informal aspect of the curriculum includes the unplanned things that happen in classes, in the hallways, on the play-ground, in the cafeteria, and on the way to and from school...

Wiles, Kimball *The Changing Curriculum of the American High School* (1963).

79. Curriculum is the whole range of formal studies and learning experiences offered by a school. In most schools, subjects studied in the classroom form the chief part of a programme. But a curriculum may also include independent study and investigation; lectures by outsiders; participation in school athletics, plays, and concerts; educational television programmes; field trips; and work or service projects in the community. A curriculum organises all learning experiences to give students the most benefit from them at each level of their school career.

The World Book Encyclopedia (1984).

2

International Commission on Education for the Twenty-First Century (1993-96)

(*Delors Commission*)

Learning the Treasure Within—Report to UNESCO of the International Commission on Education for the Twenty-First Century is the result of three years of research and debate by an international panel of fifteen educational specialists belonging to China, France, India, Jamaica, Japan, Jordan, Korea (Republic of), Mexico, Poland, Portugal, Senegal, Slovenia, United States, Venezuela and Zimbabwe.

Organised around six lines of enquiry: education and development, education and science, education and citizenship, education and culture, education and social cohesion and education and work, Commission's report is expected to guide the policy makers and implementers in the field of education at the national and international levels.

The International Commission on Education for the 21st Century had mapped out six main tensions as the central problems for the next century; the global *vs.* the local; the universal *vs.* the individual; tradition. *vs.* modernity; long-term considerations *vs.* short term; the need for competition *vs.* the concern for equality; and the "age-old tension between the spiritual and the material."

The Commission proposes four pillars for the education of the future: learning to live together by understanding others and their history, learning to know as preparation for learning throughout life, learning to do, in order to face a variety of situations; and learning to be better by understanding one's own personality.

Fundamental to these pillars is basic education, which helps develop a taste and capacity for learning throughout life.

Among the report's important recommendations are: strong encouragement for education of girls and women; allocating 25 per cent of development aid to education; introducing new "information society" technologies in all countries; and turning to the educational potential of Non-Governmental Organisations (NGOs) and local communities to supplement international cooperation.

One of the Commission's main proposals is education throughout life. "We used to think that life was divided into time for learning, a time for working and a time for resting in retirement but this would be overturned by the world ahead," noted Jacques Delors, Chairman of the Commission.

The report suggests approaches to both policy and practice which are both innovative and feasible to a great extent, while taking into account the wide diversity of situations, needs, means and aspirations existing in countries and in regions. The report is addressed primarily to governments but one of its purposes is to address issues related to the role of international cooperation and assistance in general and the role of UNESCO in particular. It also attempts to formulate recommendations which are pertinent for international bodies.

The Commission focussed its reflection on one central and all-encompassing question: What kind of education is needed for what kind of society of tomorrow? It considered the new roles of education and the new demands made on education system in a world of accelerating economic, environmental and social change and tension. It studied the implications for education of the major trends in the evolution of contemporary society. It examined the state of knowledge and experience of the best educational practices in various cultural, economic and political settings in order to identify the strengths and weaknesses of contemporary policy. In doing so it attempted to keep at the heart of its work, those most intimately involved in education, i.e., learners of all ages, first of all and those involved in fostering learning, whether they be teachers, parents, members of the community or other participants in education.

Initially the Commission attempted to identify a series of key questions which it was to examine during its work, the answers to which would be the major recommendations it would put forward the perennial issues facing governments, societies and educators and which may continue to be important during the coming years, questions raised by new configurations of society and new developments in the physical and social world implying new priorities, new needs and new action; universal questions based on inevitable and indispensable responses to a changing world, regional or nation-specific issues. It focussed on the widely differing economic, cultural and social situations prevailing in different countries.

The Commission took into account questions concerning education and education systems falling broadly into two main categories. The first category includes those questions relating to the purposes, goals and functions of education, including the aims of individuals and each person's needs and desire for self-fulfillment. The second covers self-fulfillment issues concerning providers of education including the models, structures, contents and functioning of educational systems.

The Commission carried out a broadly based analysis both of what is known about the current situation and of forecasts and trends in national policies and reforms in education in the different regions of the world over the last twenty years. On this basis the Commission reflected in depth on the major turning points in human development on the eve of the twenty-first century and the new demands these turning points will make on education. It highlighted the ways in which education can play a more dynamic and constructive role in preparing individuals and societies for the twenty-first century.

As observed by Jacques Delors, Chairman of the Commission, "Our Commission had perhaps the impossible task of overcoming the obstacles presented by the extraordinary diversity of situations in the world and trying to arrive at analyses that are universally valid and conclusions acceptable to everyone.

Nevertheless, the Commission did its best to project its thinking on to a future dominated by globalisation, to choose those questions that everyone is asking and to lay down some guidelines that can be applied both within national contexts and on a worldwide scale."

Background of the International Commission

UNESCO had on several previous occasions produced international studies reviewing issues and priorities in education worldwide. In 1968, *The World Educational Crisis: A Systems Analysis,* by Philip H. Coombs, the then Director of UNESCO's International Institute for Educational Planning (HEP), drew on the work of the Institute to examine the problems facing education, and to recommend far-reaching innovations.

In 1971, in the wake of student upheavals in much of the world during the previous three years, Rene Maheu (the then Director-General of UNESCO), asked a former French Prime Minister and Minister of Education, Edgar Faure, to chair a seven-person panel entrusted with defining 'the new aims to be assigned to education as a result of the rapid changes in knowledge and in societies, the demands of development, the aspirations of the individual, and the overriding need for international understanding and peace', and putting forward 'suggestions regarding the intellectual, human and financial means needed to attain the objectives set.' Published in 1972 under the title *Learning to Be,* report of the Faure Commission had the great merit of firmly establishing the concept of life-long education at a time when traditional education systems were being challenged.

Appointment of the International Commission

In November 1991 the General Conference invited the Director-General 'to convene an international commission to reflect on education and learning for the twenty-first century.' Federico Mayor requested Jacques Delors to chair the Commission, with a group of fourteen other eminent figures from all over the world and from a variety of cultural and professional backgrounds.

Task before the Commission

The aim of the Commission was to study and reflect on the challenges facing education in the coming years and to formulate suggestions and recommendations in the form of a report which could serve as an agenda for renewal and action for policy makers and officials at the highest levels.

Scope of the Work of the Commission

The scope of the Commission's work included the concept of education in its broadest sense, from pre-school and higher education, including both formal and non-formal education and covering the widest possible spectrum of agencies and providers.

Guiding Principles

The Commission was expected to keep in mind some underlying principles which included in the mandate proposed to it by the Director-General of UNESCO.

First, education is a basic human right and a universal human value: learning and education are ends in themselves, to be aimed at by both individuals and societies, and to be promoted and made available over the entire lifetime of each individual.

Second, education, formal and non-formal, must serve society as an instrument for fostering the creation, advancement and dissemination of knowledge and science, and by making knowledge and teaching universally available.

Third, the triple goal of equity, relevance and excellence must prevail in any policy of education, and the search for a harmonious combination of these goals is a crucial task for all those involved in educational planning and practice.

Fourth, renewal and any corresponding reform of education must be the result of profound and thoughtful examination and understanding of what is known about useful practice and policy, as well as understanding of the specific conditions and requirements relevant to each particular situation: they must be decided upon by mutual agreement through appropriate facts among the parties concerned, as a medium-term process.

Fifth, while existence of a wide variety of economic, social and cultural situations clearly calls for different approaches to educational development, all approaches must take into account basic and agreed-upon values and concerns of the international community and the United Nations system: human rights, tolerance and understanding, democracy, responsibility, universality, cultural identity, the search for peace, the preservation of the environment, the sharing of knowledge, alleviation of poverty, population control, health.

Sixth, education is the responsibility of the v hole society, all persons involved and all partnership-in addition to those incumbent on institutions — must be fully taken into account.

The Commission at Work

The task of the Commission was very difficult. The first and perhaps the main difficulty confronting the Commission's Chairman Jacques Delors concerned the extreme diversity of educational situations, conceptions and structures. Related to this difficulty was the sheer quantity of information available and the obvious impossibility, for the Commission, of digesting more than a small proportion of it in the course of its work. It was thus obliged to be selective and to single out what was essential for the future, bearing in mind both geopolitical, economic, social and cultural trends on the one hand and, on the other, the part educational policies could play.

The Commission chose six lines of inquiry which enabled it to approach its task from the angle of the aims (both individual and societal) of the learning process: education and culture; education and citizenship; education and social cohesion; education, work and employment; education and development; and education, research and science, These six lines were complemented by three transverse themes relating more directly to the functioning of education systems: communications technologies; teachers and teaching; and financing and management.

The Commission adopted a wide-ranging methodology of consultation. The Commission held eight plenary sessions, and the same number of working-group sessions, to examine both the major topics chosen, and concerns and issues particular to one region or group of countries. Participants in the working-group sessions were representative of a wide range of professions and organisations directly and indirectly related to education, formal and non-formal: teachers, researchers, students, government officials, and people active in governmental and non-governmental organizations at national and international levels.

A series of presentations by distinguished individuals enabled the Commission to hold in-depth exchanges on a wide range of topics related in various degrees to education. Individual consultations were carried out, face-to-face or in writing.

A questionnaire was sent to all the National Commissions for UNESCO, inviting them to submit documentation or unpublished material, the response was very positive and the replies were studied carefully.

Non-governmental organisations were similarly consulted and in some cases invited to participate in meetings. In the past two-and-a-half years, members of the Commission, including its Chairman, also attended a series of governmental and non-governmental meetings in which its work was discussed and ideas exchanged.

Many written submission, commissioned or unsolicited, were sent to the Commission. The Commission's secretariat analysed a considerable volume of documentation and provided the Commission's members with summaries on a variety of topics.

The Four Pillars of Education

Education throughout life is based on four pillars: learning to know, learning to do, learning to live together and learning to be.

1. *Learning to know,* by combining a sufficiently broad general knowledge with the opportunity to work in depth on a small number of subjects. This also means learning to learn, so as to benefit from the opportunities education provides throughout life.

2. *Learning to do,* in order to acquire not only an occupational skill but also, more broadly, the competence to deal with many situations and work in teams. It also means learning to do in the context of young peoples' various social and work experiences which may be informal, as a result of the local or national context, or formal, involving courses, alternating study and work.

3. *Learning to live together,* by developing an understanding of other people and an appreciation of interdependence—carrying out joint projects and learning to manage conflicts—in a spirit of respect for the values of pluralism, mutual understanding and peace.

4. *Learning to be,* so as better to develop one's personality and be able to

act with ever greater autonomy, judgement and personal responsibility. In that connection, education must not disregard any aspect of a person's potential: memory, reasoning, aesthetic sense, physical capacities and communication skills.

Formal education systems tend to emphasise the acquisition of knowledge to the detriment of other types of learning; but it is vital now to conceive education in more encompassing fashion. Such a vision should inform and guide future educational reforms and policy, in relation both to contents and to methods.

Learning throughout Life

- The concept of learning throughout life is the key that gives access to the twenty-first century. It goes beyond the traditional distinction between initial and continuing education. It links up with another concept often put forward, that of the learning society, in which everything affords an opportunity of learning and fulfilling one's potential.
- In its new guise, continuing education is seen as going far beyond what is already practised, particularly in the developed countries, i.e., upgrading, with refresher training, retraining and conversion or promotion courses for adults. It should open up opportunities for learning for all, for many different purposes—offering them a second or third chance, satisfying their desire for knowledge and beauty or their desire to surpass themselves, or making it possible to broaden and deepen strictly vocational forms of training, including practical training.
- In short, 'learning throughout life' must take advantage of all the opportunities offered by society.

From Basic Education to University

- A requirement valid for all countries, albeit in various forms and with different types of content—the *strengthening of basic education:* hence the emphasis on *primary education* and its traditional basic programmes—reading, writing; arithmetic—but also on the ability to express oneself in a language that lends itself to dialogue and understanding.
- The need, which will be still greater tomorrow, for receptivity to science and the world of science, which opens the door to the twenty-first century and its scientific and technological upheavals.
- The adaptation of *basic education* to specific contexts, the most deprived countries as well as the most deprived section of the population, starting out with the facts of everyday life, which affords opportunities for understanding natural phenomena and for different forms of socialisation.
- The pressing needs of literacy work and basic education for adults are to be kept in mind.
- In all cases, emphasis is to be placed on pupil-teacher relations, since the most advanced technologies can be no more than a back-up to the relationship (transmission, dialogue and confrontation) between teacher and pupil.
- Secondary education must be rethought in this general context of learning

throughout life. The key principle is to arrange for a variety of individual paths through schooling, without ever closing the door on the possibility of a subsequent return to the education system.

Debates on selection and guidance would be greatly clarified if this principle is accepted.

- Universities would have vested in them four key functions:
    1. To prepare students for research and teaching.
    2. To provide highly specialized training courses adapted to the needs of economic and social life.
    3. To be open to all, so as to cater for the many aspects of lifelong education in the widest sense.
    4. International co-operation.
- The universities should also be able to speak out on ethical and social problems as entirely independent and fully responsible institutions exercising a kind of intellectual authority that society needs to help it to reflect, understand and act.

3

Teachers for the Twenty-First Century

Indeed, globalisation which is affecting the economy, culture and information, internationalisation of relations and the increasing mobility of individuals, a complete revolution in the communications media and the massive advent of computerisation into daily life and into the world of work represent both a challenge and an opportunity to the education systems. At the same time, many societies and education systems are experiencing serious problems of social integration, among which should be mentioned inter-ethnic conflicts and violence, increasing unemployment—particularly among young people—a decline in moral values, the weakening of guidelines and changes in the role of family ties in the socialisation of children. If all these challenges and problems are not overcome in the short-term, there could be a risk of reinforcing feelings of uncertainty and pessimism that are particularly pernicious for future generations. Hopes on the part of societies, and especially the youth, for a more dignified, democratic and prosperous life are linked to education, which is considered to be the main instrument in the development of humanity.

While education is being transformed as a result of these changes, it is expected that teachers will educate, teach, guide and evaluate, and that they will also demonstrate their capacity to develop themselves, to participate in modernising the school and to make it more proactive and receptive to change. They should not only facilitate learning, but should also promote citizenship training and active integration into society, develop curiosity, critical thinking and creativity, initiative and self-determination. The role of the teacher will increasingly become that of a facilitator of learning within the group. Furthermore, confronted with the increasing role played by other information providers and socialization agents, it is expected that teachers will assume the role of moral and educational guide enabling learners to obtain their bearings in this mass of information and different values. It is through carrying out their functions as co-ordinator of educational activities provided by various partners—and directed towards common educational goals—that modern teachers will become effective agents of change in the community. Much is expected of education and teachers, too much perhaps, and not always for the right reasons, for, in the first place, it is society itself, clearly with the participation of the teacher, that is supposed to find a solution to its malfunctions.

It is not a question of putting forward a unique solution for all countries, but of establishing common guidelines. The variety of situations at the regional, national and local levels obviously implies that these guidelines should be adapted. There is, however, one essential condition: if this vast undertaking of educational renewal is to succeed, inevitably there has to be mutual confidence between teachers at all levels and in all sectors, all education staff and the public and private partners of education systems. In order to maintain such a climate there is a need to establish criteria which provide a clear definition of the competencies and roles of all those involved with respect to autonomy, responsibility and participation.

Various Aspects of Teacher's Role

The following is the collective view of various countries regarding what they believe to be the various aspects of the teacher's role at the current time. The teacher is expected to:

- promote skills and competency in literacy and numeracy, sensitivity to the environment and harmony between the school and its community;
- help the growth of basic skills and attitudes for proper and continued development of cognitive, social, moral and emotional development;
- transmit culture and knowledge, and help students become aware of the world community;
- nourish creative and critical abilities;
- encourage adaptability in a dynamic and ever-changing society;
- help each individual achieve full self-actualisation to become a fully functional member of society;
- provide the students and the community with an admirable role model as a professional teacher;
- ensure students' physical well-being;
- be accountable to the community and its parents.

In order to undertake these tasks, experts at regional meetings believe that teachers need to:

- ensure their continuing personal development, including the upgrading of knowledge and teaching skills;
- be aware of the values and attitudes which lead to a healthy human society;
- be involved actively in the affairs of the local community and society;
- provide effective management of the learning environment and resources;
- be skilled in linking the curriculum of the school with the needs of the community;
- be skilled in counselling individual children and the management of groups of children;
- be skilled in the use and choice of a variety of teaching methods;
- be skilled in working with parents and other members of the community;
- be skilled in a variety of appropriate research methodologies.

The general expectation is therefore that teacher education should be modified to ensure that all teachers have the knowledge, competencies and sensitivities to accommodate all these aspects of the teacher's role.

Rationale for the Modernisation of Teacher Education

"Good education requires good teachers" means that it becomes essential that the most capable and appropriate people be recruited into the teaching profession, provided with a high quality pre-service programme of teacher education, and then offered opportunities to upgrade their knowledge and skills over the full length of their professional career. It is therefore essential that there is a major reorientation of teacher education to ensure that teachers are furnished with the necessary knowledge and skills to cope with the new demands placed on them. Teacher education needs to be adequately strengthened and upgraded to accommodate the changing role of the teacher, and so that teachers can effectively address contemporary issues regarding education.

In addition, because of the impact of social and other forms of change in society and the demands placed on the school system, there is a need for the constant upgrading and modernisation of the knowledge, skills and understanding required of teachers. This has clear implications for the content and methodology of teacher education, and stresses the need to adopt an approach which emphasises the career-long professional development of teachers. Teacher education, therefore, has to be reformed in order to adequately prepare teachers for their new and more diversified functions in the school and the community. Teachers are also increasingly expected to handle, in their day-to-day work, a number of issues of critical importance in the present day context, such as education for human rights and democracy, value education and environmental education.

The move towards the democratisation of education has necessitated a large expansion of the teaching service in all countries, in order to cater to a large number and more heterogeneous groups of students.

A paper prepared by Educational International on the occasion of ICE (1996), makes the following observations on enhancing the role of teachers in the changing world:

1. Teachers are confronted by a set of changes which lead to contradictory demands on them from society. The teaching profession has become more complex and demanding. These changes in the role of the teacher have only rarely been reflected in improvements of working conditions, salaries and status.

2. The rates of public expenditure on education have declined. Enrolment may have increased over the 1980's, but in most countries fundings has not kept pace. In countries undergoing structural adjustment, education budgets have been squeezed in areas which affect quality of education. Due to low salaries or due to irregular payment of salaries many teachers have been forced to look for a second job in order to survive. Those who can find full time jobs in other sectors move away from the teaching profession and there are serious problems in recruiting new teachers.

3. Worldwide, public expenditure on education as a percentage of gross national product, was calculated to be just above 5 per cent of GNP in 1992. The 6 per cent goal set by the International Commission on Education for the Twenty-First Century would require countries to increase their funding of

education. This 6 per cent level must be seen as a minimum investment. It has to be recognised that investment in education is necessary for sustainable development.

4. Public schools are an integral component of a democratic society. The privatisation of public education presents the danger of placing young people in separate schools which are organised along religious, cultural, social and linguistic lines. Privatisation of education does not lead to lower costs than for public education, if all the associated services which are indispensable for the proper functioning of school establishments are taken into consideration.

5. An appropriate use of the new information technologies could be used as a powerful support to the educational process, but to make this into reality there is a need for investment in computer programmes, etc., in schools and in the development of teachers' competence.

6. It is of crucial importance to find ways to introduce new technologies in schools in all countries, rich and poor, in order to avoid an increased gap between the north and the south.

7. Steps have to be taken to recruit more male teachers to areas within the teaching profession that are today predominantly female and to recruit more women teachers to areas within the teaching profession that are today predominantly male. This can be achieved through improved career counselling and active encouragement of students to pursue education based on interest rather than gender.

8. Measures must be taken to increase the number of women in posts of responsibility in the educational sector. Such measures must include improved maternity leave, availability of pre-school care and innovative arrangements such as job sharing.

9. Where education is decentralised, steps have to be taken to ensure sufficient financial resources to guarantee equality between regions, municipalities, etc. Such developments also need to be carefully prepared including widespread consultations with all partners, in-service training, exchange of information and feedback.

10. There must be machinery for consultations between teacher organisations and educational authorities on curriculum, community relations, organisation and administration, budgetary allocations, etc. Equally, there must be machinery for negotiations on salaries and working conditions.

11. The individual teacher must be given a high degree of professional autonomy allowing her/him to determine which programme, teaching methods, etc., are best suited to obtain educational objectives in her/his class.

12. The importance of finding ways to offer career paths to teachers within the classroom is widely recognised. Two possible paths are to make it easier for teachers to move from one level to another in the educational system and to increase the opportunities for teachers to be involved in research.

13. Many reports show that the workload of teachers has increased during recent years. From this perspective serious steps must be taken to review class size and the distribution of working hours. Special measures might also be necessary for older teachers so that they are not forced to leave the teaching profession through ill health or enforced early retirement.

14. Teachers' salaries have decreased in most countries. In order to ensure that teachers obtain a decent salary, to maintain good teachers in the profession and to recruit new teachers there is a crucial need to up-grade teachers' salaries.

15. There is a general need to increase the status of teachers. Teachers play a key role in all educational systems and the quality of education is finally determined by the quality of teaching in the classroom.

16. All teachers must receive initial preparation for the profession at a higher education level (university or equivalent) before starting to teach. Initial teacher education should include teaching methodology/didactics, subject study in the subjects taught, general subject study and educational science, including pedagogy and educational psychology. Teachers must also receive regular in-service training, which will allow them to incorporate new developments in their teaching.

17. If teachers are to teach children and young people respect for human rights and fundamental freedoms they must enjoy these freedoms themselves. Teachers must be able to exercise, as all other citizens, freedom of thought, freedom of speech, the right to vote and to be candidates in democratic elections, and the right to join and found organisations.

Documents of the Forty-eighth session of the International Conference on Education. IBE, Geneva, 1996

4

Comparative Curriculum Scenario

(*China, Germany, Japan, Russian Federation, U.K. and USA*)

"To Know Thyself Compare Thyself to Others"

Every individual is different from every other. Similarly nations differ from each other. The fact is brilliantly brought out by Robert Bridges in the *Testament of Beauty*.

"All men differ each from each, since, neither environment, nor disposition can ever in any two men
be the same or alike...
...Again likewise it is seen
how national mentalities are mutually up
incomprehensible and irreconcilable;
since each group as it arose was determin'd apart
by conditions of life which none other could share,
by climate, language, historic tradition
estranging evermore; nor are such obstinate bonds
the weaker for any intrinsic absurdity."

It is equally true that globalisation in the present scenario exercises a tremendous impact on every type of national system and institutions. Different aspects of education bear comparison and provide a better insight into the system of one's own country.

The Table 4.1 provides a comparative state of education in select countries.

I CHINA

Basic Data (Around 1996)

1. Total Area: 9596 961
2. Population: 1232083,000
3. Percentage of Illiterate Population 15 years and above: 17.8%
4. Public Current Expenditure on Education as Percentage of GNP: 2%
5. Public Current Expenditure by level of Education
   (a) Pre-Primary: 01.3%
   (b) First Level: 36.1%
   (c) Second Level: 32.2%
   (d) Third Level: 15.6%

Table 4.1: Education and Allied Data of Select Countries

	Country	Population in Thousand (1998)	G.N.P. Percapita (US$) (1997)	Life Expectancy (1998)	Adult Literacy Rate (1996)	Primary School Enrolment Ratio (gross) (1990-96)	% of Pri. Sch. Entrants Reaching gr. 5 (1990-95)	Secondary School (1990-96) Enrolment Ratio		Higher Education Gross Enrolment Ratio (1990-95)
								Male	Female	
1	2	3	4	5	6	7	8	9	10	11
1.	Bangladesh	12400	360	58	38	69	47	28	14	–
2.	Canada	30500	19640	79	99	102	99	107 (1993)	106	102.9
3.	China	125500	860	70	80	120	94	94	74	5.3
4.	Egypt	66000	1200	67	51	102	98	80	70	20.3
5.	France	58600	26300	78	99	106	99	112	111	51.0
6.	Germany	82000	28280	77	99	–	100	103	101	44.4
7.	India	982000	370	63	50	101	59	59	39	6.5
8.	Indonesia	206000	1110	85	84	114	89	52	44	113
9.	Iran	65800	1780	69	71	90	90	79	69	16.6
10.	Iraq	21800	–	63	58	85	72	51	32	
11.	Israel	6000	16180	78	95	99	100	84	89	41.1
12.	Italy	57000	20170	78	99	99	100	87	88	41.4
13.	Japan	126000	38160	80	99	102	100	98	98	40.3
14.	Korea Dem. People's Rep	23300	970	72	–	104	100	102	102	
15.	Korea Rep. of	46000	10550	73	97	94	99	65	65	52.0
16.	Maldives	270	1180	65	95	125	93	49	49	
17.	Myanmar	44500	220	60	83	100	–	29	30	5.4
18.	New Zealand	3800	15830	77	–	103	96	117	123	58.2
19.	Pakistan	148000	500	64	39	74	48	33	17	
20.	Russian Federation	147000	2680	67	99	108	–	84	91	42.9
21.	Saudi Arabia	20200	7150	72	71	76	89	65	57	15.8

(*Contd.*)

(*Contd.*)

1	2	3	4	5	6	7	8	9	10	11
22.	Sri Lanka	18400	800	73	90	109	83	71	78	5.1
23.	Nepal	22800	220	58	36	110	52	49	25	5.2
24.	Sweden	8800	26210	79	99	107	98	126	147	46.0
25.	Switzerland	7299	43060	79	99	107	100	94	88	32.9
26.	U.K.	58600	20870	77	–	116	–	123	124	49.5
27.	USA	274000	29080	77	99	102	99	98	97	81.0

Sources: 1. *The State of the World's Children 2000,* UNICEF
2. *World Statistical Outlook on Higher Education 1980-95,* UNESCO, Paris, 1998

6. Gross Enrolment ratios by Level of Education
   (i) Pre-Primary: 29%
   (ii) First Level: 20%
   (iii) Second Level: 71%
   (iv) Third Level: 5.7 3%
   (*Educational Data relate to 1996*)

Compulsory Education

The *Law on Compulsory Education,* promulgated in 1986 stipulated, "All children who have reached the age of 6 years shall attend school for the prescribed number of years, regardless of sex, nationality or race. In areas where this is not possible, the beginning of schooling may be postponed to the age of 7 years." Hence, the age limit for primary school pupils are 6/7 to 12/13, for lower secondary school students, 12/13 to 15/16 years. The length of compulsory schooling is 8 or 9 years, including 5/6 years of primary education, and 4/3 years of lower secondary education.

Structure and Organisation of the Education Systems

Structure

Three systems co-exist for primary and lower secondary education: the "6+3" system, the "5+4" system and the "9-year" system, with the "6+3" system predominating in most areas. Thus, the length of schooling for primary education is six or five years and for lower secondary education, four or three years. Children start school at the age of 6 or 7 years and enter lower secondary school at the age of 12 or 13 years.

The starting age for upper secondary school is 15 or 16 years, and the length of schooling is three years.

The Educational Process

The Education Law stipulates that Chinese is the basic instructional language for schools and other educational institutions. In schools and educational institutions mainly attended by ethnic minority students, the ethnic minority language or the local language can be used in teaching activities.

Pre-primary Education

Pre-school education is a one-year course before the primary stage and is the preparation for school education. The State Education Commission has been preparing a Regulation concerning the kindergarten curriculum. For pre-school classes, instructional time is no more than twelve periods per week and each period is no longer than 30 minutes. No tests or examinations are conducted at the pre-school level.

Primary Education

The curriculum of primary education is comprised of both academic subjects and practical activities, determined at State and province levels. The curriculum set forth by the State is the compulsory core curriculum, including: moral education, Chinese language, mathematics, study of the society, study of the nature, sports, music, arts and labour. Some schools with the necessary capacities also offer teaching of foreign languages. The local curriculum mainly aims at facilitating the local economic and cultural development and is arranged by the educational authorities of provinces, autonomous regions and municipalities directly under the Central Government. Schools are authorised to arrange the local curriculum, both in academic and activity aspects, as compulsory or alternative courses.

According to the two systems of 6+3 and 5+4 nine-year compulsory education, the State determines the number of teaching periods by subject for the full-time primary education programme as follows:

Number of Class Periods in Full-time Primary Schools

Subject	*Six-year System No. of Periods*	*Five-year System No. of Periods*
Moral Education	204	170
Language	1,666	1,598
Maths	986	952
Society	204	170
Nature	272	238
Sports	544	340
Music	408	340
Arts	408	340
Labour	136	102

(Length of teaching periods, expressed in minutes, and the average number of periods in each grade, are not specified).

At the compulsory education stage, namely in primary and junior secondary schools, qualification examinations are conducted at the end of each term, at the end of the school year and for graduation.

Primary graduation includes an examination in language and mathematics and only check-ups for the other courses. When students pass exams in language and mathematics and are up to the standard in physical education, they graduate. The primary graduation exams are under the guidance of the county educational departments. Normally, schools will design the examination papers; in rural townships the education department will be responsible for designing of examination papers. In the areas where the nine-year compulsory education is achieved, there is no entrance examination for junior secondary education.

Promotion Rate (%)

	1993	1994	1995
Primary to junior secondary	81.8	86.6	90.8
Junior secondary to upper secondary	44.1	86.6	90.8
Upper secondary to higher education	43.3	46.7	49.9

Drop-out Rate at the Primary and Junior Secondary Levels(%)

Year	*Primary*	*Junior Secondary*
1993	2.27	7.08
1994	1.85	5.11
1995	1.49	3.98

Repetition Rate

	1993	1994	1995
Primary schools	3.8	2.9	2.2
Junior secondary	1.0	0.7	0.5

Average Number of Pupils in Each Class at the Primary Level

Year	*Number of Classes*	*Number of Pupils*
1993	3,976,406	31.2
1994	4,013,617	31.9
1995	4,038,547	32.7

Secondary Education

At the junior secondary level, the following subjects are taught: morality and politics, Chinese language, mathematics, foreign language, history, geography, physics, chemistry, biology, sports, arts and labour, as well as short-term vocational guidance.

According to the two systems of 6+3 and 5+4 nine-year compulsory education, the State determines the number of teaching periods by subject for the full-time junior secondary education programme as follows:

Number of Class Periods in Full-time Junior Secondary Schools

Subject	*Three-year System No. of Periods*	*Four-year System No. of Periods*
Morality and Politics	200	268
Language	534	636
Mathematics	468	536
Foreign language 1	204	272
Foreign language 2	400	536
History	200	204
Geography	153	204
Physics	164	164
Chemistry	96	132
Biology	153	204
Sports	200	302
Music	100	134
Arts	100	134
Labour skills	200	268

[Length of teaching periods, expressed in minutes, and the average number of periods in each grade, are not specified).

At the general senior secondary level, subjects include: politics, Chinese, mathematics, foreign language, physics, chemistry, biology, history, geography, sports, arts and labour skills. All subjects are determined by the State and politics, mathematics, language, sports, arts and labour skills are compulsory. Other subjects could be either compulsory or alternative.

Number of Class Periods in General Senior Secondary Schools

Subject	*No. of Periods (Compulsory)*	*No. of Periods (Alternative)*
Morality and Politics	184	
Language	380	
Mathematics	390	
Foreign language	289	96
Physics	187	120
Chemistry	187	96
Biology	102	72
History	136	120
Geography	102	
Sports	184	
Arts	68	
Labour skills	4 weeks per year	12 weeks in 3 years

The subjects of junior secondary graduation examinations are selected among those of the graduating grade; other subjects are only checked. Design of examination papers is determined by education departments and education commissions of provinces, autonomous regions and municipalities directly under the central government.

The qualification examination system is adopted at the general secondary stage. Exams and checks are combined. The subjects for the examination are: language, mathematics, foreign language, politics, physics, chemistry, biology, history and geography. The subjects for check-ups are: labour skills, experiment and operation of physics, chemistry, and biology. Examination in physical education is conducted in accordance with a uniform syllabus. The examination papers are prepared by provinces, autonomous regions and municipalities. Their responsibilities also cover exam organizing, paper correcting, collecting and analysing of statistics, and results reporting. The check-up papers are prepared by the county and city education departments according to the examination norms.

Average Number of Pupils in Each Class at the Junior Secondary Level

Year	*Number of Classes*	*Number of Students*
1993	826,332	49.4
1994	857,898	50.3
1995	899,355	51.8

At present there are five types of *vocational schools* in China: higher education vocational schools (86); specialised secondary schools (4,049); schools for skilled workers (4,507); senior secondary vocational schools (8,612); and junior secondary vocational schools (1,535). Among them, the secondary technical and vocational schools (specialized secondary schools, skilled workers' schools and senior secondary schools) are the main stream of vocational education and their total number is 17,168. In addition, there are more than 2,000 pre-service training centres throughout the country.

The specialties in vocational schools cover the main positions and jobs in the first, second and third industries such as: engineering, agriculture, forestry, health and medicine, finance, management, politics, arts, physical education and others. There are 186 and 518 specialties in higher education vocational schools and specialised secondary schools, respectively. The number of specialties in skilled workers' schools and secondary vocational schools is over 3,000.

II GERMANY

Compulsory Schooling: It begins for all children at the age of six and usually lasts nine years of full-time schooling (ten years in Berlin)

Educational Structure

Preschool Education: It is provided by institutions catering to children between the ages of 3 and 6 years (mainly Kindergarten). Attendance is usually voluntary.

Primary Education: It covers grades 1 to 4, or grades 1 to 6 in Berlin. All children in Germany attend the primary school as part of their compulsory schooling between the ages of 6 and 10 years.

Secondary Education: It breaks down into lower secondary level—Secondary level I, which comprises the courses of education from grades 5 to 10 or 7 to 10 of school, and Upper Secondary level—Secondary level II which comprises all the courses of education that build on the foundations laid in lower secondary. Lower Secondary level covers the age group of pupils 10-16 years and Upper Secondary level the pupils between 16 and 19 years old. Both age groups are required to attend school.

Length of School Year: In primary schools, the number of weekly periods increase from 17-23 in the first grade to 23-27 in grade four depending upon the particular province. Each period is 45 minutes. At lower secondary level, pupils generally have 28 weekly periods in compulsory and optional subjects in grades 5 and 6 of all types of schools and 30 periods in grades 7 to 10. At upper secondary level as well, there are around 30 periods of which 20 are spent on compulsory subjects and 10 on optional subjects.

Notes

Diagram 4.1 of the basic structure of the education system. Lower secondary education (secondary level I) is portrayed in line with the distribution of the school population in 1994 taken as a national average: *Hauptschule* 25,6%, *Realschule* 26,5%, *Gymnasium* 31,5%, *Integrierte Gesamtschule* 9,0%. Unlike

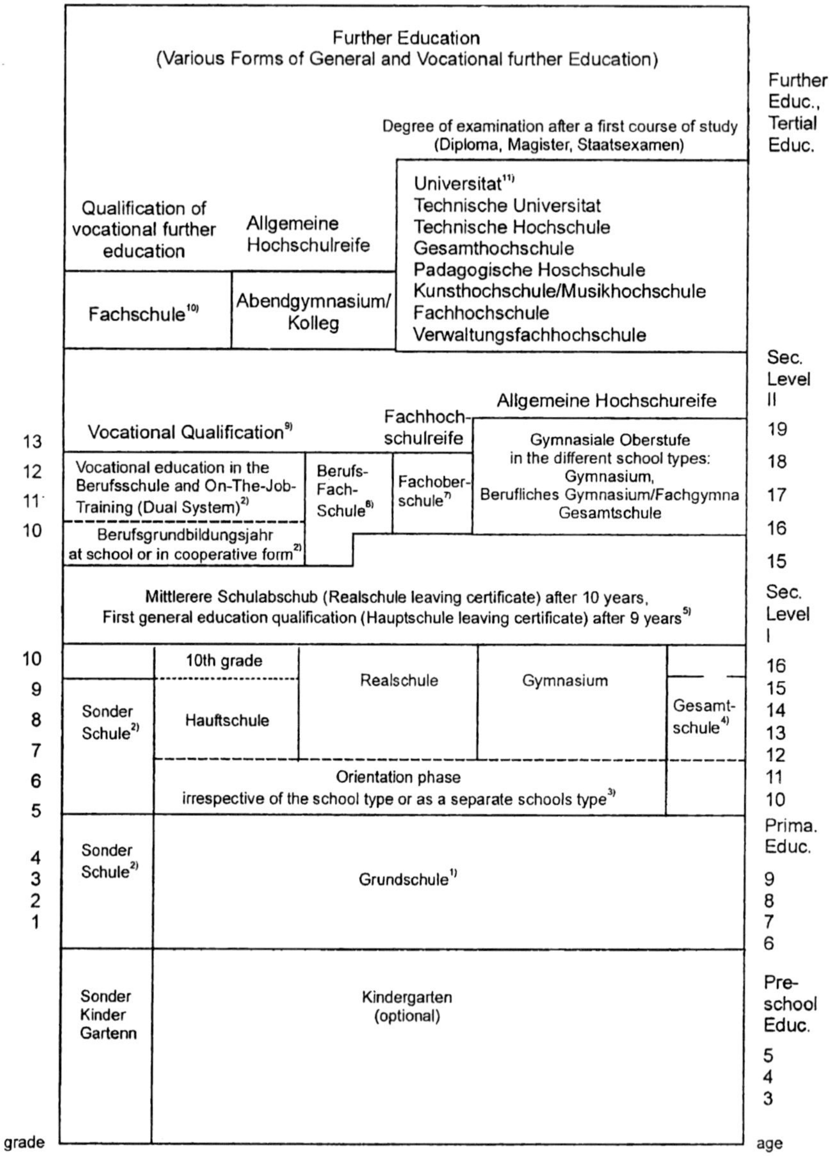

Fig. 4.1: Educational Structure

the basic structure presented here, the provision of schools at secondary level 1—with the exception of *Sonderschulen*—varying in the different Lander includes:

- separate schools which prepare pupils for one of the three school-leaving qualifications, namely *Hauptschule, Realschule* or *Gymnasium* and offered in most Lander;
- unified schools which prepare pupils for any one of the three school-leaving qualifications. *Hauptschule, Realschule* and *Gymnasium* are

either united into a single administrative unit with pupils being streamed according to their intended final qualification *(kooperative Gesamtschule, Schukentrum)* or the three school types are united administratively and educationally with pupils being taught in mixed-ability groups while setting is gradually phased in for some subjects *{Integrierte Gesamtschule);*

- unified schools which prepare pupils for one of two leaving certificates *{Hauptschule* and *Realschule)* with various names in the different Lander, such as *Mittelschule* (Sachsen), *Regelschule* (Thuringen), *Sekundarschule* (Sachsen-Anhalt, Saarland), *Integrierte Haupt-und Realschule* (Hamburg), *Verbundene Hauptund Realschule* (Hessenl and *Recionale Schule* (Rheinland-Pfalz).

The ability of pupils to transfer between school types and the recognition of school-leaving qualifications is basically guaranteed if the preconditions agreed between the Lander are fulfilled. The duration of full-time compulsory education (compulsory general education) is 9 years (10 years in four of the Lander) and the subsequent period of part-time compulsory education (compulsory vocational education) is 3 years.

1. In some Lander special types of transition from pre-school to primary education *{Vorklassen, Schulkindergarten)* exist. In Berlin and Brandenburg the primary school comprises 6 grades.
2. The disabled attend special forms of general-education and vocational school types (in some cases integrated with non-handicapped pupils) depending on the type of disability in question. Designation of schools varies according to the law of each Land.
3. Irrespective of school type, grades 5 and 6 constitute a phase of particular support, supervision and orientation with regard to the pupil's future educational path and its particular focusses. In some Lander, the orientation stage *(Orientierungsstufe)* is organised as a separate organisational unit independent of the standard school types.
4. The provision of comprehensive schools *{Gesamtschulen)* varies in accordance with the respective educational laws of the Lander.
5. The general education qualifications that may be obtained after grades 9 and 10 carry particular designations in some Lander. These certificates can also be obtained in evening classes.
6. Admission to the *Gymnasiale Oberstuie* requires a formal entrance qualification which can generally be obtained after grade 10. Sachsen-Anhalt and Thuringen have ruled that the formal entrance qualification can be awarded after grade 9 at the *Gymnasium. The Allgemeine Hochschulreife* can generally be obtained after the successful completion of 13 school years, i.e. consecutive grades. In four Lander (Sachsen, Sachsen Anhalt, Thuringen, Mecklenburg-Vorpommern), *the Allgemeine Hochschulreife* can, for a transitional period, be acquired after 12 years of schooling.
7. The *Fachoberschule* is a school type lasting two years (11th and 12th grades) which takes pupils who have completed *the Realschule* and which qualifies them for higher education *Fachhochschulreife.* Pupils

who have successfully completed the *Realschule* and have been through initial vocational training can also enter the *Fachoberschule* directly in the 12th grade. Alternative routes for acquiring the *Fachhochschulreife* are e.g. the *Berufsfachschule* and *Fachschule.*

8. Full-time vocational schools differing in terms of entrance requirements, duration and leaving certificate. Certain two-year *Beruisfachschulen* requiring a *Realschule* certificate for admission lead to a state-recognised examination as technical assistant. One-year courses at *Beruisfachschulen* offer basic vocational training.
9. Extension courses are offered to enable pupils to acquire qualifications equivalent to the *Hauptschule* and *Realschule* leaving certificates.
10. *Fachschulen* are schools at the upper level of secondary education offering courses of between 1 and 3 years duration.
11. Including institutions of higher education offering courses in particular disciplines at university level (e.g., theology, philosophy, medicine, administration, science, sport).

Glossary

Abendgymnasium: General secondary night school for employed adults providing university entrance qualification.

Allgemeine Hochschulreife: Qualification obtained as a rule by taking a final examination *(Abitur-prulung)* after 13 years of schooling, including upper secondary education, normally at a *Gymnasium.* The holder has in general the right to study at all institutions or higher education without restrictions with regard to subject areas.

Berufliches Gymnasium: Upper level of the *Gymnasium* with a career-oriented or technical bias (grades 11 to 13) which leads to a general university entrance qualification. Career oriented-subject areas and focusses such as economics and engineering are added to the subjects otherwise available at the general education *Gymnasium.*

Berufsfachschule: Full-time vocational school at the upper level of secondary education that prepares students for jobs or provides them with vocational training promoting at the same time general education. Depending on the objective of training, the requirements for admission *(Hauptschule* or *Realschule* certificate) and the period of training vary from 1 year to 3 years.

Berufsgrundbildungsjahr: Basic vocational training year as the first stage of vocational training either in a full-time school or in the cooperative form of part-time school and on-the job training (dual system).

Berufsschule: Part-time vocational school at the upper level of secondary education providing general and vocational education for pupils in initial vocational training, special attention is paid to the requirements of training in the dual system (part-time school and on-the job training).

Fachhochschule: Institution of higher education offering degree programmes, particularly in engineering, economics, administration, social work, agriculture and design. The preparation for employment on the basis of applications-oriented teaching and research is the specific training purpose of the *Fachhochschulen.*

Fachoberschule: Technical secondary school (grades 11 to 12) specializing in various areas and providing access to *Fachhochschulen.*

Fachschule: Technical school providing advanced vocational training.

Gesamthochschule-Universitat: Institution of higher education existing in two Lander combining functions of the universities, *Fachhochschulen* and, in some cases, colleges of art and music. The institution offers courses of study of varying duration and leading to different degrees.

Gesamtschule: Comprehensive school existing in two forms: the cooperative comprehensive school combines the schools of the traditional tripartite system under one roof and harmonizes the curricula in order to facilitate the transfer of pupils between the different coexisting types; the integrated comprehensive school admits all pupils of a certain age without differentiating between the traditional school types. A number of the integrated comprehensive schools also have the upper secondary level, organized as the *Gymnasiale Oberstufe.*

Grundschule: Primary school marks the beginning of compulsory education, to which all children go once they have reached the age of six (in general grades 1-4). The aim of the primary school is to provide its pupils with the basis for their subsequent education at the lower level of secondary education.

Gymnasiaie Oberstufe: Upper level of *Gymnasium* (normally grades 11, 12, 13) preparing for the final examination *(Abiturprufung)* and the general university entrance qualification.

Gymnasium: Secondary school (normally grades 5 to 13) providing intensified general education and conferring at the upper level the general university entrance qualification. See also *Gymnasiale Oberstuie.*

Hauptschule: Secondary school—lower level, normally grades 5 to 9—providing fundamental general education. The leaving certificate is primarily used as a basis for vocational training in the dual system. In most Lander where compulsory education covers 9 grades, pupils have the option of attending a voluntary tenth grade at the *Hauptschule* to acquire a further qualification.

Kolleg: Institution of general education offering day school courses for adults with work experience.

Realschule: Secondary school—lower level, normally grades 5-10, providing extended general education.

Curriculum at the Primary Stage

Lessons at the primary school initially focus on reading, writing and arithmetic. Teaching takes place both in lessons concentrating on a specific subject or area and in cross-disciplinary classes. As a rule, subjects include: German, mathematics, *Sachunterricht,* art, music, sport and, in most Lander, religious instruction. Several areas, especially German, *Sachunterricht,* drama, music, art and handicrafts, are often brought together to produce lively and varied work on topic focusses or lesson units.

As for a first encounter with foreign languages at primary school age the Lander have developed various approaches. Foreign language teaching in grades 3 and 4 in the *Grundschule* is understood as a distinct course with its own specific didactic methods. It is characterised by play-based learning methods which permit each individual child to make his or her own progress.

Primary Education. Average Number of Class Hours Per Year in Each Grade

grade 1	561 hours
grade 2	613 hours
grade 3	689 hours
grade 4	712 hours

Prescribed Time Allocated to Each teaching Subject in Each Grade (on average for all Lander

Grade1	▪ German:	152 hours per year
	▪ Mathematics:	129 hours per year
	▪ Artistic Activities:	89 hours per year
	▪ Sport:	67 hours per year
	▪ Religion/Ethics:	53 hours per year
	▪ Social and Natural Sciences:	59 hours per year
	▪ Others:	12 hours per year
Grade 2	▪ German:	147 hours per year
	▪ Mathematics:	135 hours per year
	▪ Artistic Activities:	102 hours per year
	▪ Sport:	75 hours per year
	▪ Religion/Ethics:	56 hours per year
	▪ Social and Natural Sciences:	81 hours per year
	▪ Others:	17 hours per year
Grade 3	▪ German:	162 hours per year
	▪ Mathematics:	138 hours per year
	▪ Artistic Activities:	120 hours per year
	▪ Sport:	85 hours per year
	▪ Religion/Ethics:	62 hours per year
	▪ Social and Natural Sciences:	102 hours per year
	▪ Others:	20 hours per year
Grade 4	▪ German:	160 hours per year
	▪ Mathematics:	135 hours per year
	▪ Artistic Activities:	125 hours per year
	▪ Sport:	85 hours per year
	▪ Religion/Ethics:	62 hours per year
	▪ Social and Natural Sciences:	120 hours per year
	▪ Others:	25 hours per year

Alternative forms of learning in the *Grundschule* are contributing towards a new understanding of what is conducive to learning, and of assessing pupils' performance. The focus has shifted to encouraging each individual pupil to achieve all that he or she is capable of—guided by the learning requirements for the respective school grade. In order to do this, it is necessary to monitor the individual development and performance of each pupil on a constant basis, as well as their working and social behaviour, and assess these factors comprehensively. Educational progress is examined by constant monitoring of the learning processes and by the use of oral and written controls. In primary grades 1 and 2, the focus is on direct observation of the pupils. In grade 3, pupils also begin to be familiarised with written class tests in certain subjects (especially German, mathematics and *Sachunterrichi).* Assessment is always based on syllabus requirements and the knowledge, abilities and skills acquired in class. Assessment is carried out by the teacher responsible for lessons, who is responsible educationally for his or her decision. In the first two grades of primary school this assessment takes the form of a report at the end of the school year describing in detail a pupil's progress, strengths and weaknesses in the various fields of learning. At the end of the second grade, or sometimes later, pupils receive their first certificates with marks placing the individual pupil's performance more in the context of the group and enabling a comparative assessment. There is currently a trend towards learning processes and performance being assessed in the form of reports in grades 3 and 4 as well.

There is no leaving examination at the end of primary school, and pupils are not awarded a school-leaving certificate. However, at the end of grade 4 (or grade 6) pupils do receive a report for that year. The transition from primary school to one of the secondary school types is regulated differently according to Land law. The vote of the school which the pupil is leaving is either taken as a basis for the decision or guidance in the decision concerning the pupil's future school career. In all cases, this is combined with detailed consultations with the parents. The final decision is taken either by the parents or by the school or by the school supervisory authority.

Secondary Education

General education schools in secondary level I (lower secondary) build on the work of the *Grundschule,* which is compulsory for all pupils. Most Lander offer the *Hauptschule, Realschule, Gymnasium* and *Gesamtschule.* Some Lander have also begun to offer new school types in recent years. These are given various names in the different Lander and combine the educational paths offered in the *Hauptschule* and *Realschule* in one organisational and educational unit; they include the *Mittelschule* (Sachsen), the *Regelschule* (Thuringen), the *Enveiterte Realschule* (Saarland), the *Sekundarschule* (Saarland, Sachsen-Anhalt), the *Integrierte Haupt- und Realschule* (Hamburg), the *Verbundene Haupt-und Realschule* (Hessen) and the *Regionale Schule* (Rheinland-Pfalz).

The types of schools and educational paths at secondary level I are based on the idea of providing all pupils with a basic general education, combined with an element of individual specialisation in line with support and advancement of the pupil according to his/her performance and interests. Irrespective of school type, grades 5 and 6 constitute a phase of particular support, supervision and orientation with regard to the pupil's future educational path and its particular focuses. This orientation stage in grades 5 and 6 is also organised as an educational stage independent of the different school types in some Lander. From grade 7 onwards, the types of schools and educational paths increasingly differ in terms of the subjects they offer, their requirements with regard to individual specialisation and the leaving qualification they aim at. As pupils progress through the grades, the shaping of the educational path and ensuring that this takes on a qualification-related form is accorded increasing importance with respect to the development of each pupil's individual school career.

The agreement reached on December 3, 1993, amended on September 27, 1996, by the Standing Conference of the Ministers of Education and Cultural Affairs of the Lander, concerning the types of schools and courses of education in lower secondary level, lays down a framework schedule for grades 5-9/10, requiring certain core subjects in every type of school and course of education: German, mathematics, one foreign language, natural and social sciences. Music, art and sport, at the very least, have to be among the other compulsory or elective subjects offered. A second foreign language is compulsory at *Gymnasium* in grades 7-10, and may be offered as an elective course at other types of schools. An introduction to the professional and working world is a compulsory component of every course of education and is provided either in a special subject such as *Arbeitslehre* (work orientation) or as part of the material covered in other subjects. Religious education is subject to the respective regulations in each Land, according to which religion is a standard subject in nearly every Land.

The development of syllabi for secondary education, as well as for the primary school, are the responsibility of the Ministries of Education and Cultural Affairs in the Lander.

The education and training establishments for 16 to 19-year-olds at *upper secondary level* include general education schools, full-time vocational schools, as well as training companies and part-time vocational schools as part of the dual training system.

The *Gymnasiale Oberstufe* (upper level of the *Gymnasium)* covers grades 11 to 13 (in four Lander, grades 10-12 or 11 and 12). After a transitional period, pupils are no longer taught in the class unit but follow courses in their chosen subjects. Although pupils are still required to take certain subjects or subject combinations; they now have extensive scope for individual specialisation with a wider range of subjects to choose from. Related subjects are grouped together into three main areas: languages, literature and the arts; social sciences; mathematics, natural sciences and technology. Every single pupil is required to study subjects from each of these three areas right up to the completion of the upper level of the *Gymnasium,* including *Abitur* examinations. Religious education and sport are also compulsory.

III JAPAN

Curriculum Organisation

Pre-primary Education

Kindergartens are non-compulsory schools intended to help infants develop their minds and bodies by providing them with an appropriate educative

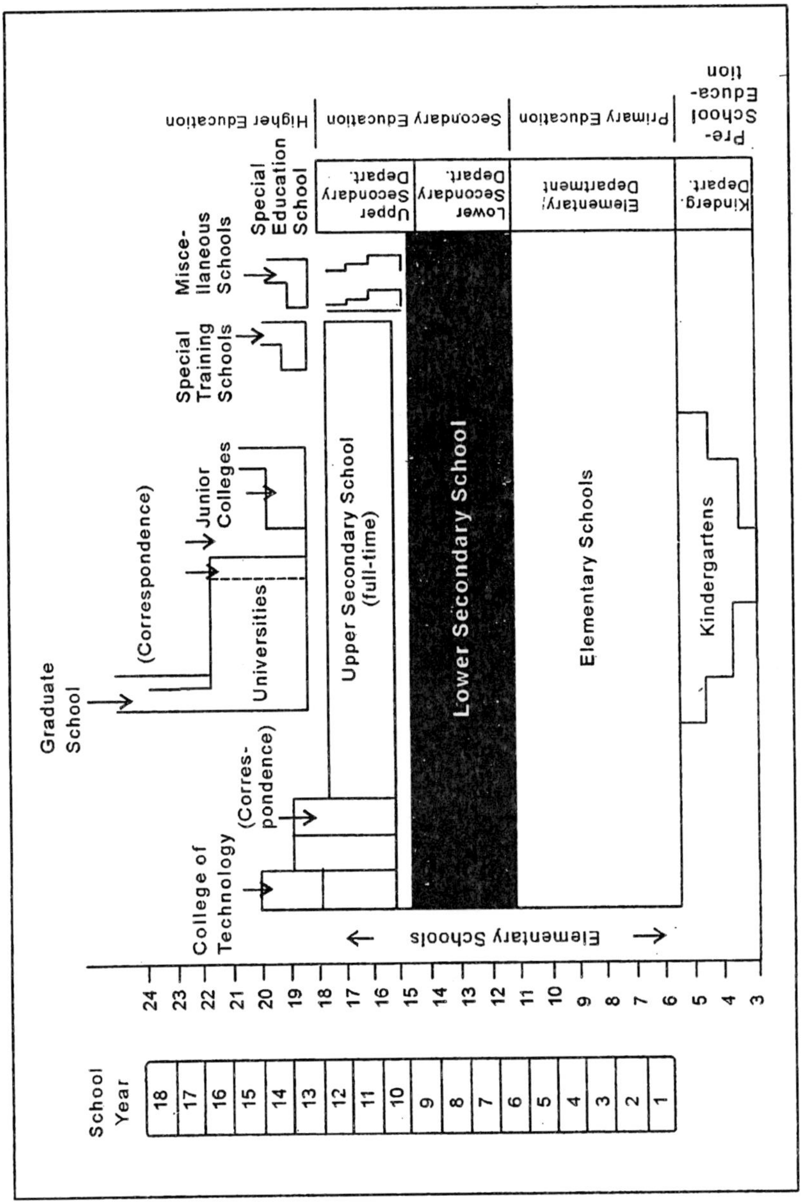

Fig.: Educational Structure in Japan

environment. The Course of Study for Kindergartens (put into effect in 1990) sets forth specific objectives to be achieved by children by the end of a kindergarten course with regard to their emotions, willingness and attitudes, as well as the specific content to be taught to achieve each objective. These objectives and corresponding content are set forth in each of the five aspects of children's development: health, human relations, environment, language, and expression. All objectives and related content are to be achieved through children's play and other activities.

It is also specified that the standard number of daily school hours should be four and that the number of school weeks per year should be not less than 39.

Primary Education

The elementary school is intended to provide children with elementary general education suited to the relevant stages of their mental and physical development.

The following table presents the subjects to be taught in elementary schools, as well as the national standard number of yearly school hours to be devoted to each subject, as specified in the current Course of Study, which was put into effect in the school year 1992. Each school is expected to develop its activities for teaching respective subjects with due regard to the provisions of the Course of Study.

In September 1992, a five-day school week began to be introduced once every month, and in April 1996 the five-day week began to be implemented twice every month. The five-day school week is intended to contribute to an overall review of the educational functions of the school, the home and the community. It is also aimed at bringing about the sound character formation of children.

Standard Number of Yearly School Hours(1) in Elementary Schools(1)

	1st Year	*2nd Year*	*3rd Year*	*4th Year*	*5th Year*	*6th Year*
Japanese language	306	315	280	280	210	210
Social Studies	–	–	105	105	105	105
Arithmetic	136	175	175	175	175	175
Science	–	–	105	105	105	105
Life environmental studies	102	105	–	–	–	–
Music	68	70	70	70	70	70
Drawing and Handicrafts	68	70	70	70	70	70
Homemaking	–	–	–	–	70	70
Physical education	102	105	105	105	105	105
Moral education(2)	34	35	35	35	35	35
Special activities(3)	34	35	35	70	70	70
Total	**850**	**910**	**980**	**1,015**	**1,015**	**1,015**

1. One school hour is defined as a class period of 45 minutes.
2. In private elementary school, a part or all of the school hours for moral education may be replaced by religious education.

3. "Special activities" include "class activities" (including guidance on school lunch), pupils' councils, club activities, and "school events" (e.g., ceremonial events, sports events, school excursions, and community services). In this table, however, the number of hours for special activities includes that for "class activities" (other than guidance on school lunch) and club activities only.

The enrolment ratio for compulsory schools in Japan has always been nearly 100 per cent, and grade-to-grade promotion is practically automatic.

Secondary Education

The lower secondary school aims to provide children between the ages of 12 and 15 years with general secondary education suited to the level of their mental and physical development, based on the education given in the elementary school.

The following table presents the subjects to be taught in lower secondary schools, as well as the national standard number of yearly school hours to be devoted to each subject, as specified in the current Courses of Study, which was put into effect in the school year 1993.

Standard Number of Yearly School Hours in Lower Secondary Schools[1]

Subjects	*1st Year*	*2nd Year*	*3rd Year*
Japanese language	175	140	140
Social Studies	140	140	70/105
Mathematics	105	140	140
Science	105	105	105/140
Music	70	35/70	35
Fine Arts	70	35/70	35
Health and Physical education	105	105	105/140
Industrial Arts and Homemaking	70	70	70/105
Moral education[2]	35	35	35
Special activities[3]	35/70	35/70	35/70
Elective subjects, etc.[4]	105/140	105/210	140/280
Total	**1,050**	**1,050**	**1,050**

1. One school hour is defined as a class period of fifty minutes.
2. In private lower secondary school, a part or all of the school hours for moral education may be replaced by religious education.
3. "Special activities" include "class activities" (including guidance on school lunch), pupils' councils, club activities, and "school events". In this table, however, the number of hours for special activities includes that for "class activities" (other than guidance on school lunch) and club activities only.
4. The number of school hours for elective subjects shall be allotted to elective subjects and may be allotted to additional hours of Special Activities. Regarding elective subjects, the standard school hours of Foreign Language shall be 105 to 140 in each year, and the standard school hours of other subjects are as prescribed in the Course of Study.

In 1995, the total number of lower secondary schools was 11,274 with 4,570,390 students enrolled and 271,020 teachers. The average pupil-teacher ratio was 16.9:1. In the same year, 96.7 per cent of students completing lower secondary courses entered upper secondary schools and colleges of technology.

Upper secondary schools may offer a number of elective subjects at their discretion, so that the curriculum in each school may be adapted to the aim of the courses offered in the school and to the differing abilities, aptitudes and future prospects of individuals, and so that students may choose appropriate subjects suited to their own abilities, aptitudes and future prospects. In 1995, 74.2 per cent of upper secondary school students were enrolled in general academic courses, and the rest in vocational and other specialised courses.

The revised Course of Study for upper secondary schools became effectively progressive from 1994 (specifically, it took effect in 1994 for the first year of the upper secondary school, in 1995 for the second year, and 1996 for the third year).

The Course of Study specifies the subjects both in general education and in specialised education, as well as the objectives and the standard content of teaching in each subject. In addition, it lays down the standard number of credits to be acquired for most of the general education subjects.

General Education Subjects in Upper Secondary Schools

1. Japanese Language
2. Geography and History
3. Civics
4. Mathematics
5. Science
6. Health and Physical Education
7. Art
8. Foreign Languages (not compulsory
9. Home Economics

List of Specialised Subjects in Secondary Schools

1. Home Economics
2. Agriculture
3. Industry (Including Information Technology)
4. Business
5. Fisheries
6. Nursing
7. Mathematical Science
8. Physical Education
9. Music
10. Art
11. English
12. Foreign Languages

Each school organises its own curriculum in accordance with the provisions of the relevant statutes and courses of study, taking into account the actual circumstances of the locality in which it operates as well as the characteristics of children enrolled and the stage of their mental and physical development.

Evaluation and Examination

There is no external examination in Japan. Promotion and certification of completion are made on the basis of internal assessment. Certificate of graduation (from the Upper Secondary School) is issued by the individual school principal.

IV UNITED KINGDOM

Structure and Organisation of the Education System

Preschool Education: It is available for ages 2 to 4/5 through playgroups and nursery schools.

Compulsory Education: It begins at 5 in England, Wales and Scotland and 4 in Northern Ireland and ends at 16, though many pupils stay on beyond the minimum leaving age.

Curriculum Organisation

Primary Education

In 1988 the National Curriculum was introduced into schools in **England** and **Wales,** making for a broader, more balanced and coherent schooling system. The curriculum sets out what pupils should study, what they should be taught and the standards that they should achieve, the National Curriculum is statutory in England and Wales. It accounts for approximately 80 per cent of a pupil's time in school, the remaining 20 per cent being left to the discretion of the school itself. It defines four key stages and ten statutory subjects:

- key stage 1; up to age 7;
- key stage 2: seven to 11;
- key stage 3: 11 to 14 (pre-GCSE);
- key stage 4: 14 to 16 (preparation for GCSE and equivalent vocational qualifications).

Key stages one and two are the primary phase. Key stages three and four constitute the secondary phase. There are three "core" subjects, which are: English, mathematics and science (in Wales, Welsh is a core subject in Welsh-speaking schools). There are seven other "foundation" subjects which are: technology, history, geography, music, art, physical education and a modern foreign language (in Wales, Welsh is a foundation subject in non-Welsh speaking schools).

All children in key stages one to three must study the first nine of these subjects. In key stage three, they must also study a modern foreign language. Pupils aged 14 to 16 must study the core subjects, technology, a modern foreign language and physical education, plus either history or geography or short courses in both. All National Curriculum and assessment matters are overseen by two independent statutory bodies: The School Curriculum and Assessment Authority (SCAA) in England; and The Curriculum and Assessment Authority for Wales.

In **Scotland,** the curriculum is not determined by statute or legislation, but by advice from the Scottish Office Education and Industry Department

(SOEID). The aim of the curriculum is to provide breadth, balance, coherence and progression and, to attain this, the curriculum has been divided into a number of broad curricular areas, set in an appropriate balance. Progression through the curriculum is integrated with assessment as it is recognised that pupils learn at different rates. The curricular areas are: language, mathematics, environmental studies, expressive arts, religious, moral and social education. The Scottish Consultative Council on the Curriculum (SCCC) advises the Secretary of State on curriculum development.

In general terms, the purpose of primary schooling is to provide a broad basic education. Through reading, writing and counting, it introduces children to ways of examining and understanding their environment. It helps them to express themselves through art, music, and physical activity, and develops their awareness of religious, moral and social values.

The class teacher is expected to be able to teach all aspects of the curriculum, but in practice may well receive support from visiting teachers of art, drama, music and physical education. All primary school classes contain both boys and girls and cover the full range of abilities, there is no selection or streaming by ability. The approach to teaching reflects this with a mixture of whole-class, group and individual pupil techniques. The use of group methods is particularly characteristic and trains the pupils to work co-operatively as well as independently, following a programme set out by the class teacher. Curriculum integration is also an important approach followed in primary schools; linking different curricular areas or subjects to each other by means of project work, generally of an environmental studies nature. All pupils are admitted to secondary education after completing seven years of primary education.

In **Northern Ireland,** pupils study a common curriculum made up of religious education and six broad areas of study: English, mathematics, science and technology, creative and expressive studies, language studies (for Irish-medium schools). The school curriculum also contains six compulsory cross-curricular themes: education for mutual understanding, cultural heritage, health education, information technology, economic awareness (in secondary schools), careers education (in secondary schools). The Northern Ireland Council for Curriculum, Examinations and Assessment is responsible for curriculum development and assessment.

The most common age for pupils to transfer from state primary to state secondary schools in the UK is 11 (12 in Scotland). No form of examination has to be undertaken in order for them to do so. Entrance to independent secondary schools is by way of a Common Entrance Examination, taken at the ages of 11, 12 or 13. The introduction of the National Curriculum allowed the implementation in England and Wales of Standard Assessment Tasks (SATs), which mean that pupils are assessed at various stages throughout their compulsory education. The ages for assessment are 7, 11 and 14 years. SATs are used as a form of national external testing, to complement teachers' own assessments and schools' internal tests and examinations. They enable each pupil's progress to be measured against national standards, providing pupils, parents and teachers with a measurable achievement. In Northern Ireland, several schools are currently piloting a similar scheme, although their main focus is on teacher assessment.

In **England** and **Wales,** towards the end of the first three key stages, there is statutory assessment through national tests and teacher assessment. Results are published for each child, each school and the national averages for comparison purposes. In **Scotland,** national tests in language and mathematics were developed in 1990 by the Scottish Examinations Board for pupils aged 5 to 14 in support of the Government's 5-14 Development Programme. The tests are arranged at five levels of difficulty and take the form of a large bank of test units from which teachers may choose test materials to fit their own teaching programmes and contexts In **Northern Ireland,** there is statutory assessment at key stages 1 and 2 in English, mathematics and Irish (in Irish-medium schools). Pupils study for the same range of public examinations as their counterparts in England and Wales.

Secondary and Further Education

In **England** and **Wales,** secondary school usually admit pupils aged 11 years, but in areas where three-tier systems exist, pupils may transfer from middle schools at 12 or 13 years or from junior high schools at 14 years. Schools may be organised in a number of ways, including those that the full secondary school age range from 11 to 18; middle schools whose pupils move on to senior comprehensive schools at 12, 13 or 14, leaving at 16 or 18; and schools with an age range of 11 or 12 to 16 combined with a sixth form or a tertiary college for pupils over 16. In England, over 90 per cent of secondary pupils attend comprehensive schools, which admit pupils without reference to ability or aptitude, and provide a wide range of secondary education for all or most of the children of a district. Most other children receive secondary education in grammar or secondary modern schools, to which they are allocated on the basis of their performance in selection tests, taken at the age of 11: *grammar schools* provide a mainly academic course for selected pupils from the age of 11 to 18 or 19; *secondary modern schools* provide a general education up to the minimum school-leaving age of 16, although their pupils can stay on beyond that age and are tending to do so in increasing numbers.

In addition, the Education Reform Act 1988 provided for the setting up of *City Technology Colleges (CTCs)* and *City Technology Colleges of the Arts (CTCAs),* in order to extend choice of school locally, and to pioneer new approaches to delivery of the curriculum. They are required to offer free education to pupils of all abilities accepted within their catchments areas. They are funded by central government directly and by industrial sponsors. These new schools have to teach all the core and foundation subjects of the national curriculum to all pupils. *CTCs,* however, put considerable emphasis on science and technology across the curriculum, while *CTCAs* will specialise in arts, technology, film, video and a range of technical skills related to the arts world.

Young people over the age of 16 have a number of education and training options open to them. They may stay on in sixth form of their school or they may transfer to a *Sixth-form college, a tertiary college* or a *further education college,* depending on take system operated in the area they live in. (The three latter types of establishment offer a range of academic and vocational courses for young people over the age of 16. There are differences in the range and number of courses available and in the regulations which govern them. *Sixth-form colleges* are part of the schools' system, while *tertiary colleges* are part of the further education system. Young people may choose to join the Government-backed *Youth Training Scheme.*

Further education is deemed as full-time or part-time education after statutory school age—normally in a local college-leading to a qualification no higher than the standard of *GCE 'A' level* (Advanced level of the General Certificate of Education, the main external examination offered in schools at upper secondary level).

In **Scotland** at the end of four years of lower secondary education pupils are eligible to receive the *Scottish Certificate of Education,* Standard Grade. This certificate, intended to be attainable by all pupils, is gained by examination with an element of assessment within the school itself. Pupils in S3 and S4 can also take modules from the catalogue of the Scottish Vocational Education Council (SCOTVEC), and by completing them successfully receive credit towards the National Certificate which is a "non-advanced" vocational qualification.

The aim of upper secondary school education (16-18 years) is to equip pupils to profit from vocational training and higher education, which is the next stage in their education. All 16 year olds must be given two weeks of work experience in local firms as part of their general pre-vocational training. Many pupils will continue to study the same subjects studied in previous years, but the level of study will be higher and the number of subjects studied for the Higher Grade of the Scottish Certificate of Education is likely to be no more than five. The broad range remains with freedom of choice being greater than in previous years.

The most significant curricular difference is the offer of a wide range of short, modular courses offered by SCOTVEC, as an alternative to those leading to the Higher Grade and Certificate of Sixth-Year Studies examinations organised by the Scottish Examination Board (SEB). Some schools will have pupils studying combinations of courses offered by both the SEB and SCOTVEC. A new broadly based qualification, the *General Scottish Vocational Qualification* (GSVQ), has been developed. It is aimed at the age range 16-19 in schools and further education.

The Higher Grade of the Scottish Certificate of Education, taken in the fifth year of secondary education at about age 17, is the target for many school pupils who aim to enter professions or to go into higher education. The examinations are externally set by the SEB using teachers and lecturers from higher education and mainly consist of written paper. The *Certificate of Sixth-year Studies* is available for pupils who obtain a pass at Higher Grade in their fifth year and wish to continue their studies for another year

V. UNITED STATES OF AMERICA

Education in the United States is organised on three principle levels: the elementary (including pre-school and primary), the secondary, and the post-secondary. Vocational training is available at the secondary and post-secondary levels. In addition, formal and informal programmes of adult education and continuing education are offered widely to U.S. citizens in virtually any part of the country and throughout their lives.

The Structure of Education in the United States

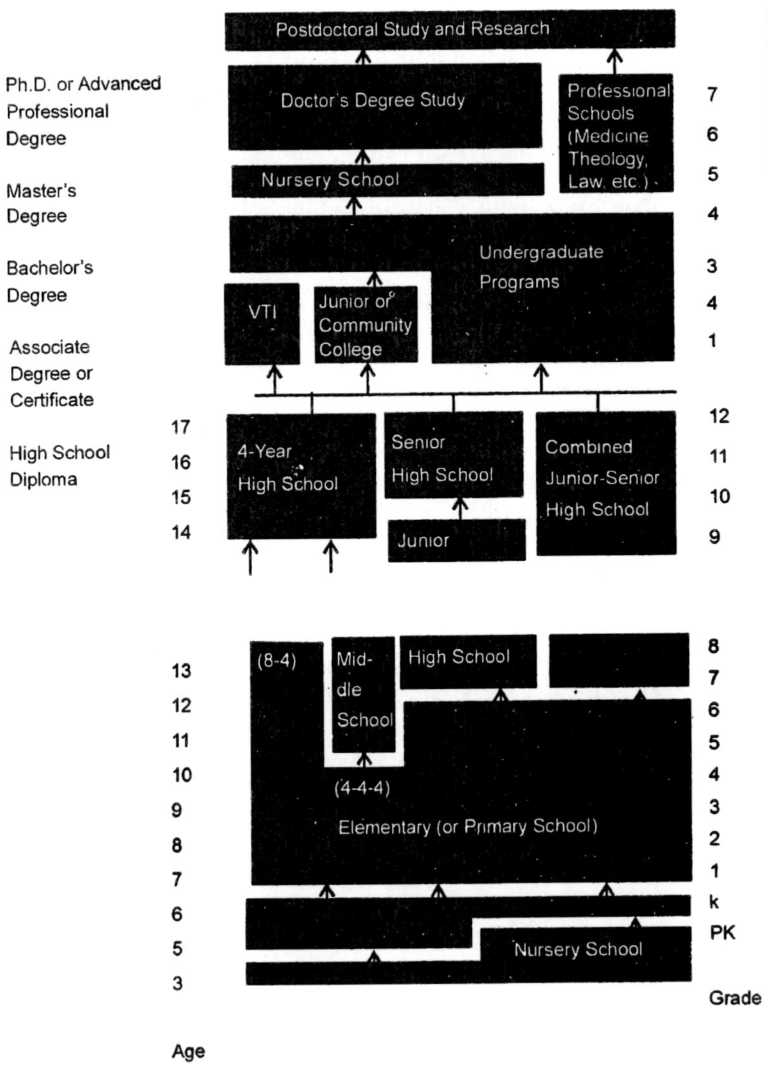

Education is compulsory, beginning at age seven in 21 states, at age six in 18 states, at age five in 9 states, and at age eight in two states (data refer to 1996). Usually a person is required to attend school until age 16. Because of the different State laws governing the structure and organisation of education programmes, length of compulsory school attendance may vary: nine years in 16 states; ten years in 19 states; eleven years in seven states; twelve years in six states; and 13 years in two states (data refer to 1996). Schooling is free, through completion of secondary school (grade 12) for those who attend public schools.

Primary Education

Although primary education may consist of six or eight grades, the six-grade school is most common. The main purpose of primary school is the general development of children from 6 to 12 or 14 years of age (depending on whether the school-is a six-or eight year elementary school).

Secondary education begins at grade 7 or grade 9, depending on whether elementary education in the system extends through grade 6 or grade 8. In some systems, junior high school follows elementary school, and includes grades 7 and 8 or 7 through 9, followed by high school, which can include grades 9-12 or 10-12. At this level of education, students normally complete the 12th grade by ages 17 or 18.

By the end of grade 10, most students have decided whether they will follow a primarily academic programme leading to further education at the college level, a vocational training programme leading to employment or specialised post-secondary training, or a general programme combining elements of both the academic and the vocational programmes.

All secondary programmes lead to the high school diploma and in most school districts are offered in the same comprehensive institution. A comprehensive institution offers a combined curriculum like the general programme, allows students to transfer easily from one programme to another, and provides flexibility for students to develop individual schedules to meet their own personal goals. It is not unusual for a medium-sized comprehensive high school to offer 200 or more separate courses. A comprehensive high school also provides the opportunity for young people with different career interests, as well as diverse social and economic backgrounds to have regular contact with each other. However, in recent years many school districts have introduced *magnet schools,* which are designed to attract students from all over the school districts with a special interest in a particular area of study, such as science, the arts or languages. Thus, magnet schools, while retaining economic and cultural diversity, deliberately sacrifice some curricular variety in order to achieve a more concentrated academic focus.

Vocational education typically begins at the secondary level and continues through the second year of the post-secondary level. Vocational programmes are also designed to retrain and upgrade the skills of adult workers in order to keep them current with the changing needs of the market place. These programmes are usually grouped under the seven traditional headings of vocational education: agriculture, marketing and distribution, health occupations, occupational home economics, business and office occupations, technical education, and trade and industrial education.

Certain programmes, logically continue from the secondary to the post-secondary level. These include office occupations, marketing and distribution education, health occupations, and other non-technical programmes. Because of the academic foundation required at the secondary level, technical education usually begins with post-secondary schooling. However, some special-purpose high schools and large vocational/technical schools offer technical programmes at the secondary level. Generally, a two-year post-secondary programme is required for minimal competency in any of the physical sciences. If the post-secondary programme permits, at this point a student may choose to terminate his or her technical education and transfer credits to study at a four-year college or university. Thus, among institutions that offer technical programmes, there is a logical progression from sub-professional to professional technical occupations.

High school graduates who decide to continue their education may enter a technical or vocational institution, a two-year college, or a four-year college or university. A two-year college normally offers the first two years of a standard four-year college curriculum and a selection of terminal-vocational programmes. Academic courses completed at a two-year college are usually transferable for credit at a four-year college or university. A technical or vocational institution offers post-secondary technical training leading to a specific career.

An associate degree requires at least two years of college-level work, and a bachelor's degree normally can be earned in four years. At least one year beyond the bachelor's necessary for a master's degree, while a doctoral degree usually requires a minimum of three or four years beyond the bachelor's. Some institutions have post-doctoral programmes for advanced study, generally based on an individualised study or research plan.

Professional schools differ widely in admission requirements and in programme length. Medical students, for example, generally complete a four-year programme of premedical studies at a college or university before they can enter the four-year programme at a medical school. Law programmes normally require three years of course work beyond the bachelor's degree level.

Academic Year: Duration

On the primary and secondary levels, the academic year usually begins in September and continues through the first or second week in June, though some school districts prefer to begin and end the school year earlier. Most states require a school year of 180 school days. The school day usually lasts from 8:30 a.m. to 3:30 p.m.—six hours long, excluding recess and lunch periods. In most instances, and particularly at the secondary level, students are given assignments to complete in the afternoon or evening, after the official school day has ended. Most classes are taught in English. However, in schools where there is a high concentration of students whose first language is not English, courses are sometimes taught in a foreign language until students are sufficiently conversant in English to enter regular classes.

On the post-secondary level, the academic calendar is much more flexible. The norm for a full-time student is two semesters of 15-16 weeks each per academic year, but many institutions vary this pattern. Some, for example, adopt a trimester system, which divides the academic year into three segments of 15-16 weeks; and others adopt a quarter system, with the school year divided into four 11-week segments. In the latter two systems, the student normally does not attend school the entire year, but two out of three trimesters or three out of four quarters.

Instructional Hours Spent on Curriculum
(Grades 1 to 4—Primary Education)

State	*Length of School Week in Hours*	*Hours per Week Spent on Core Curriculum*	*Percent of Time Spent on Core Curriculum*	*Length of School Year in Days of Instruction*
1	2	3	4	5
Alabama	34.0	22.5	66.3	175
Alaska	32.2	21.3	67.2	180
Arizona	32.4	21.6	66.9	175
Arkansas	34.1	22.0	64.7	178
California	30.5	21.0	69.1	175
Colorado	33.1	23.1	71.5	172
Connecticut	30.9	22.2	72.0	180
Delaware	33.3	19.8	60.1	—
District of Columbia	32.4	19.8	60.1	180
Florida	31.1	21.4	69.1	180
Georgia	33.1	21.6	66.0	180
Hawaii	31.0	19.9	64.5	184
Idaho	30.4	21.9	73.4	180
Illinois	30.8	20.6	67.1	180
Indiana	32.7	22.6	69.1	180
Iowa	33.6	20.6	61.6	180
Kansas	33.0	21.9	67.6	186
Kentucky	33.2	22.8	69.4	175
Louisiana	33.1	23.1	70.0	175
Maine	30.8	21.1	68.8	175
Maryland	31.5	22.1	69.6	180
Massachussets	30.5	21.1	69.6	180
Michigan	30.6	21.3	69.5	180
Minnesota	32.2	19.8	61.8	—
Mississippi	34.7	24.9	72.7	180
Missouri	32.5	21.2	65.3	174
Montana	32.1	23.2	71.6	180
Nebraska	33.2	21.8	65.3	—
Nevada	31.1	22.5	72.2	180
New Hampshire	31.3	20.9	67.3	180

(Contd.)

(Contd.)

1	2	3	4	5
New Jersey	29.9	21.7	72.2	180
New Mexico	32.0	22.0	69.4	180
New York	31.3	22.2	71.5	180
North Carolina	32.1	21.5	66.3	180
North Dakota	31.5	21.2	67.6	173
Ohio	31.3	20.8	63.3	182
Oklahoma	32.5	20.8	64.3	180
Oregon	31.7	20.7	65.4	—
Pennsylvania	31.5	22.7	72.3	180
Rhode Island	30.0	22.5	76.1	180
South Carolina	33.2	21.2	63.9	180
South Dakota	33.3	21.9	66.1	175
Tennessee	33.9	22.8	67.6	180
Texas	35.3	23.2	66.3	187
Utah	31.9	21.7	67.7	180
Vermont	31.9	20.7	66.9	175
Virginia	31.9	21.5	67.6	180
Washington	31.6	20.6	65.3	180
West Virginia	33.3	23.8	71.5	180
Wisconsin	33.5	21.9	66.4	180
Wyoming	31.8	22.3	70.4	175
US average	**32.1**	**21.7**	**68.2**	**180**
American Samoa	—	—	—	180
Puerto Rico	—	—	—	180
Virgin Islands	—	—	—	180

VI. RUSSIAN FEDERATION

Basic Law on Education

The *Law on Education* adopted by the Parliament in 1992, set the basic foundations for a radical change of the educational system. The government adopted the *Typical Provision on Comprehensive Educational Establishments:* primary, basic, secondary comprehensive schools, *'lyceums'* and *gymnasia.*

Compulsory Schooling

Under the current legislation, education is free and compulsory for all children aged between 6 (or 7) and 15 years (the so-called basic secondary education, which includes primary and lower secondary education and usually lasts nine years

Educational Structure

Pre School Education: It is not compulsory and normally caters to children between the ages of 3 and 6 (or 7) years.

Primary Education: It is usually incorporated in the general education structure. It covers three to four years and most children enter primary school at the age of 7 (about 20 per cent at the age of 6, as they follow the eleven-year Secondary School course).

Secondary Education: It includes: basic secondary education (lower secondary), which lasts five years and completes the compulsory schooling cycle. Complete secondary education (two-year course following basic secondary education); initial vocational education (normally a three year course after basic secondary).

Upper Secondary Education is also provided in *gymnasia.*

Length of the School Year

The official length of the school year is 30 weeks in grade I of primary education and not less than 34 weeks in grades 2-11(12).

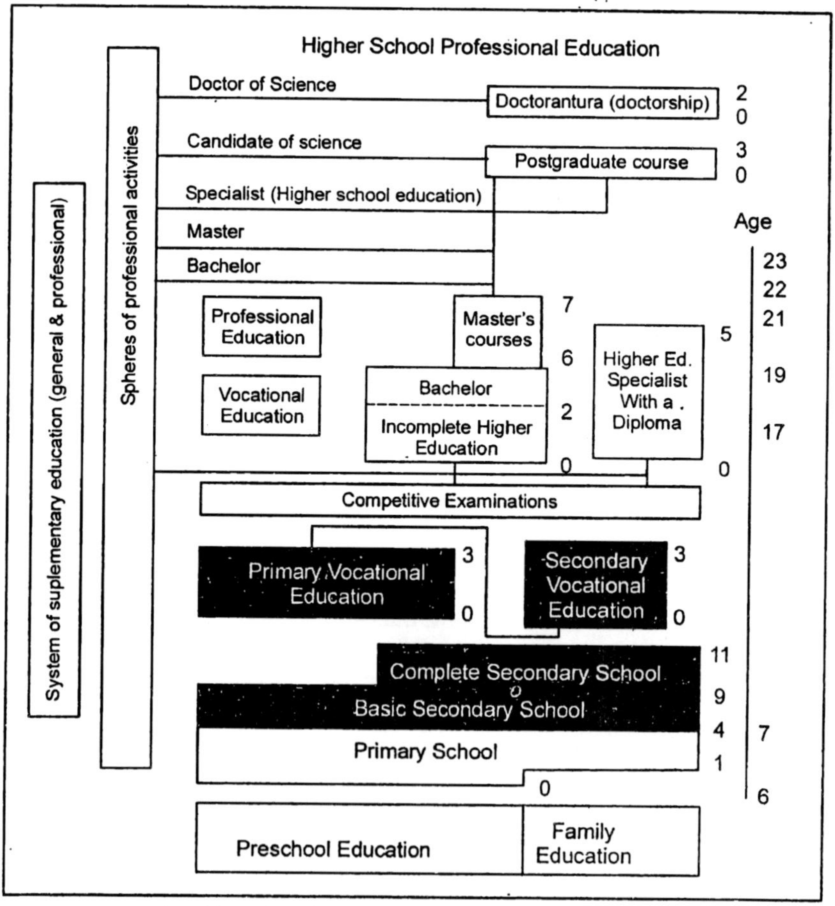

Fig.: The education system in the Russian Federation

Curriculum

The new *Basic Curriculum* introduced in 1993 contains the following programme:

The education system in the Russian Federation is organised as an uninterrupted continuity of levels or stages of education. General secondary education is the core of the system, and it includes: basic secondary schools, offering elementary and basic (lower) secondary education; and complete secondary schools, offering elementary, basic and complete (upper) secondary education.

Curriculum

The invariable part of the basic plan consists of the following educational areas:

Russian language; languages and literature; arts; social studies; natural sciences; mathematics; physical training; and technology. In the changeable part of the plan there are compulsory classes that learners choose and optional classes (not compulsory). A new course called "Environment" has been introduced. It helps learners to get adjusted to the social environment and to form the right attitude towards nature, along with providing them with elementary knowledge of democracy and human rights. Optional foreign language courses are also being introduced. Integrated courses such as "Introduction to the life of people and nations" or "Your Universe" have been created.

Study Plan of the First Three Years of General Secondary Education

Subject	*Average Weekly Hours*		
	1st grade	*2nd grade*	*3rd grade*
Russian language	4	4	4
Languages and Literature	4	3	2
Arts	2	2	2
Social studies	–	1	2
Natural sciences	–	1	2
Mathematics	5	5	5
Physical training	2	2	2
Technology	2	2	2
Additional compulsory classes	5	4	3
Total	**24**	**24**	**24**
Optional classes	2	3	3
Total	**26**	**27**	**27**

(each teaching period lasts 45 minutes).

Secondary Education

The main goals of general secondary education are: providing favourable conditions for mental, moral, intellectual, physical and emotional development of the individual and for his/her realisation; integrating the individual into the national and world culture; moulding a personality and a citizen who is well integrated into his/her society. State educational standards and basic curricula are under preparation and will be adopted in the near future. General educational establishments are free to choose the system of grading, forms, procedure and regularity of intermediate certification of learners according to their charter and requirements of the Law on Education.

The final certification is conducted in grade 9 and grade 11 in the form of oral and written examinations. In grade 9, four subjects are considered, two of them (Russian language and mathematics) are compulsory, and the other two are chosen by the student. The written exam concerns the Russian language and the mother tongue. In grade 9, the learner can choose between a composition, a reproduction with elements of a composition, and a dictation. The written examination in mathematics is conducted on the basis of the open texts published in the "Book for written exams on mathematics in grade 9 of the general educational establishments of the Russian Federation". Graduates of the ninth grade of a general educational establishment with State accreditation, who have been allowed to participate in the final examination and have passed it, receive a Certificate of Basic General Education (certificate of incomplete secondary education). This is the decision of the pedagogical council of the general educational establishment. Ninth grade learners that failed to master general educational programmes, or failed to pass the final examination, do not receive any certificate.

Programmes concerning natural sciences have become less abstract; priority is given to the experiment and there is integration on an interdisciplinary basis. With introduction of areas of knowledge into the basic curriculum and specialisation of schools, integrated courses such as natural history, natural sciences, physics and astronomy, ecology and dialectics, etc., are becoming very popular. A natural sciences course is being developed for grades 10-11 of the humanities branch schools. Geography serves as a link that helps to understand the close relationship of scientific and social disciplines, the nature and society. A cultural approach to studying countries and regions is becoming very popular, and more attention is paid to the influence of the history of a region on its current situation and to the comprehensive study of the environment, population and economy of specific territories and of the world as a whole. New integrated courses are being developed, such as Mathematics and Design, Natural History and Agriculture, Physics and Fundamentals of Industrial Production, Art and Crafts, Man-Labour-Profession.

In the senior school there is a greater differentiation of vocational training, and an extensive polytechnic training at different levels, including specialisations in different variants and directions. Learners acquire basic knowledge and skills in fundamentals of applied economics, management and marketing, and they receive pre-professional and elementary professional training.

A new concept of education in the field of humanities is being developed, based on transition from the monopoly of the State ideology to ideological pluralism. It is closely connected with the development of Russia's national doctrine. Currently there is a stage-by-stage transition from the linear structure to a concentric one. The content of education in the field of social sciences is

Study Plan of General Secondary Education (grades 4-11)

Subject	*Average Weekly Hours*							
	4th	5th	6th	7th	8th	9th	10th	11th
Russian language	3	3	3	3	3	3	–	–
Languages and Literature	4	8	8	6	5	5	4	4
Arts	2	2	2	2	2	–	–	–
Social studies	–	2	2	2	3	4	4	4
Natural sciences	2	2	3	6	8	8	4	4
Mathematics	4	5	5	5	4	5	3	3
Physical training	2	2	2	2	2	2	3	3
Technology	2	2	2	2	3	3	2	2
Additional compuls classes	5	3	3	4	2	3	12	12
Total	**24**	**29**	**30**	**32**	**32**	**33**	**32**	**32**
Optional classes	3	3	3	3	3	3	6	6
Total	**27**	**32**	**33**	**35**	**35**	**36**	**38**	**38**

shaped taking into account the changes in the society and recent developments in social sciences. A "Man and Society" course has been created, selecting and systematising knowledge in philosophy, sociology, political science, economic theory, law and culture. The course *Grazhdanovedenie* (Introduction to civics) is gaining popularity as it focusses on the problems of socialisation, civic education, human rights and democracy. The course "What School Children Should Know about Law" has been introduced in general schools. Within the framework of this course learners study the Constitution of Russia, major international laws and acts and, in the first place, the Universal Declaration of Human Rights. Courses such as Religious Studies, World Religions, Monuments of Religion, and Human Values of European Civilization and the Modern World, have become popular optional subjects.

The content of linguistic native and foreign language courses has been revised. The major focus in studying the Russian language is on communicative functions of the language, the culture of communication and basic linguistic competence. The most important challenge is to introduce learners to the cultural and historical legacy of the nation, its culture and the culture of the modern society through the language. The interest in learning foreign languages has grown significantly. New textbooks on foreign languages are being developed on a social, cultural and linguistic basis; native speakers participate in creating textbooks. Pilot textbooks based on intensive methods of training have been released.

The concept of ecological education has been spelled out and its status has been determined with due regard to global trends in the development and establishment of information society and ecological society. Economic education has a greater role in laying foundations for economic culture, changing stereotypes of economic beheviour and becoming adjusted to life.

Courses such as Fundamentals of Economics, Introduction to Economics, Fundamentals of Business, etc., are being introduced.

Role of Different Authorities in Education

According to the Law on Education, the federal bodies are responsible for:

- shaping and implementing the federal policy and providing legal regulations in the field of education;
- establishing the procedures of setting up, reorganising and liquidating educational institutions, their licensing, certification and state accreditation;
- establishing the lists of professions concerning vocational training and professional education;
- establishing and adopting standard regulations on educational institutions;
- establishing procedures concerning certification of educational staff;
- establishing labour rates and federal norms of payment at educational institutions, as well as minimum wage and salary rates in the state educational institutions;
- establishing federal components of state educational standards;
- determining the annual share of federal income for the financing of education and establishing federal funds for the development of education;
- providing information and scientific support, developing modern curricula and courses, producing texts and other teaching aids, establishing a unified system of educational information within the Federation;
- creating a federal system of training and in-service training of teachers and educational managers;
- providing control over the implementation of the law, and ensuring the realisation of the federal standards.

The main responsibilities of local authorities are:

- the development and implementation of the educational policy, in accordance with the policy of the Federation, and the financial support to compulsory education;
- the elaboration and implementation of republican and regional programmes of educational development taking into account their own peculiarities;
- the establishment, reorganisation and liquidation of educational institutions;
- the establishment of national and regional components of state educational standards;
- the introduction of local taxes to support educational development;
- the establishment, in addition to federal ones, of social incentives, types and forms of material support for students and teachers;
- the elaboration and adoption of local regulations and norms;

- the construction of infrastructures and facilities.

The Law also emphasises the responsibility of each individual educational institution for the results obtained, and the importance of its Council (an elective, representative body which provides general guidance and is responsible for the implementation of the educational, staff and financial policy of the institution).

5

A Brief History of Educational Reconstruction in India

(*Committees and Commissions*)

After independence the first action of great significance in the field of education taken by the Government of India was the appointment of the University Education Commission in December, 1948, under the Chairmanship of Dr. S. Radhakrishnan, an eminent scholar and former Vice-Chancellor of Banaras University, who later on became the second President of India. The Commission submitted its report in August 1949. The report of the Commission is a unique document of great importance as it has guided the development of university education in India till the formation of the National Policy on Education, 1968. While outlining the aims of university education, the Commission said, "The greatness of a country does not depend on the extent of its territory, the length of its communications or the amount of wealth, not even on widespread education or equitable distribution of wealth, important as all these things are. If we wish to bring about a savage upheaval in our society, a *raksasa raj,* all that we need to do is to give vocational and technical education and starve the spirit. We will have a number of scientists without conscience, technicians without taste who find a void within themselves, a moral vacuum and a desperate need to substitute something, anything, for their lost endeavour and purpose. Society will then get what it deserves. If we claim to be civilised we must develop thought for the poor and the suffering, chivalrous regard and respect for women, faith on human brotherhood regardless of race or colour, nation or religion, love of peace and freedom, abhorrence of cruelty and ceaseless devotion of the claims of justice."

The second most significant document in the history of the development of education is the Report of the Secondary Education Commission 1952-53.

Writing about the aims of the secondary education in accordance with the needs of democratic India, the Commission observed, '...we shall have to formulate our aims with reference to these broad categories—the training of character to fit the students to participate creatively as citizens in the emerging democratic social order; the improvement of their practical and vocational efficiency so that they may play their part in building up the economic prosperity of their country, and the development of their literary artistic and cultural interests, which are necessary for self-expression and for the full development of the human personality, without which a living national culture cannot come into being'. The recommendation of the Commission, unfortunately remained unfulfilled by and large.

In 1966, an important event in the history of education in India took place. This was the publication of the report of the Education Commission 1964-66, popularly known as the Kothari Commission after the name of its Chairman D.S. Kothari. The report went into all aspects of education and at all levels and suggested a blue-print of educational reforms to be carried out during the coming twenty years. The report appropriately subtitled *Education and National Development* begins with these words, 'The destiny of India is now being shaped in our classrooms. This, we believe, is no more rhetoric. In a world based on science and technology, it is education that determines the level of prosperity, welfare and security of the people.' It concludes with these remarks, 'We must either build a sound, balanced, effective and imagined educational system to meet our developing needs and respond to challenging aspirations or be content to be swept aside by the strong currents of history.'

The Commission identified the three important facets of the big programme that would bring about the desired 'educational revolutions'

- internal transformation so as to relate it to the life, needs and aspirations of the nation;
- qualitative improvement so that the standards achieved are adequate, keep continually rising, and at least in a few sectors become internationally comparable; and
- expansion of educational facilities broadly on the basis of manpower needs and with an accent on equalisation of educational opportunities.

For the internal transformation of the system of education the following programmes urged high priority.

1. Work experience as an integral part of general education; vocationalisation of education at the secondary level; improvement of professional education and research, promoting national consciousness;
2. Introducing a common school system, making social and national service compulsory; developing all modern Indian languages;
3. making science education an integral part of all school education and developing scientific research; and
4. Inculcation of high values—social, moral and spiritual—at all stages of education.

The Report received wide attention and aroused great hopes. Its recommendations had been the major base for the declaration of the National Policy on Education (1968); and the Fourth, Fifth and Sixth Five-Year Plans. More than two decades have passed since the publication of the Report and yet many of its significant recommendations, especially on vocationalisation of secondary education, common school system and educational planning on manpower needs have not been implemented.

The Commission recommended that the Government of India should issue a statement on the National Policy on Education which should provide guidelines to the State Governments and the local authorities in preparing and implementing educational plans in their areas. Therefore, in 1967, the

Government of India constituted the Committee of Members of Parliament on Education to prepare the draft of a statement on the National Policy on Education. Dr. Triguna Sen, the Union Education Minister, was the chairman of the Committee which included 29 leading members of all the different political parties in the country. A Drafting Committee under the chairmanship of Shri Ganga Saran was constituted from among the members of the Committee. The Committee arrived 'at the greatest common measure of agreement' and evolved the draft of a National Policy on Education. It was placed before the Central Advisory Board of Education (CABE) which met in 1967 and discussed the formulation of a National Policy. During the discussion it was realised that the policy should be as brief as possible and should define clearly and realistically the new directions of the changes proposed for education at all levels in the country. A general consensus emerged in the course of the Board's deliberations. Thereafter the Government of India passed the resolution on National Policy on Education (1968). The Resolution *inter alia* states, 'The Government of India is convinced that a radical reconstruction of education on the broad lines recommended by the Education Commission is essential for economic and cultural development of the country, for national integration and for realising the ideal of a socialistic pattern of society.' The Government of India accordingly resolved to promote the development of education in the country in accordance with seventeen principles.

About the educational structure, the policy statement said, 'It will be advantageous to have a broadly uniform educational structure in all parts of the country. The ultimate objective should be to adopt the 10 plus 2 plus 3 pattern, the higher secondary stage of two years being located in schools, colleges or both according to local conditions'.

Resolution also envisaged that the Government of India would 'also review every five years, the progress made and recommend guidelines for future development.'

In 1972, the Ministry of Education and Social Welfare appointed a Committee consisting of 11 members to suggest practical steps to be taken for implementation of the pattern for the school and college classes in all States, and Union Territories of the country and to estimate the cost of implementing the programme. The Committee was headed by Dr. P.D. Shukla as Chairman and Dr. R.P. Singhal, Secretary, Central Board of Secondary Education as Member-Secretary. The Committee submitted its report in November 1973.

The Report of the Committee provided guidelines for the implementation of the new pattern of education.

In November 1974, the CABE adopted a resolution recommending the introduction of the 10+2+3 pattern of education all over the country during the Fifth Plan Period. By the end of 1976-77, this pattern had been introduced in 19 States and Union Territories. It has now been accepted in all parts of the country. According to the modified National Policy on Education, 1992, efforts will be made to have the +2 stage accepted as a part of school education throughout the country.

With the coming of the Janata Government in power in 1977 at the Centre, the first question in the field of education to be raised was whether the Resolution on National Policy on Education (1968) should be reviewed. The new Government declared that it would review all educational programmes including the National Policy. The Government appointed the Ishwarbhai Patel Committee and the Adiseshiah Committee to review the educational programmes in classes I to X and classes XI to XII respectively. The University Grants Commission was also requested to review all its programmes. The draft of the revised National Policy on Education which the Government had promised to the people was released in 1979.

The New Pattern of Education 10+2 had been introduced in several schools of the country. The NCERT had prepared new curriculum and textbooks which came under heavy criticism, and it was felt that the curriculum was overloaded. The Ishwarbhai Patel Review Committee (1977) scrutinised the scheme of studies and suggested some modifications. The Review Committee also defined the concept of Socially Useful Productive Work (SUPW). This, by and large, replaced the concept of Work Experience and Craft Based education.

The National Review Committee (1978-79) on Higher Secondary Education, headed by Dr. Malcolm S. Adiseshiah, Vice-Chancellor, Madras University, reviewed the NCERT's document 'Higher Secondary Education and its Vocationalisation' and recommended a plan of action for vocationalisation of education at the secondary/higher stage. The Report of the Committee is entitled *Learning To Do—Towards a Learning and Working Society.*

The 1968 National Policy on Education had stipulated a review of progress every five years. Such a review was overdue. In the meanwhile there had been a change of Government at the Centre. The Janata Government, in pursuance of its election manifesto decided to frame a new national education and for this purpose a Draft National Policy on Education (1979) was issued. Since the Janata Dal Government was short-lived, the policy could not be finalised.

In 1985, the NCERT prepared a 'National Curriculum for Elementary and Secondary Education: A Framework'. The document covered four broad areas—emerging concerns and imperatives, curriculum organisation, evaluation and implementation.

education policy. It also formed the basis of discussions in the conference of State Ministers of Education, held on August 29-30, 1985. It was translated practically into all regional languages of the country and given wide circulation. In addition, 5,80,000 copies of the document in English, 2,40,000 in Hindi and 4,000 in Urdu were distributed by the Ministry in response to requests received from and also to different organisations. As a part of the nationwide debate, 12 National Seminars and 17 Sponsored Seminars were organised by the Government of India and its agencies.

More than 8,000 communications were received by the Ministry of Education. In 1986, the Ministry of Education, now renamed the Ministry of Human Resource Development, Government of India, brought out a revised document *National Policy on Education, 1986—A Presentation* which was discussed in meetings of the State Ministers of Education, the National Development Council and the Central Advisory Board of Education. The document was again revised in the light of discussions and the *Draft National Policy on Education, 1986,* was placed on the table of Parliament in the first week of May, 1986. The draft was debated and finally adopted by the Lok Sabha on May 8 and Rajya Sabha on May 12, 1986. Thus, the National Policy on Education, 1986 emerged.

The National Policy on Education (NPE) 1986 marks a significant step in the history of education in post Independent India. It contains XII parts and 157 Paragraphs (i) Introductory; (ii) The Essence and Role of Education; (iii) National System of Education; (iv) Education for Duality; (v) Reorganisation of Education at Different Stages; (vi) Technical and Management of Education; (vii) Making the System Work: (viii) Re-orienting the Content and Process of Education; (ix) The Teacher; (x) The Management of Education; (xi) Resources and Review; and (xii) The Future.

With a view to implementing the NPE, the Ministry of Human Resource Development undertook an extensive exercise to prepare a programme of Action. Twenty-three Task Forces were constituted and each was assigned a specific subject covered by the NPE. The Task Forces submitted their reports in July 1986. These reports were discussed in a series of meetings taken by the Minister of Human Resource Development. After these discussions were completed, a conference of Education Secretaries of the State Governments and Union Territories Administrators was convened on 20 July, 1986. Suggestions received during this meeting were considered and the Programme of Action was prepared with reference to the main areas covered in NPE. The CABE met at New Delhi on August 1 and 2, 1986.

The document on the Programme of Action was discussed at this meeting.

The final Programme of Action was presented to Parliament on August 8, 1986.

The Lok Sabha and the Rajya Sabha discussed and approved the Programme of Action on August 22 and 23, 1986 respectively.

It was the first time in the history of Independent India that a National Policy on Education was prepared at the initiative of a Prime Minister, and that a Programme of Action was planned for bringing about educational reforms.

Among the most important programmes initiated at the school stages are: Blackboard Operation at the primary stage, Pace-Setting of Navodaya Vidyalayas and the Vocationalisation of Education at the secondary stage. In the field of Teacher Education, District Institutes of Education and Training have been set up, and selected Secondary Teacher Education Institutions upgraded into Colleges of Teacher Education/Institutions of Advanced Study in Education (CTEs/IASEs).

In the field of Higher Education, some of the major thrust areas are: Strengthening Autonomous Colleges, Redesigning Courses, Academic Staff Colleges for Orientation of Teachers and Eligibility Tests for Recruitment of Lecturers, etc.

In 1988, NCERT developed syllabi at the school stage. In this context it is hardly necessary to stress that a detailed syllabi form an important link in the process of curriculum development. The new syllabi were meant for serving as an effective instrument for initiating the desired educational goals. The syllabi were finalised in a national level meeting attended by representatives of State Boards of School/Secondary Education, Kendriya Vidyalaya Sangathan and SCERTs/SIEs.

With a view to implementing the directions contained in the National Policy on Education, 1986 regarding 'Reorienting the Content and Process of Education', the NCERT revised the curriculum in 1988. The revised curriculum was the outcome of the deliberations of a large member of seminars, participated by eminent educationists, curriculum specialists, subject experts, principals of schools, teacher educators, legislators, journalists and representatives of teachers' organisations. The publication incorporated in it emerging concerns and imperatives, curriculum concerns, basis for the national system of education, factors related to the organisation of the curriculum, allocation of time to different areas, evaluation and examination, etc. It also suggested the strategy of implementation.

Two reports on teachers also deserve attention in the context educational reforms in India. For the first time two National Commissions on Teachers were appointed by the Government of India in 1983. The reports though submitted in 1985 and published in 1986 were made public only in 1987. It is sad to note that these reports have received very little attention of the concerned authorities.

Of course, the recommendations of the Commission on School Teachers regarding the pay scales have led to agitations by the teachers. Mention may be made of the two important observations made by the Commission on Teachers. The Commissions on School Teachers concluded Chapter II with these words, "Status, by reason of a title or position will become increasingly difficult to come by, we feel. Status, in other words, will have to be earned by the teacher as any other professional worker.... So must the new teacher earn status through achievement'. The other Commission concluded Chapter II by stating. 'The National Commission on Teachers in Higher Education would therefore make a fervent plea on the one hand to the Government to appreciate how potent the teacher is in engineering social change and hence to provide him status, encouragement and resources for the purpose, and on the other to the teachers to open their minds and hearts to the new possibilities and to discharge their responsibilities with an urgent sense of social purpose'.

The political scenario has adversely affected the implementation of the NPE.

In the November 1989 Lok Sabha poll, Shri Rajiv's Congress Party lost and in December, the Janata Dal Government was formed with Shri V.P. Singh as Prime Minister. The BJP and the Left Parties decided to give outside support to Janata/NF Government.

In pursuance of its election manifesto, the National Front Government appointed on May 7, 1990,, a Committee with Acharya Ramamurti as its Chairman, to review the National Policy on Education (NPE), 1986. The Committee submitted its report to the Minister of State in the Ministry of Human Resource Development on December 26, 1990. The report was tabled in Parliament on January 9, 1991. During this period political changes of far-reaching consequences took place. Shri VP. Singh's Government was voted out on November 7, 1990 and Shri Chandra Shekhar became Prime Minister on November 10. Shri Chandra Shekhar's Government lasted for a very brief period between November 10, 1990 to March 6, 1991. Thereafter he worked as a caretaker Prime Minister till June 20. Shri P.V. Narasimha Rao assumed office of the Prime Minister of India on June 21, 1991, after the victory of his party at the polls. It was, therefoie, natural that under the changed situation, the Ramamurti Report could not receive government patronage.

The recommendations of the Ramamurti Review Committee Report were examined by the Janardhana Committee appointed by the Central Advisory Board of Education in July, 1991. The Janardhana Committee submitted its recommendations in January, 1992. The C ABE considered the Janardhana Committee Report in the first week of May, 1992, and finalised the Revised NPE.

The Revised NPE was presented in both Houses of Parliament on May 7, 1992, by the Human Resource Development Minister Shri Arjun Singh. Apart from tabling the Revised NPE, Shri Singh also presented the Report of the Janardhana Committee (Central Advisory Board of Education's Committee). In his statement, the Minister said the NPE, 1986 has stood the test of time and enunciated a comprehensive framework to guide the development of education. He further observed that while that framework continues to be relevant, the development during the last few years and the experience in implementation of the policy have necessitated certain modifications.

In the field of higher education also, a number of committees have made recommendations for carrying out the directions contained in the NPE.

Two Committees have reviewed the load of the 'school bag'.

The National Council of Teacher Education has published a number of documents during the period 1995 to 1999.

January 2000 saw the publication of National Curriculum Framework for School Education—A Discussion Document.

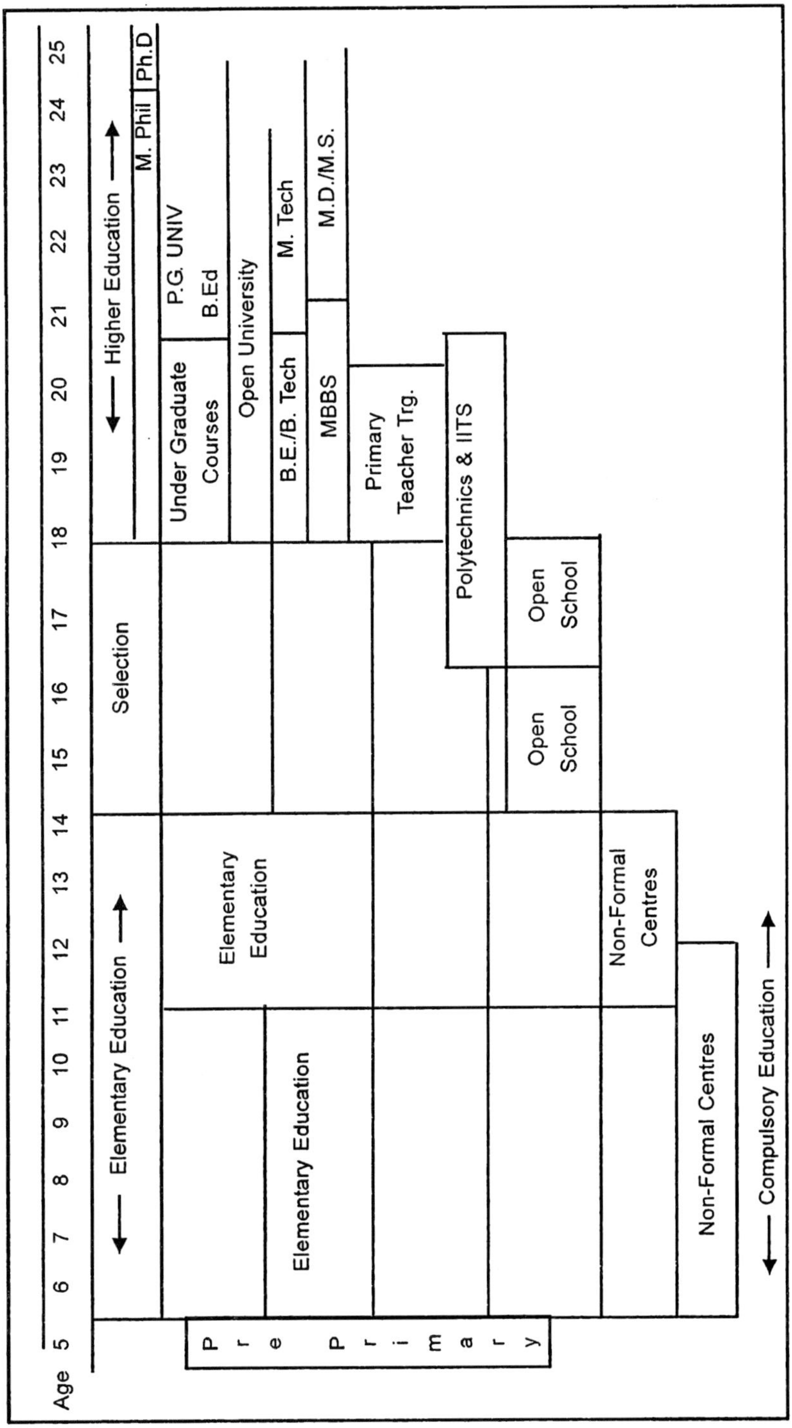

Fig.: Structure of Education in India

Select List of National Committees and Commissions and Working Groups on Education (1947 to 2005)

1947 : Overseas Scholarship Committee, 1947, Ministry of Education, Bureau of Education, Pamphlet No. 62. New Delhi, 1947.

1948 : Committee on Secondary Education in India, 1948, Ministry of Education, Bureau of Education, Pamphlet No. 52, New Delhi, 1948.

1949 : Indian University Education Commission, 1948, Manager of Publications, New Delhi, 1949.

1950 : Committee on the Ways and Means of Planning Educational Development in India, 1948, Manager of Publications, Bureau of Education, Pamphlet No. 64, New Delhi, 1950.

1951 : Committee on Relationship between State Government and Local Bodies in the Administration of Primary Education, 1951, Manager of Publications, 1954.

1952 : First Five Year Plan, Planning Commission, Government of India, New Delhi, 1952.

1953 : Secondary Education Commission, 1952-1953, Ministry of Education, 1953.

1954 : Committee on Higher Education for Rural Areas, 1954, Ministry of Education, New Delhi, 1954.

1955 : Study Team on General Education, Ministry of Education, New Delhi, 1955.

- Committee to Study and Report on the Question of Establishing Uniform Standards in respect of Education and Practice of *Vaids, Hakims* and *Homoeopaths,* 1955, Ministry of Health, 1956.

1956 : Assessment Committee on Basic Education, 1956, Manager of Publications, New Delhi, 1956.

- Education Committee for the Andaman and Nicobar Islands, 1956, Manager of Publications, New Delhi, 1956.
- Second Five Year Plan, Planning Commission, New Delhi, 1956.
- Sanskrit Commission, 1956, Ministry of Publications, New Delhi, 1958.
- Three-year Degree Course Committee, 1956, Manager of Publication, New Delhi, 1956

1957: Committee on Rural Education, 1957, Ministry of Education, New Delhi, 1959.

- Examination Committee, 1957, University Grants Commission, New Delhi, 1957.
- Banaras Hindu University Enquiry Committee, 1957, Ministry of Education, New Delhi, 1957.
- Committee for the Integration of Post Basic and Multipurpose Schools, 1957, New Delhi, 1960.

1958 : Committee on Fisheries Education, 1958, Ministry of Food and Agriculture, New Delhi, 1959.

- National Committee on Women's Education, 1958, Manager of Publications, New Delhi, 1959.

- Committee on General Education, 1958, UGC, New Delhi, 1961.
- Special Committee on Commerce Education, 1958. AH India Council for Technical Education, New Delhi, 1961.

1959 : Review Committee for Mathematics in Indian Universities, 1959, UGC, New Delhi, 1959.

- Committee on Religious and Moral Instruction, 1959. Ministry of Education, New Delhi, 1960.
- Committee for Coordination and Integration of Schemes Operating in the Field of Physical Education, Recreation and Youth Welfare, 1959, Ministry of Education, New Delhi, 1960.
- Committee on Problems of Students Indiscipline in Indian Universities, 1959, UGC, New Delhi, 1960.
- Committee on Post-Graduate Engineering Education and Research, 1959, Ministry of Scientific Research and Current Affairs, New Delhi, 1961.
- Review Committee on Bio-Chemistry, 1959, UGC, New Delhi, 1963.
- Review Committee on Botany, 1959, UGC, New Delhi, 1963.

1960 : Rural Committee on Social Work, U.G.C., New Delhi, 1960.

- Review Committee for Education in Indian Universities, 1960, UGC, New Delhi, 1963.
- Review Committee for English in Indian Universities, 1960, UGC, New Delhi, 1963.
- Review Committee for Chemistry in Indian Universities, 1960, UGC, New Delhi, 1963.

1961 : Committee on Plan Projects: Study Team for Selected Educational Schemes, 1961, Report on Social Education, Ministry of Education, New Delhi.

- Committee on Model Acts for Universities, 1961, Ministry of Education, New Delhi, 1961.
- Expert Committee on Correspondence Courses and Evening Colleges, 1961, Manager of Publications, New Delhi, 1961.
- Review Committee for Sociology in Indian Universities, 1961, UGC, New Delhi, 1961.
- Third Five Year Plan, Planning Commission, New Delhi, 1961.
- Review Committee on Philosophy in Indian Universities, 1961, UGC, New Delhi, 1961.
- Committee on Plan Projects, Panel for Science Laboratories and Equipment, 1961, New Delhi, 1962.
- Committee on Plan Projects Study Team for Selected Educational Schemes, 1961, Ministry of Education, New Delhi, 1963.
- Committee on Differentiation of Curricula for Boys and Girls, 1961, Ministry of Education, New Delhi, 1964.
- Indian Parliamentary and Scientific Committee, 1961, Manager of Publications, New Delhi, 1964.

1962 : Committee on Residential Accommodations for Students and Teachers, 1962, UGC, New Delhi, 1966.

1963 : Committee on Setting up a University for the North Eastern Region of India, 1963, UGC, New Delhi, 1965.

- Committee to Look into the Causes for Lack of Public Support Particularly in Rural Areas for Girls Education and to Enlist Public Cooperation, 1963, Ministry of Education, New Delhi, 1965.
- Committee on Education on Elective Subjects at The Undergraduate Stage, 1963, UGC, New Delhi, 1966.

1964 : Committee on Plan Projects Panel for Science Education in Secondary Schools, 1964, Government of India Press, 1964.

- Mathematics Reforms Committee, 1964, UGC, New Delhi, 1966.
- Education Commission, 1964 to 1966, Manager of Publications. New Delhi, 1966.
- Committee to Examine the Extent of Malpractices in the Universities, 1964, UGC, New Delhi, 1967.
- Committee on Plan Projects: Study Team for Selected Educational Schemes, 1964. Report on Teacher Training, New Delhi, 1969.

1965 : Committee on Physical Education, 1965, UGC, New Delhi, 1965.

- Report of the Committee on Student Welfare and Allied Matters, UGC, New Delhi, 1967.

1966 : Committee on Improvement of Art Education, 1966, NCERT, New Delhi, 1967.

- Review Committee on Political Science in Indian Universities, 1966, UGC, New Delhi, 1967.
- Committee on Examination Reform in Central Universities, 1966, UGC, New Delhi, 1969.
- Committee on School Textbooks, 1966, Ministry of Education, New Delhi, 1969.

1967 : Committee of Members of parliament on Education, 1967, Government of India Press, Faridabad, 1969.

- Committee on Workers Education, 1967, Manager of Publications, Delhi, 1968.
- Committee on Rural Education, 1967, Ministry of Education, New Delhi, 1970.
- Committee on Audio-Visual Aids in Higher Education, 1967, UGC, New Delhi, 1969.

1968 : National Policy on Education, Ministry of Education, New Delhi, 1968.

- Review Committee on Future Development of National Council of Educational Research and Training, 1968, NCERT, New Delhi, 1969.

1969 : Banaras Hindu University Inquiry Committee, 1969, Ministry of Education and Youth Services, New Delhi, 1969.

- Study Group on Supervision and Inspection, 1969, NCERT, New Delhi, 1969.
- Committee on Governance of Universities, 1969, UGC, New Delhi, 1971.

1970 : Fourth Five Year Plan, Planning Commission, New Delhi, 1970.

- Committee on Examinations, 1970, NCERT, New Delhi, 1971.
- Special Committee on Reorganisation and Development of Polytechnic Education in India, 1970, Ministry of Education, New Delhi, 1971.
- Committee on School Buildings, 1970, Ministry of Education, New Delhi, 1972.
- Committee on Calcutta University, 1972, UGC, New Delhi, 1972.
- Review Committee on Regional Colleges, 1972, Ministry of Education and Social Welfare, New Delhi, 1974.
- Committee on the Status of Teaching of Sociology and Social Anthropology, 1974, UGC, New Delhi, 1974.
- Committee on Vishva Bharati, 1974, Government of India Press, Faridabad, 1975.
- Review Committee on the University Grants Commission, 1974, Ministry of Education and Social Welfare, New Delhi, 1977.

1976 : Fifth Five Year Plan, Planning Commission, New Delhi, 1976.

1977 : Review Committee on Education—Ishwarbhai Patel, NCERT, New Delhi, 1977.

- Working Group on Organisation of Vocational Education, 1977, Ministry of Education, New Delhi, 1977.
- Working Group on Universalisation of Elementary Education, 1977, Ministry of Education and Social Welfare, New Delhi, 1977.
- Committee on Adult Education Programmes for Women, 1977, Ministry of Education and Social Welfare, New Delhi, 1978.

1978 : National Review Committee on Higher Secondary Education with Special Reference to Vocationalisation, 1978, Ministry of Education and Social Welfare, New Delhi, 1978.

- Development of Higher Education in India—A Policy Framework, UGC, New Delhi, 1978.
- Fourth All India Educational Survey 1978, NCERT, New Delhi, 1982.

1979 : Draft National Policy on Education, 1979, Ministry of Education, New Delhi, 1979.

1980 : Sixth Five Year Plan, Planning Commission, New Delhi, 1980

- Report on Autonomous Schools, Central Board of Secondary Education, New Delhi, 1981.

1983 : National Commission on Teachers I, (School Teachers), 1983 to 1985. Controller of Publications, New Delhi, 1986.

- National Commission on Teacher II, (Higher Education), 1983 to 1985, Controller of Publication, New Delhi, 1986.

1984 : Report of the Committee to Look into the Working of the Central Universities, UGC, New Delhi, 1984.

1985 : Curriculum Load at the School Level: A Quick Appraisal. NCERT, New Delhi, 1985.

- Challenge of Education—A Policy Perspective. Ministry of Human Resource Development, Government of India, New Delhi, 1985.
- Seventh Five Year Plan, Planning Commission, New Delhi, 1985.
- National Working Group on Vocational Education, Ministry of Human Resource Development, New Delhi, 1985.

- Report of the UGC Committee on the Involvement of the Universities and Colleges in the Promotion of National Integration, 1985 to 1986. UGC, New Delhi, 1986.

1986 : National Policy on Education, 1986, Ministry of Human Resource Development, New Delhi, 1986.

- Programme of Action, NPE 1986, Ministry of Human Resource Development, New Delhi, 1986.
- Report of the Committee on Revision of Pay Scales of Teachers in Universities and Colleges, 1986, UGC, New Delhi, 1986.
- Report of the Committee on Revision of Pay Scales of Librarians and Directors of Physical Education in Universities and Colleges, 1986, UGC, New Delhi, 1986.

1987 : Report of the UGC Committee Towards New Educational Management, 1987, UGC, New Delhi, 1990.

1988 : Report of the Task Force on Performance of Appraisal of Teachers, UGC, New Delhi, 1988.

- Report of the Committee on Setting up State Councils of Higher Education, UGC, New Delhi, 1988.
- National Curriculum for Elementary and Secondary Education, A Framework, NCERT, New Delhi, 1988.
- College/University Buildings, UGC, New Delhi, 1986.
- UGC Review Committee on University System and Extension as the Third Dimension, UGC, New Delhi, 1986.
- NCERT Committee on Transformation of Regional Colleges of Education into Regional Institutes, NCERT, New Delhi, 1987.
- National Commission on Self Employed Women and Women in the Informal Sector (1987-88), Department of Women and Child Development, Ministry of Human Resource Development, New Delhi, 1988.
- Science Education for the Ten Years of Schooling, NCERT, New Delhi, 1988.
- Guidelines for Upper Primary and Secondary Classes, NCERT, New Delhi, 1988.
- Detailed Syllabus of Science for the Upper Primary Level (11 + 13+), NCERT, New Delhi, 1988.
- Detailed Syllabus of Mathematics for Upper Primary Level (11 + to 13+), NCERT, New Delhi, 1988.
- Detailed Syllabus of Science for the Secondary Level (14+ to 16+), NCERT, New Delhi, 1988.
- Guidelines and Syllabi for Secondary Stage Classes IX-X, NCERT, New Delhi, 1988.
- Guidelines and Syllabi for Social Science, NCERT, New Delhi, 1988.

1989 : Fifth All India Educational Survey, Selected Statistics, NCERT, New Delhi, 1989.

1990 : Report of the Seventh Plan Visiting Committees for Mid Term Review of Bihar State Universities, 1989, UGC, New Delhi, 1990.

- Report of the Committee for Review of National Policy on Education 1986, Recommendations Ministry of Human Resource Development, New Delhi, 1990.
- Committee for Review on National Policy on Education, Towards an Enlightened and Humane Society: NPE, 1986. A Review. Ministry of Human Resource Development, New Delhi, 1990.

1991 : Report of the CABE Working Group on Adult Education, New Delhi, March 1991, Ministry of Human Resource Development, New Delhi, 1991.

- Report of the CABE, Working Group on Elementary Education, Ministry of Human Resource Development, New Delhi, 1991.
- Report of the CABE Working Group on Secondary Education, Ministry of Human Resource Development, New Delhi, 1991.
- Report of the CABE Working Group on Technical Education, Ministry of Human Resource Development, New Delhi, 1991.
- Report of the CABE Working Group on Education of Women and Other Disadvantaged Groups like SC, ST, Minorities, etc. Ministry of Human Resource Development, New Delhi, 1991.
- Objectives, Thrusts and Macro-Dimensions of the Eighth Plan, Planning Commission, New Delhi, 1991.
- Report of the Committee on Minimum Levels of Learning at the Primary Stage, NCERT, New Delhi.

1992: Report of the CABE Committee on Policy Department of Education, Ministry of Human Resource Development, New Delhi, 1992.

- National Policy on Education (NPE), 1986, Revised Policy Formulations. Department of Education, Ministry of Human Resource Development, New Delhi, 1992.
- Report of the Conference of Chairmen of Boards of School Education on Semesterisation and Examination, NCERT, New Delhi, 1992.
- Report of the National Colloquium on Right to Education as a Fundamental Right, Sponsored by UGC and Association of Indian Universities, September 1992, AIU, 1992. Journal of Higher Education, Autumn 1992.
- Eighth Five Year Plan (1992-97), Planning Commission, New Delhi, 1992;.

1993 : Learning Without Burden: Yash Pal Committee (1993) Central Advisory Board of Committee on Decentralisation of Educational Planning: Panchayati Raj: Veerapan Report (1993). Ministry of Human Resource Development, New Delhi, 1993.

- Report of the Group on the Reduction of Academic Burden on School Education (1993-94), Ministry of Human Resource Development, New Delhi, 1993.
- Report of the Committee on Vocationalisation of Higher Education, UGC, (1993).
- Report of the Justice Punnya Committee on UGC Funding of Higher Education (1992-93), UGC, 1993.

- Performance and Accountability in Higher Education: Discussion Papers and Summary.
- Record of Discussions on the Workshop, UGC, New Delhi, 1994. UGC Occasional Papers.
- Resource Mobilisation for ERA., NIEAP, New Delhi, 1993.
- Report of Expert Committee for Developing a Performance Appraisal System, Ministry of Human Resource Development, Government of India, New Delhi, 1993.

1994 : Report of the Expert Group on National Literacy Mission (1993-94), Literacy Mission, Ministry of Human Resource Development, New Delhi, 1994.

1995 : Sixth All India Educational Survey: Provisional Statistics, NCERT, New Delhi, 1995.

- Report of the IIT Synergy Sub-Group, 1995, Ministry of Human Resource Development, New Delhi, 1995.

1996 : Curriculum Framework for Teacher Education—Discussion Document, National Council for Teacher Education, New Delhi, 1996.

1997 : Report of the Committee of State Education Ministers on Implications of the Proposal to make elementary Education a Fundamental Right, Ministry of Human Resource Development, New Delhi, 1997.

1998 : Restructuring and Revitalising Teacher Education (National Report on the Role of CTE/IASES, National Council of Teacher Education, New Delhi (1998).

1999 : Expert Group Report on Financial Requirements for Making Elementary Education a Fundamental Right. Ministry of Human Resource Development, New Delhi, 1999.

- Report of the Chief Justice J.S. Verma Committee to Operationalize the suggestions to teach the Fundamental Rights to the Citizens of India, New Delhi, 1999.
- Human Values in Education: Chavan Committee Report, Rajya Sabha Secretariat, Eighty First Report on Value Based Education, New Delhi, 1999.
- Ninth Five Year Plan on Education (1997-2000). Planning Committee, New Delhi, 1999.

2000 : National Curriculum Framework for School Education: A Discussion Paper, NCERT, New Delhi, 2000.

- National Curriculum Framework for School Education, NCERT, New Delhi, 2000.
- Census of India, 2001. Registrar, General and Census Commissioner, India, Census of India, 2001, Delhi.

2002 : Education Rights of Minorities: Supreme Court Judgment (2002), P.D. Mathews, S.J. Indian Social Institute, New Delhi, 2002.

- Tenth Five Year Plan (2002-2007), Planning Commission.
- The Constitution (Eighty-Sixth Amendment) Act, 2002.

2005 : Draft National Curriculum Framework, 2005, NCERT, New Delhi, 2005.

- Autonomy of Higher Education, Central Advisory Board of Education (CABE), MHRD, Govt. of India, 2005.
- Free and Compulsory Education Bill and Other Issues Related to Elementary Education, (CABE) 2005
- Regulatory Mechanism for Textbooks and Parallel Textbooks Taught in Schools Outside the School System, CABE 2005
- Integrating of Culture Education, CABE 2005.
- Universalisation of Secondary Education, CABE, 2005
- National Curriculum Framework, 2005 NCERT, New Delhi

6

Educational Reforms for the Twenty-First Century

The first attempt in India for educational reforms was made on January 5, 1985 when the then Prime Minister Rajiv Gandhi declared that a new education policy would be formulated that would equip the country both scientifically and economically to enter the twenty-first century. This statement resulted in the National Policy on Education (1986). With a view to implementing the NPE, a Programme of Action (1986) was prepared and followed.

In 1992, the Policy was reviewed and slightly revised in the light of the experience gained in the implementation of the Policy. Accordingly a new Programme of Action (1992) was planned.

The National Council of Education Research and Training, New Delhi, usually called the academic wing of the Ministry of Human Resource Development, Department of Education, Government of India, published in 1986 a book entitled *School Education in India: Present Status and Future Needs,* which contained the views of the eminent educators of the country.

Notwithstanding the time gap, these views are still relevant and provide useful pointers. Here, they are briefly reviewed.

Prof. Malcolm S. Adiseshiah, a great scholar and educationist, in an article 'Educational Perspectives' described the position in the beginning of the 21st century as "Education of the future will be life-long—a glimpse of a great and revolutionary truth will emerge that education is not a spatial monopoly of something called the school and college; that it is not a time-bound learning experience; that there is no such thing as childhood education, adolescent education, youth education, or adult education. There is just education which is a way of life, a life-long way of life. Every year, every month, everyday, from the cradle to the grave, a person will be learning, open to learning and given the opportunity to learn in the home, school, university, factory, farm, hospital, office, co-operative, temple, trade union, political party, cinema and club. Education will be open. Schools without walls, polyvalent classes, integrated schools, universities of the air, will be juxtaposed with firms, farms, factories and business houses as education extension agents with their survey documentation and research facilities. The whole wide-open area of self-instruction, similar to what is taking place in our rural areas, will be operative. Let us not forget that for the farmer and his wife the farm is the school, what they do in their daily life is their curriculum of learning. Their experience in dealing with their daily survival problem is the substance of their evaluation. Life-long education will be a fact of life."

Suggestive Educational Model

Prof. Adiseshiah suggested the following educational model for meeting the future needs:

1. Launching the non-formal education sub-system for the two priority groups—school drop-outs in the age group 6-14 and working adult illiterates in the age group 15-40, evolving, devising functional curricula, producing learning materials, mobilising teaching resources from trained teachers as well as progressive farmers, engineers, musicians, dramatists and sportsmen and using existing buildings, labs and workshops for running the concentrated courses.
2. Reorganising the existing formal education sub-system into multiple entry and exit points at its different levels so that students could enter, leave and re-enter the school and university system at anyone of several points to answer the call of work in the home, farm, factory or office; continue their education through organised non-formal programmes.
3. Establishing the relationship between the two sub-systems involving the nexus between their educational content, methods and technologies of teaching and learning.
4. Vocationalising the second level of education.

Things like computerised instruction, open learning systems undifferentiated curricula for rural-urban and male-female population, inter-disciplinary approaches to teaching, integration of education and work and establishment of a value system which would promote international understanding, peace and harmony will become some of the important components of education in the beginning of the 21st century.

Prof. S.V.C. Aiya, a former Director of NCERT in an article 'School Science Curriculum Dynamics' visualised the scenario for 2000 A.D. as, "Inadequate control of population will create serious problems on the food and health fronts, requiring a specific orientation of school science towards agriculture and preventive medicine".

"Even in agriculture, the demand for unskilled and illiterate labour will decrease. Skilled workers must be mentally prepared to learn, even on their own, new jobs and move to them. Apart from similar qualities, technicians must have proficiency in an international language like English and must be capable of innovating to fill gaps between old and new techniques, etc. Technologists including management personnel, must be familiar with the use of computers, statistical methods, etc. It is their responsibility to reduce pollution, prevent upsetting of the ecological balance and more generally, everything that harms society. They have to instill in society a sense of duty and of social purpose. They have to persuade those concerned to move to new technologies and guard against obsolescence.

"Capacity for logical, orderly and exact expression, ability to properly comprehend technical literature, often in a language other than their mother tongue, and proper realisation of social responsibilities appear to be prerequisites for skilled workers, and to a much greater extent for technicians and technologists. These qualities have to grow from education at the school level. Hence, the humanities and social sciences will go together with science. So far as science is concerned, the forecast indicates that much greater attention has to be paid to application. In addition there is need to move children at school even directly into technology

Dr. P.N. Kirpal, a former Secretary, Ministry of Education, Government of India, in an article under the caption "Towards an Education for the 21st Century" that also appeared in the same book as referred to earlier noted the three great explosions of a accelerated development, three crucial issues contending for mastery, three deep conflicts requiring peaceful resolution and balanced synthesis and three poignant gaps portending grave dangers and fateful challenges. Dr. Kirpal further observed, "Some of these twelve problems have plagued several civilisations of the past, but in the 21st century they can threaten the entire humanity and consequently call for global efforts to overcome the evil and nurture the good implicit in the choices and solutions that may be offered and taken."

Three Explosions

1. Explosion of Population;
2. Explosion of Knowledge; and
3. Explosion of Expectations.

Three Issues

1. Issues of War and Peace;
2. Issues of Man and Environment; and
3. Issues of Culture and Technology.

Three Conflicts

1. Conflict between the Inner Man and the Outer Man;
2. Conflict between Freedom and Social Organisation; and
3. Conflict between Tradition and Modernity.

Three Gaps

1. Gap between Developed and Developing Countries;
2. Gap between Knowledge and Wisdom; and
3. Gap between Power and Love.

Dr. Kirpal suggests ten principles for a profound renewal and transformation of education:

1. Our thinking should be hard and without rhetoric.
2. Education is synonymous with life.
3. Education is a comprehensive national task involving all people and all society.
4. Integrated education should serve man and social development.
5. Value-oriented education is essential for balanced personality and harmonious society.
6. Indian education should draw upon the growing corpus of international education and enrich it by its own contributions.

7

Curriculum Reviews and Implementation in India

The first major attempt in Curriculum Reconstruction in India was made in 1937 when Gandhiji propounded the idea of basic education and Dr. Zakir Hussain Committee elaborated the scheme of studies of basic education. However, much work in this direction could not be done as India was under the British rule. After independence, Basic System of Education was accepted as the National System of Education at the primary stage. The entire instructional programme was to centre round a craft. Besides craft, physical and social environment were also considered to be important factors in the curriculum. Correlation of various subjects was to be achieved through craft and social and physical environment.

Immediately after independence a University Education Commission was set up under the Chairmanship of Dr. Radhakrishnan. The Commission recommended the adoption of 3 years degree course and recommended suitable curriculum for this stage.

The third step in curriculum reconstruction in India was taken with the appointment of the Secondary Education Commission, 1952-53.

The Secondary Education Commission noticed the following criticisms regarding school curriculum in, India:

1. The present curriculum is narrowly conceived.
2. It is bookish and theoretical.
3. It is overcrowded, without providing rich and; significant contents.
4. It makes inadequate provision for practical and other kinds of activities which should reasonably find room in it, if it is to educate the whole of the personality.
5. It does not cater to various needs and capacities of the adolescents.
6. It is dominated too much by examinations.
7. It does not include technical and vocational subjects which are so necessary for training the students to take part in the industrial and economic development of the country.

The Commission took note of the democratic needs of free India and accordingly made recommendations for bringing about reforms in the existing curriculum at the school stage. The Secondary Education Commission realised that there was a great need for providing technical education in the country and, therefore, it recommended multipurpose schools. The Commission also made recommendations regarding the duration of the secondary stage of education. The Commission thoroughly studied the prevailing curriculum and suggested far-reaching changes in it. A core curriculum at the Higher Secondary Stage was also recommended.

The Secondary Education Commission highlighted the following principles of Curriculum Construction:

1. Principle of totality of experience.
2. Principle of variety and elasticity.
3. Principle of core subjects.
4. Principle of linking with community life.
5. Principle for me use of leisure.
6. Interrelation, of subjects.

Curriculum at the Middle Stage

The Secondary Education Commission pointed out that the function of the middle school curriculum is to introduce the pupil in 'a general way' to certain broad fields of human knowledge and interest. The middle school is not the place for specialisation but the stage when a general introduction to all the broad and significant fields of knowledge can and should be given. The purpose is two-fold:

(i) The child as the inheritor of the treasures of human civilization has the right to know what its main components are.

(ii) As a result of acquiring that knowledge to choose at a later stage, the particular field in which he can, in his own way, contribute his share to this fund of human culture.

Great discrimination will be required in selecting from this vast treasure such elements as the child can understand and appreciate at this stage.

Again it is in this middle stage that the special abilities and interests of the individual child tend to crystallise and take shape. In view of this, the middle school curriculum has to be exploratory in character. This can be done by providing a broad-based and general curriculum and an appropriate environment in the school.

Keeping in view these considerations, the Commission suggested the following broad outline of the middle school curriculum:

1. Languages,
2. Social Studies,
3. General Science,
4. Mathematics,
5. Art and Music,
6. Craft, and
7. Physical Education.

Languages include the mother-tongue, the natural medium of self-expression or the regional languages, and the official language of the Republic, *i.e.*, Hindi. Where Hindi is the mother-tongue, the pupil may study another language. English is also to be provided for but not to be treated as a compulsory subject.

Curriculum at the High and Higher Secondary School Stages

The Commission stated that the following considerations should be kept in mind while constructing the curriculum:

(i) The curriculum at the Higher Secondary stage should be, as far as possible, framed on the basis of the abilities and interests of the students.
(ii) Varied courses with a fairly wide latitude for choice should be provided for.
(iii) The educational programme should not be narrowly vocational but should have a definite vocational bias.
(iv) The curriculum should provide for certain core subjects, common to all, and certain optional subjects.

The curriculum, as envisaged by the Secondary Education Commission, consists of the following:

A. (i) Mother-tongue or regional language or composite course of the mother-tongue and a classical language.
   (ii) One other language to be chosen from among the following:
      (a) Hindi (for those whose mother-tongue is not Hindi).
      (b) Elementary English (for those who have not studied it in the middle stage).
      (c) Advanced English (for those who had studied English in the earlier stage).
      (d) A modern Indian language (other than Hindi).
      (e) A modern foreign language (other than English).
      (f) A classical language.

B. (i) Social Studies—general course (for the first two years only).
   (ii) General Science including mathematics—general course for two years only).

C. One craft to be chosen from the following list (which may be added according to needs):
   (a) Spinning and weaving
   (b) Wood-work
   (c) Metal work
   (d) Gardening
   (e) Tailoring
   (f) Typography
   (g) Workshop practice
   (h) Sewing, needlework and embroidery.

D. Three subjects from one of the following groups:
   Group I. Humanities
   Group II. Sciences
   Group III. Commercial *Group IV.* Agriculture *Group V.* Fine Arts *Group VI.* Home Science

E. Besides the above, a student may take at his option one additional subject from any one of the above groups irrespective of whether or not he has chosen his other options from that particular group.

School Curriculum and the Education Commission, 1964-66

Need for a Radical Reform of School Curriculum

The Commission stated: "The explosion of knowledge in recent years and the reformulation of many concepts in the sciences have highlighted the inadequacy of existing school programmes and brought about a mounting pressure for a radical reform of school curriculum. A unified approach should be taken to the framing of the entire school curriculum, a new definition of the content of general education and a new approach to the place of specialisation."

Major Steps of Curricular Improvement

The Commission suggested that school curricula should be upgraded by:

I. (a) Research in curriculum development undertaken by University Departments of Education, Training Colleges, State Institutes of Education and Boards of School Education.
   (b) Revision of curricula based on such research.
   (c) The preparation of textbooks and teaching-learning materials.
   (d) The orientation of teachers to the revised curricula through in-service education.

II. Schools should be given the freedom to devise and experiment with new curricula suited to their needs. A lead should be given in the matter by training colleges and universities through their experimental schools.

III. Advanced curricula should be prepared by State Boards of School Education in all subjects and introduced in a phased manner in schools which fulfil certain conditions of staff and facilities.

IV. The formation of Subject Teachers Associations in the different school subjects will help to stimulate experimentation and the upgrading of curricula. The State Education Departments, State Institutes of Education and NCERT should help the associations in their educational activities and co-ordinate their work.

Organisation of the Curriculum

The Commission made the following recommendations:

1. *Common Curriculum for Ten Years*: In general or non-vocational schools, a common curriculum of general education should be provided for the first ten years of school education, and diversification of studies and specialisation should begin only at the higher secondary stage. Moreover, standards of attainment should be clearly defined at the end of each sub-stage.

2. *Curriculum at the Lower Primary Stage*: At the lower primary stage, the curriculum should be simple with reduced load of formal subjects and emphasis on language and elementary mathematics.

A study of problems relating to beginning of reading accompanied by a vigorous programme of improving reading instruction at the lower primary stage should receive great emphasis.

At the lower secondary stage, study of subjects should gain in vigour and depth.

3. *Curriculum at the Higher Primary Stage*: At the higher primary stage, the curriculum will broaden and deepen, teaching methods will become more systematic, and standards of attainment more specific.

4. *Curriculum at Higher Secondary Stage*: At the higher secondary stage of general education, courses to be diversified in such a manner as to enable pupils to study a group of any three subjects in depth with considerable freedom and elasticity in the grouping of subjects. A student, for example, may specialise in any three subjects of the science group or in combination of subjects from the science and the humanities. In order to ensure the balanced development of the adolescent's total personality, the curriculum at this stage should provide half the time to the electives, one-fourth of the time to the language, and one-fourth to physical education, arts and crafts, and moral and spiritual education.

5. *Provision for Ordinary and Advanced Course*: Wherever possible courses should be provided at two levels—ordinary and advanced-beginning with Class IX. For the lower classes beginning with Class V, enrichment programmes should be provided for the talented children. It may take the form of additional subject or greater depth in the same subject. The programme may be done within or outside school hours or on a self-study basis. A beginning may be made with advanced courses in mathematics, science and languages at the lower secondary stage and in all the specialised subjects at the higher secondary stage.

Subject Areas in the Higher Secondary Classes (XI and XII)

1. Any two languages, including any modern Indian language, and any classical language.
2. Any three subjects from the following:
   (a) An additional language, (b) History, (c) Geography, (d) Economic, (e) Logic, (f) Psychology, (g) Sociology, (h) Art, (i) Physics, (j) Chemistry, (k) Mathematics, (I) Biology, (m) Geology, (n) Home Science,
3. Work Experience and Social Service.
4. Physical Education.
5. Art or Craft.
6. Education in Moral and Spiritual Values.

Difference in Organisation of the Curriculum as Recommended by the Kothari Commission and Secondary Education Commission

1. *Curriculum of the First Ten Years*: In the Kothari Commission's recommendations for the vast majority of pupils there would be a single curricular stream from Class I to Class X, ending with the first external or public examination, and there would be no 'streaming' or specialisation in this general course.

2. *Scheme of Multipurpose Schools*: On the recommendations of the Secondary Education Commission a number of multipurpose higher secondary schools were opened offering different groups of elective subjects to students in the last three classes. The scheme of multipurpose schools did not work and was scrapped. Students were divided into streams according to their optional groups, and the opportunities for further education were determined, by and large, in terms of the groups selected in the Secondary Schools.

3. *Specialisation*: One of the major weaknesses in the scheme as suggested by the Secondary Education Commission is that specialisation of studies begins too early. At the age of 13 or 14, the students are classified as belonging to the pre-engineering or the pre-medical section. The streaming of pupils in this way into specialised groups from Class IX upwards is undesirable. The recent world trends in secondary education are in the direction of lengthening the period of general education and postponing diversification and specialisation to the second cycle or senior stage of secondary education.

4. *Emphasis on Science and Mathematics*: The Kothari Commission laid emphasis on these two subjects on account of their special importance in the technological age.

5. *Work Experience*: This has been included to initiate students into the 'world of work'.

The recommendations of the Kothari Commission led to the introduction of 10+2+3 pattern of education.

Subject Areas in the Higher Secondary Courses According to Education Commission

1. Two years course instead of one at present. Subjects like Logic, Psychology, Sociology, Geology, Work-Experience and Social Services, Craft, Education in Moral and Spiritual Values were the new subjects recommended for teaching.
2. Provision for advanced courses for talented and gifted children.
3. No diversification favoured at Secondary Stage.
4. Organisation of courses at two levels-ordinary and advanced.

Implementation of Recommendations

The Government of India considered the recommendations of the Education Commission and adopted a National Policy on Education in 1968 which identified National goals of education. The Policy Resolution stated that the educational system must produce young men and women of character and ability committed to National service and development. The following five goals were clearly mentioned:

1. Relating Education to the Needs of the Society.
2. Promotion of National Integration.
3. Equalisation of Educational Opportunity.
4. Linking Education with Productivity and National Development.
5. Acceleration of Social Transformation.

It was thought that a new programme of curriculum development should be undertaken by the adoption of a broadly uniform pattern popularly known as 10+2+3 pattern throughout the country. This pattern meant 10 years of general education followed by diversified Higher Secondary Education and then 2 or 3 years of University Education (2 years pass course and 3 years honours course).

In 1975, the NCERT published an "approach paper" which outlined the salient features of the proposed model curriculum for classes I to X. There was a Nation-wide consultation and ultimately, there was "the curriculum for the 10 years schools".

The new pattern of education was introduced in some of the States. In 1977, the Government of India appointed a Committee known as the Ishwarbhai Patel Committee to review the working of the new pattern and it suggested certain modifications in the scheme in the light of its working during the previous years. One of the important recommendations regarding curriculum reconstruction was the introduction of the concept "Socially Useful, Productive Work" at the High School stage.

In 1977, another Committee known as Plus 2 Committee under the Chairmanship of Dr. Malcolm S. Adiseshiah, then Vice-Chancellor, University of Madras, was appointed to review the curriculum of the Plus 2 stage of school education with special reference to vocationalization of education.

National Policy on Curriculum

The National Policy on Education 1986, is formulated on the fundamental principle that "education is a unique investment in the present and the future". This implies that education is for all and it must promote the goals of socialism, secularism and democracy enshrined in our Constitution and that education develops manpower for different levels of economy. Accordingly curriculum is to be formulated. The National Policy has laid down guidelines in this context in Parts III, V, and VIII. Significant features are as under:

1. *Common Core Curriculum*: The National System of Education will be based on a national curricular framework which contains a common core along with other components that are flexible. The common core will include the history of India's freedom movement, the constitutional obligations and other content essential to nurture national identity. These elements will cut across subject areas and will be designed to promote values such as India's common cultural heritage, egalitarianism, democracy and secularism, equality of the sexes, protection of the environment, removal of social barriers, observance of the small family norm and inculcation of the scientific temper. All educational programmes will be carried on in strict conformity with secular values.

2. *Minimum Levels of Learning*: Minimum levels of learning will be laid down for each stage of education. Steps will also be taken to foster among students an understanding of the diverse cultural and social systems of the people living in different parts of the country.

3. *The Cultural Perspective*: The existing schism between the formal system of education and the country's rich and varied cultural traditions need to be bridged. The preoccupation with modern technologies cannot be allowed to sever new generations from the roots in India's history and culture. De-culturisation, dehumanisation and alienation must be avoided at all costs. Education can and must bring about the fine synthesis between change-oriented technologies and the country's continuity of cultural traditions.

The curricula and processes of education will be enriched by cultural content in as many manifestations as possible. Children will be enabled to develop sensitivity to beauty, harmony and refinement.

4. *Value Education*: The growing concern over the erosion of essential

values and an increasing cynicism in society has brought to focus the need for readjustments in the curriculum in order to make education a forceful tool for the cultivation of social and moral values.

In our culturally plural society education should foster universal and eternal values, oriented towards the unity and integration of our people. Such education should help eliminate obscurantism, religious fanaticism, violence, superstition and fatalism.

5. *Languages*: The Education Policy of 1968 had examined the question of the development of languages in great details; its essential provisions can hardly be improved upon and are as relevant today as before. The implementation of this part of the 1968 Policy has, however, been uneven. The Policy will be implemented more energetically and purposefully.

6. *Media and Educational Technology*: Modern communication technologies have the potential to bypass several stages and sequences in the process of development encountered in early decades. Both the constraints of time and distance at once become manageable. In order to avoid structural dualism, modern educational technology must reach out to the most distant areas and the most deprived sections of beneficiaries simultaneously with the areas of comparative affluence and ready availability.

The media has profound influence on the mind of children as well as adults; some of it has encouraged consumerism, violence etc., and thus had a deleterious effect. Radio and TV programmes which clearly militate against proper educational objectives will be prevented. Steps will be taken to discourage such trend in the films and other media also. An active movement will be started to promote the production of children's films of high quality and usefulness.

7. *Work Experience*: Work experience, viewed as purposive and meaningful manual work, organised as an integral part of the learning process and resulting in either goods or services useful to the community, is considered as an essential component at all stages of education, to be provided through well-structured and graded programmes. It would comprise activities in accordance with the interests, abilities and needs of students, the level of skills and knowledge to be upgraded with the stages of education. The experience would be helpful on entry into the workforce. Pre-vocational programmes provided at the lower secondary stage will also facilitate the choice of the vocational courses at the higher secondary stage.

8. *Education and Environment*: There is a paramount need to create a consciousness of the environment. It must permeate all ages and all sections of society, beginning with the child. Teaching should include environmental consciousness in schools and colleges. This aspect will be integrated in the entire educational process.

9. *Mathematics Teaching*: Mathematics should be visualised as the vehicle to train a child to think, reason, analyse and to articulate logically. Apart from being a specific subject, it should be treated as a concomitant to any subject involving analysis and reasoning.

With the recent introduction of computers in schools, educational computing and the emergence of learning through the understanding of cause-effect relationships and the interplay of variables, the teaching of mathematics will be suitably redesigned to bring it in line with modern technological devices.

10. *Science Education*: Science education will be strengthened so as to develop in the child well defined abilities and values such as the spirit of inquiry, creativity, objectivity, the courage to question, and an aesthetic sensibility.

Science education programmes will be designed to enable the learner to acquire problem solving and decision making skills and to discover the relationship of science with health, agriculture, industry and other aspects of daily life. Every effort will be made to extend science education to the vast numbers who have remained outside the reach of formal education.

11. *Sports and Physical Education*: Sports and physical education are an integral part of the learning process, and will be included in the evaluation of performance. A nation-wide infrastructure for physical education, sports and games will be built into the educational edifice.

The infrastructure will consist of playfields, equipment, coaches and teachers of physical education as part of the School Improvement Programme. Available open spaces in urban areas will be reserved for playgrounds, if necessary by legislation. Efforts will be made to establish sports institutions and hostels where specialised attention will be given to sports activities and sports-related studies along with normal education. Appropriate encouragement will be given to those talented in sports and games. Due stress will be laid on indigenous traditional games. As a system which promotes an integrated development of body and mind, Yoga will receive special attention. Efforts will be made to introduce Yoga in all schools; to this end, it will be introduced in teacher training courses.

12. *Education for International Understanding*: India has always worked for peace and understanding between nations, and treating the whole world as one family. True to this age old tradition, education has to strengthen this world view and motivate the younger generations for international cooperation and peaceful co-existence. This aspect cannot be neglected.

13. *Curriculum at Pre-elementary Stage*: Recognising the holistic nature of child development, *viz.*, nutrition, health and social, mental physical, moral and emotional development, Early Childhood Care and Education (ECCE) will receive high priority and be suitably integrated wherever possible. Day-care centres will be provided as a support service for universalisation of primary education, to enable girls engaged in taking care of siblings to attend school and as a support service for working women belonging to poorer sections.

Programmes of ECCE will be child-oriented, focussed around play, and the individuality of the child. Formal methods and the introduction of the 3Rs will be discouraged at this stage. The local community will be fully involved in these programmes.

A full integration of child care and pre-primary education will be brought about, both as a feeder and a strengthening factor for primary education and for human resource development in general. In continuation of this stage, the School Health Programme will be strengthened.

14. *Curriculum at the Elementary Stage: Child-centred Approach*: A warm, welcoming and encouraging approach, in which all concerned share a solicitude for the needs of the child, is the best motivation for the child to attend school and learn. A child-centred and activity-based process of learning should be adopted at the primary stage. First generation learners should be allowed to set their own pace and be given supplementary remedial instruction.

15. *Curriculum at the Secondary Stage*: Secondary education begins to expose students to differentiated roles of science, the humanities and social sciences. This is also an appropriate stage to provide children with a sense of history and national perspective, and give them opportunities to understand their constitutional duties and rights as citizens. Conscious internalisation of a healthy work ethos and of the values of a humane and composite culture will be brought about through appropriately formulated curricula. Vocationalisation through specialised institutions or through the refashioning of secondary education can, at this stage, provide valuable manpower for economic growth.

National Curriculum for Elementary and Secondary Education (1988)

For carrying out the directives in the policy, the National Council of Educational Research Training, New Delhi, prepared a National Curriculum for Elementary and Secondary Education. Some of the emerging curricular concerns and imperatives based on socio-cultural, political and economic considerations, which have a strong bearing on the school curriculum included the following:

1. Equality of Educational Opportunity.
2. Preservation of Cultural Heritage.
3. Constitutional Obligations.
4. Strengthening of National Identity and Unity.
5. Character Building and Inculcation of Values.
6. A Global Perspective.
7. Protection of the Environmental and Conservation of Natural Resources.
8. Observation of Small Family Norms.
9. Future-Oriented Education.
10. Education for All-round Development.
11. Evolving a Child-Centred Approach to Education.
12. Facilitating Creative Expression.
13. Inculcation of the Scientific Temper.
14. Interface between Education and the World of Work.
15. Continuous and Comprehensive Education.
16. Utilisation of Media and Education Technology.
17. Minimum Levels of Learning.
18. Core-Curriculum.

Scheme of Studies (Classes I to X)

Subject and Stages	*Percentage of Time*
1. Elementary Education (8 years)	
1. *Primary-Stage* (5years)	
(a) One language-the mother-tongue/the regional language	30%
(b) Mathematics	15%
(c) Environmental Studies I and II	15%
(d) Work Experience	20%
(e) Art Education	10%
(f) Health and Physical Education	10%
Total	**100%**
2. *Upper Primary Stage* (3 years)	
(a) Three Languages	32%
(b) Mathematics	12%
(c) Science	12%
(d) Social Science	12%
(e) Work Experience	12%
(f) Art Education	10%
(g) Health and Physical Education	10%
Total	**100%**
3. *Secondary Stage* (2 years)	
(a) Three Languages	30%
(b) Mathematics	13%
(c) Science	13%
(d) Social Science	13%
(e) Work Experience	13%
(f) Art Education	9%
(g) Health and Physical Education	9%
Total	**100%**

8

Salient Features of the National Curriculum Framework for School Education (2000)

The National Curriculum for School Education is the outcome of the initiative of NCERT Chairman J.S. Rajput. His paper on *"School Curriculum in India: A Case for Transformation"* became the starting point. A Task Force, constituted for the purpose, deliberating with Departments of NIE, RIES, CIET interacted with some key academicians like Prof. J.N. Kapur, Dr. (Mrs.) Kapila Vatsayan, Prof. Yogender Singh, Dr. Ravindra Kumar, Dr. Sugata Mitra, Dr. Arvind Kumar, Prof. Mukhopadhyaya, Shri M. Varadarajan and Prof. D.P. Pattanayak. This was the first phase of a curriculum design which resulted in the preparation of the present document. The activity flow chart of the programme is given at page 87.

Chief Features of the National Curriculum Framework

The Curriculum Framework, second in the series since the formulation of the National Policy on Education-NPE 1986, provides a framework for all the stages of school education—Elementary to Senior Secondary. The whole idea according to the framers of the curriculum is to provide continuity and sequence between all the stages of school years, and thereby ensure a holistic approach to all the years of school curriculum.

The curriculum, it is claimed has been evolved through a variety of strategies by looking into theoretical and research materials including consultations and discussions with educationists and experts.

I. *New Panchsheel as the Essence of Curriculum*

The function of the curriculum is to ensure the realisation of the new 'Panchsheel' in the present context which would duly emphasizes learner centred education, women centred family, human being centred development, knowledge centred society and innovation centred India.

II. Curriculum Concerns

The curriculum which is envisaged to stand on three pillars—*'relevance'*, *'equity'* and *'excellence'*, must look after the following concerns:

(1) Education for a cohesive society, which implies providing equality of access and opportunity-taking note of the special requirements of the first generation learners, physically, mentally and visually challenged pupils as well as pupils coming from the disadvantaged sections of society.

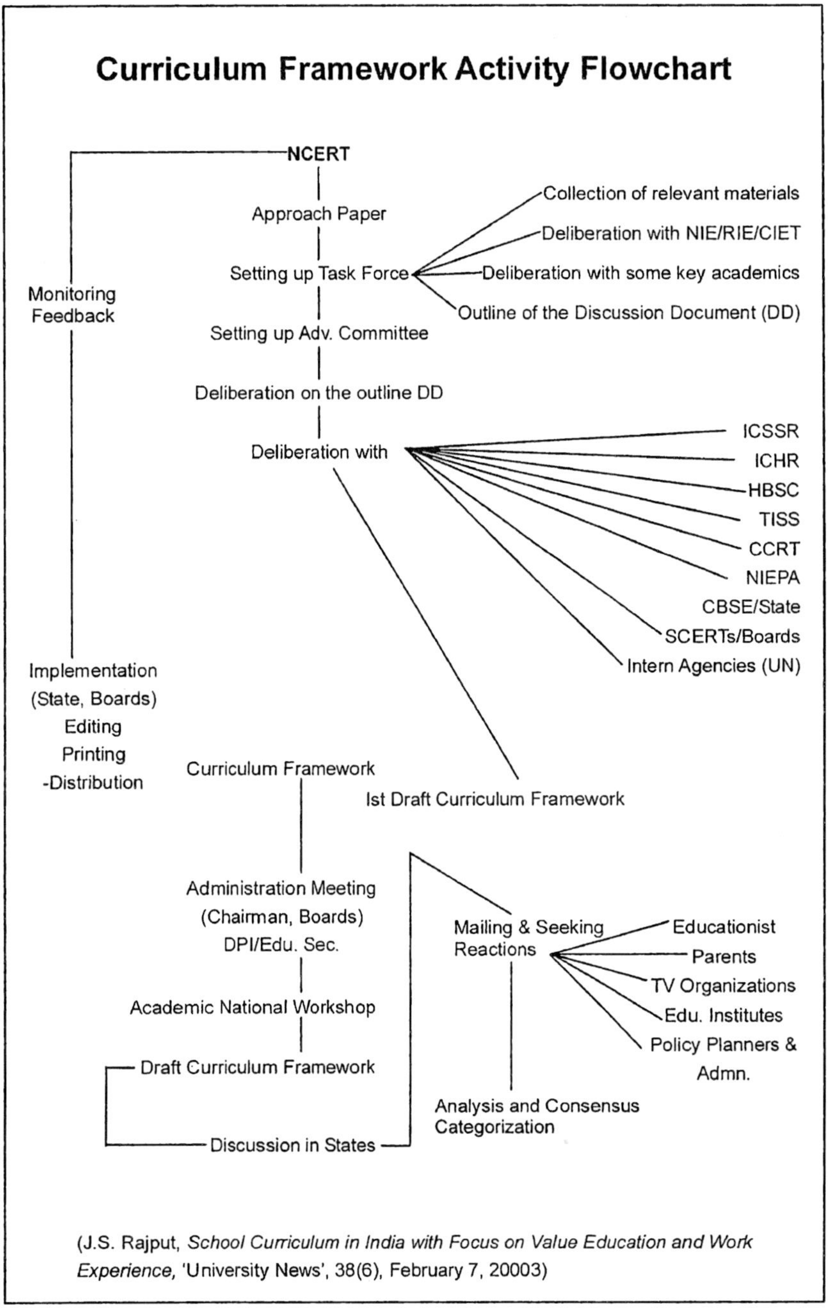

Fig.: Curriculum Framework Activity Flowchart

(J.S. Rajput, *School Curriculum in India with Focus on Value Education and Work Experience,* 'University News', 38(6), February 7, 2000)

(2) Strengthening national unity and preserving cultural heritage.
(3) Improving indigenous knowledge and India's contribution to mankind.
(4) Responding to the impact of globalisation.
(5) Meeting the challenge of information and communication technologies.
(6) Linking education with life skills.
(7) Education for value development.
(8) Spreading fruits of literacy to a large group of children through non-formal/alternative schooling.
(9) Integrating diverse curricular concerns.
(10) Relating education to world of work.
(11) Reducing the curriculum load.
(12) Making child as a constructor of his knowledge.
(13) Recognising interface between cognition and emotion.
(14) Using culture-specific pedagogies.
(15) Developing aesthetic sensibilities.
(16) Making continuous and comprehensive evaluation.
(17) Treating education as a life-long process.

III. ***Organisation of Curriculum at Elementary and Secondary Stages***

Curriculum renewal should lay emphasis on the following points:

(1) Provision of a common core curriculum.
(2) Introduction of the norms of minimum levels of learning or the essential levels of learning outcomes for each stage of school education in order to bring about a broad commonality in the standards of education throughout the country.
(3) A common scheme of studies for classes I to X: Pre-primary Education (2 years), Elementary Education (8 years), divided into two stages of Primary Stage (5 years) and Upper Primary Stage (3 years). Primary Stage is further divided into two stages: A. Classes I and II, B. Classes III-V The Upper Primary Stage comprises (3 years) and the Secondary Stage (2 years).
(4) Issues and themes drawn from the areas—history, geography, economics, civics and geography to be organised from simple to complex ideas as well as immediate to remote.
(5) After taking into account the number of days required for organising evaluation activities/tests/examinations, school functions, etc., a minimum of 180 days in a year to be made available for effective instruction.
(6) The duration of class period to be around 40 minutes.
(7) The existing groupings like arts, science, commerce, and agriculture not to be treated as water-tight compartments. Students to have the freedom, within practical limits, to offer courses simultaneously from more than one group according to their needs, interests and aptitude.
(8) Over a period of time the mental inhibitions setting barriers between academic and vocational and between various traditional groupings to be dismantled.
(9) Semesterisation of senior secondary stage to be made operative.
(10) Credit system to be introduced.

(11) Common Foundation Course to be introduced at the senior secondary stage and this course to consist of (i) Language and Literature (ii) General Studies (iii) Work Education and (iv) Health and Physical education.
(12) Accepting universalisation as an essentiality.

IV. *Evaluation and Examination*

(a) There is a need to revamp the whole system of examinations and evaluation from primary grades to senior secondary stage if proper benefit is to be derived out of precious inputs provided through resources drawn from the country's economy.
(b) No common strategy of evaluation may suit all levels of education.
(c) Minimum Levels of Learning (MLLs) to be accepted not only as a concept but as an approach.
(d) Emphasis to be laid on deformalisation of both internal and external examinations with a view to reducing the anxiety and fear experienced by the learners at all stages of education.
(e) Grading system to be adopted.
(f) The elements of subjectivity to be reduced by employing multiple criteria and multiple sources from where the assessment should come.
(g) Educational Testing Service to be established.

Implementation and Managing the System

Curriculum renewal is an on-going process and it calls for multipurpose activities involving the following agencies and programmes:

1. Professional support from agencies like SCERTs.
2. Professional support from teacher education/training institutions.
3. Resource centres at the school complexes.
4. In-service training programmes.
5. Net work of technical support structure from institutions like National Institutes of Educational Planning and Administration (NIEPA), Central Institute of English and Foreign Languages (CIEFL). Boards of Secondary Education etc.
6. National Council for Information Technology.

V. *Education for Value Development*

Curriculum being an expression of the school philosophy, to contain components that communicate essential values relating to physical environment, organisational health, human relations, such as discipline, cleanliness, punctuality, democratic functioning/commitment, responsibility for maintaining order, decorum, environment protection, respect for others religion, caste, creed and community.

Textbooks content to be developed in such a manner that these values get represented in an explicit manner and not remain as hidden agenda.

Teacher training programmes to clarify teachers' role in value orientation.

Co-curricular activities like NCC, NSS, Scouts and Guides, Games, Plays/Drama, Exhibition, Bal Melas, etc. to be utilised as very potent medium to communicate values.

The philosophy of guidance and counselling which involves among students open-mindedness, sensitivity, caring, empathy, problem-solving skills etc., to be made use of in the learning of values.

VI. *Development of Evaluation Materials*

A variety of evaluation materials to be developed by the organisations like the NCERT, SCERTs and DIETs for the use of teachers, teacher educators and parents.

VII. *Boards of Secondary Education*

The Boards to shift gradually their focus from merely conducting the examinations to upgrading the quality of school education and strengthening school based evaluation.

VIII. *Provision of the Minimum Essential Facilities*

The Government at the Central and the state level should make adequate provisions to ensure that all schools have basic inputs for teaching-learning, i.e. school building with classrooms, drinking water and toilet facilities, teachers', instructional materials and teaching aids.

The document ends with these remarks, "Mechanisms should be devised in consultation with the community (including professionals) to extend intersectoral cooperation in augmenting the resources of the school."

Basic Thrusts of Organisation of Curriculum at Elementary and Secondary Stage

In keeping with our development priorities of today and the foreseeable future, the basic thrusts and objectives of the New Framework have been rightly visualised as detailed below:

(i) Emphasis on the development of human resources to put the young men and women of India on the forefront of development for the realisation of the national goals of education, prosperity and social cohesion.

(ii) Broad-based general education to all learners at the elementary (5 years of primary and 3 years of upper primary) and secondary (2 years) stages. It will help them become life-long learners and develop in themselves basic life skills and emotional intelligence for sustenance and coping with the challenges of day-to-day life.

(iii) A broad-based common scheme of studies for the elementary and secondary stages with emphasis on the skill of "learning how to learn".

- At this point, however, there may arise a question whether uniformity of structure and scheme of studies is desirable, especially at the elementary stage, in view of the school grade system and single teacher schools.
- Another issue that merits consideration is whether the scheme of studies at this stage has to be common, ignoring a sizeable number of those learners who are either disabled (about 10% of the total number of learners), slow learners or the gifted ones. If yes, ways to cater to the needs of these special groups of learners under a common scheme of studies at this stage will have to be found.

(iv) The 1976 addition (Part IV A, Article 51 A) to the Constitution of India laid down some Fundamental Duties which exhorted all Indian citizens to (a) abide by the Constitution and respect its ideals and institutions, the *National Flag* and the *National Anthem;* (b) cherish and follow the noble ideals that inspired our national struggle for freedom; uphold and protect the sovereignty, unity and integrity of the country; defend the country and render national service when called upon to do so; (e) promote harmony and the spirit of common brotherhood among all the people of India transcending religious, linguistic and regional or sector diversities; (f) renounce practices derogatory to the dignity of woman; (g) value and preserve the rich heritage of one composite culture; (h) protect and improve the natural environment and have compassion for living. creatures; (i) develop scientific temper, humanism and the spirit of enquiry and reform; (j) safeguard public property and abjure violence, and (k) strive toward excellence in all spheres of individual and collective activity so that the nation constantly rises to higher levels of endeavour and achievement.

The National Policy on Education 1986 reflected almost every element included in the Fundamental Duties. All these elements were spelt out in the *National Curriculum Framework,* 1988 as the common core and, hence need to be reaffirmed.

(v) The common core components comprise the following:

(a) The history of India's freedom movement.
- However it is also felt that this should appropriately lead on to India's struggle for development and growth after independence.

(b) The Constitutional obligations.

(c) Content essential to nurture national identity

(d) India's common cultural heritage.
- Some interpretation of 'common culture' excludes India's ancient and medieval cultures. The real spirit of this element must be understood and accordingly it should be decided whether 'uniformity of cultures' or 'unity of cultures' is intended here.

(e) Egalitarianism, democracy and secularism.
- **Secularism, in the present educational parlance, has wrongly been misunderstood as rejection of religion.** There has now emerged an opinion that the term ought to mean equal understanding of and respect for all religions 'Sarvadharma Samabhava' or 'Panthanirapekshata'. This interpretation, as also accepted by the Sriprakasa Committee (1960), facilitates the view that religion in its basic form (devoid of myth dogma and ritual) would draw younger generation to basic moral and spiritual values.

In this context Mahatma Gandhi also asserted,

"The education which leads to the negation of God cannot make for the service of the country nor of humanity". (*The Hindu,* 21 July 1927)

(f) Equality of sexes

(g) Protection and preservation of the environment
(h) Removal of social barriers
(i) Observance of the small family norm, and
(j) Inculcation of scientific temper.

There, however, seems room for some more components that may claim the status of 'core components' in the changed and fast changing national scenario even if we do not follow the 'panic approach'. These may be:

(a) Human Rights including Rights of the Child and those of the Girl Child.
(b) Inculcation of personal and social values such as cleanliness, compassion, truthfulness, integrity, responsibility, justice, respect for law and order, courage and the values cherished for the functioning of democracy.

(vi) Emphasis on ensuring minimum essential level of acquisition of knowledge, understanding and skill in all subjects at all stages, commensurate with the learners' abilities and learning experiences.

(vii) Provision of flexibility in terms of selection of content/components and learning experiences which could facilitate the attainment of minimum essential level of knowledge/skill laid down for each stage of school education.

(viii) Emphasis on learner centred and activity-based processes rather than the teacher-centred content-based approach during curriculum transaction.

(ix) Recasting of the examination system and introduction of continuous and comprehensive evaluation that incorporates both—scholastic and non-scholastic aspects of education spread over the total span of instructional time.

(x) Provision of remedial teaching as well as counselling services for carrying out the diagnosis of learning problems and providing support to the needy learners' groups.

(xi) Setting up an appropriate system of National Testing Service (NTS) for the selection and development of norms of comparable competence across the nation.

(xii) Applicability of the curriculum to all learners irrespective of their modes/channels of learning in order to ensure comparability of attainment and to facilitate horizontal and vertical mobility of the learners.

- However, one has to re-examine the assumption that comparability of attainment and applicability of the curriculum to all learners despite difference in their modes/channels of learning could be possible.

(xiii) Provision of essential facilities or the minimum conditions for learning through effective transaction of curriculum in all schools and centres of alternative schooling centres.

Formulation of Objectives of Curriculum

Curriculum organisers, would indicate, at the outset, the overall objectives of curriculum which would coincide with the overall aim of school education. Then stage-wise objectives are to be carefully formulated keeping in view the developmental characteristics and level associated with different stages of education. Each subject area would have its own specific objectives clearly defined in behavioural terms. However, it must be remembered that human learning makes one unified whole and that separate subject areas have been created only for the sake of convenience.

General Objectives of Education

School curriculum should aim at enabling the learners to acquire knowledge, develop understanding and inculcate skills, positive attitudes, values and habits conducive to the all-round development of their personality. Learners are a nation's assets and they are to be empowered through education to increase their scope and capability to do and to be. Simultaneously, school curriculum has the onus of minimising and, if possible, eradicating the country's 'liabilities' like ignorance, poverty and moral weaknesses. Paradigm shifts are therefore necessary to support a curriculum that values the interaction of process and content. Besides, the development of intrinsic values and emotional intelligence of learners are also crucial.

School curriculum should, therefore, help to generate and promote among the learners:

1. Language abilities (listening, speaking, reading and writing) needed for social living and further learning;

2. Communication skills (verbal and visual) for effective participation in day-to-day activities;

3. Mathematical abilities to develop a logical mind and enable learners to perform simple mathematical operations and their application in every day life;

4. Scientific temper characterised by spirit of enquiry, courage to question and objectivity leading to elimination of obscurantism, superstition and fatalism;

5. Knowledge of scientific methods of enquiry and its use in solving problems;

6. Understanding of the environment in its totality (natural and social, and their interactive processes), the environmental problems and the ways and means to preserve the environment;

7. Abilities to investigate into various issues and problems at the local, regional, national and global levels and to make one's own independent assessment;

8. Appreciation of sacrifices and contributions made by the freedom fighters and social workers in India's freedom struggle and social regeneration, and readiness to follow their ideals;

9. Qualities that make a person humane and socially effective giving meaning and direction to life. These values may be clustered around social/ economic and personal/spiritual values;

10. Understanding the diversity in lands and people living in different parts of the country and the country's composite cultural heritage;

11. Appreciation for the need of a balanced synthesis between the change oriented technologies and the continuity of the country's traditions and heritage;

12. Knowledge of and respect for our national symbols and desire and determination to uphold the ideals of national identity and unity;

13. Understanding the positive and the negative impact of the processes of globalisation, liberalisation and localisation in the context of our own country;

14. Knowledge, attitude and habits necessary for keeping physically and mentally fit and strong in conformity with the normal developmental pattern;

15. An awareness of the inherent equality of all and the need for global fraternity with a strong commitment to human values and to social justice;

16. Application of and readiness to practise in life the national goals of socialism, secularism, healthy democracy and non-violence;

17. Qualities and characteristics necessary for self-learning, self-directed learning and life-long learning leading to the creation of a learning society;

18. Pre-vocational/vocational skills, willingness to work hard, entrepreneurship and dignity of manual work necessary for increasing productivity, obtaining job-satisfaction and creating wealth generating systems;

19. Ability to discover and appreciate beauty in different life situations, and integrate it into one's own personality;

20. Capacity not only to accumulate factual information but also to understand, reflect and internalise and develop insight;

21. Capability of appreciating and tolerating difference and diversities of various sorts/ideologies and the capacity to choose between alternative value systems;

22. Appreciation of various consequences of large families and over population and need for checking population growth; and

23. Cultivating proper understanding of and attitude towards healthy sex related issues and healthy, respectful attitude towards members of the opposite sex.

9

A Critique of the NCERT Curriculum Framework

General Observations

The present document is an excellent one as a series of well-prepared learned discourses for the students of education preparing for their examinations. It can serve as an important source of suitable quotes. It may also prove very helpful to progressive schools having fairly large resources.

One of the greatest tragedies in the field of educational reforms is that the advisory bodies enjoy a large measure of autonomy but very little responsibility.

Specific Observations

At the very outset, a few comments may be made on the observations contained in the preface of the document. It states, "The National Policy on Education', 1986 categorically recommended the revision of the policy and the curriculum after every five years". The exact words used in the NPE are, "The implementation and parameters of the New Policy must be reviewed every five years". Apparently there is a difference between 'review' and 'revision'. The present revision also seems to be lop-sided and slip-shod. After 1992, no review has been undertaken.

The preface further observes, "The National Council of Educational Research and Training also realises that every curriculum has an expiry date and needs to be revised at regular intervals". This appears to be a very restricted view of curriculum. Curriculum has no expiry date. Curriculum renewal is an on-going process. The Central Board of Secondary Education revises its curriculum every year. A dynamic and progressive classroom teacher, in a way, daily revises the curriculum and attempts to incorporate the latest knowledge and innovation in his work. He does not wait for twelve years as is being done by the NCERT in bringing out its curriculum. 'Expiry date' connotes a somewhat fixed curriculum.

Thirdly, it is said the "document has been evolved through a variety of strategies—by looking into theoretical and research materials." In this context it does not throw any light as to what specific research studies have been undertaken in the parameters of the NPE, 1986 as amended in 1992.

Fourthly, it is said to have been evolved "...consulting practically all the faculty members of the Council, whether at its headquarters in Delhi or at other constituent units, and discussing with them issues that have some bearing on the different aspects of curriculum and its transaction. Eminent educationists and experts were invited to speak to the Curriculum Group and other faculty members. An attempt has been made to integrate all such ideas in the document". Regretfully, the Curriculum Group did not think it prudent to interact with class room teachers, educational administrators and supervisors, parents and students— the real users of the curriculum.

Fifthly, the document is to be taken up for extensive as well as intensive discussions at various levels to evolve a consensus. It is common knowledge that consensus on such issues is elusive.

Lastly, the new 'Panchsheel' of the curriculum emphasizes women centred family but the working group includes just one presentation of an eminent women educationist and ten from men educationists. A very discriminatory approach on the part of path makers!

There is nothing new in the document which has not been said earlier and seriously debated and consensus arrived at. On the other hand the document tends to rake up old controversies like the Three Language Formula, Religious policy, flexible courses, etc.

If we want to do things at a slightly deeper level, than of the clitches of the day, we must allow our enthusiasm, however, justified to subside, and start looking at things pragmatically and rationally.

The document is full of sweeping charges regarding the implementation of NPE. It reads, "While reviewing the situation with regards to the implementation of these areas, a dismal picture emerges. Of the eleven thrust areas, only a few could be implemented, that too in a limited manner." This is doing injustice to lakhs of devoted teachers who are working under heavy strain on account of the non-availability of basic facilities.

The financial aspect of the educational reform is totally missing.

There is absolutely no basis in the charge levelled by the so called votaries of secularism that attempts are made in the document to saffronise the curriculum. After going through it thoroughly, one does not find any such element in this criticism. On the contrary, NCERT Social Studies and History Text books reflect somewhat distortion of ancient Indian History. For instance, NCERT textbooks invariably mention the term 'Coming of the Aryans/advent of the Aryans'. An appropriate and objective approach would be to delete the words 'coming of and 'advent of. This is a contentious issue. Views of historians representing both sides should be given. Let the students derive their own conclusion. Value judgement should be avoided. Another point may be stated regarding this. It is rather surprising that whereas so many material objects have been discovered regarding the Harappan Culture which is said to have flourished about 1000 years before the Aryan Civilization but no such material on the later civilization is discovered. This is an issue to be looked into.

Summing Up

As already observed, it is an excellent Paper but only for discussion. Theoretically speaking all suggestions are worth implementation.

We have more important and pressing tasks in educational reconstruction than discussing such theoretical papers which raise contentious issues already settled. In this regard special mention may be made of the Three Language Policy, Religious Policy. Such efforts are likely to distract the attention of field workers and others engaged in carrying out programmes in accordance with the accepted policies.

It appears, the NCERT has run short of meaningful and purposeful programmes and this exercise is meant to keep die staff occupied. In this context one is reminded of the famous remarks of an internationally known economist that digging of holes may be resorted to for providing employment when a country is faced with unemployment.

The writer is acutely aware of the fact that his views are likely to raise a howl of protests from vested sections and he is dubbed as a cynic, conservative, ignorant, reactionary and skeptic etc.

All said and done, perhaps some miracle may happen and a workable programme for revitalising education may emerge out of this document. Let us hope so!

Parawise Observations

The key points contained in the Discussion Paper are followed by observations.

New 'Panchsheel'. The new curriculum framework has to ensure the realisation of the new 'Panchsheel' in the present context which duly emphasize learner centred education, women centred family, human being centred development, knowledge centred society and innovative centred India.

[Observations. The proposed concept seems to be a little lopsided. It may be rephrased as: The new curriculum framework has to ensure the realization of the new 'Panchsheel' in the present context which duly emphasise Learner centred education, Women equality centred family, Human being centred development, Knowledge, wisdom and value centred Society, and Constructive innovated centred India.

Alternatively the new Panchsheel may be described as:

Each letter of the word 'Panch' may denote:

P - stands for productive and purposeful curriculum A-stands for action based curriculum

N - New knowledge oriented curriculum

C - Child centred education

H - Humane centred development Indian Society

Curriculum for the 21st century may be expressed in terms of 'Sapth Sheel' i.e. 7R's.

R - Reading

R - Writing

R - Arithmetic
(signify discipline/school subjects)

R - Rights

R - Responsibilities (Duties)

R - Relationships (among Subjects and Rights and Responsibilities)

R - Recreation.

International community did not pay due heed to the religious 'Panchsheel' of Buddha.

China disregarded political 'Panchsheel'.

Now it is to be seen to what extent educational 'Panchsheel' works.]

Scheme of Studies

A common scheme of studies is advocated for Classes I to X. The general objectives of education will be realised through the content and learning experiences related to different subject areas. However, the emphasis would shift from factual knowledge to the process of understanding, thinking and internalising. Besides, personality development, value education, health and physical education, art education and work experience, should be given appropriate importance in the school curriculum. The inter-connections among various subject areas should be clearly established.

The core component areas and values should form an integral part of the curriculum at all the stages of school and may suitably be integrated in different subject areas. Flexibility in selection of content and learning experiences should be built in the system.

Pre-Primary Education (2 Years)

This stage of education would help children prepare for school later through group activities, play-way techniques, language games, number games and activities directed to promote socialisation and environmental awareness. Perception, pleasure and participation are to be emphasised. No formal teaching of subjects or reading and writing are to be undertaken at this stage.

- Although it is understood that a National Curricular Framework aims at providing a uniform stage structure for the whole country, it is found that the Pre-Primary Stage of education is not available to children in many States. In many others, it is not available in the rural sector. In some States the 'Aanganwadis' exist but these do not function as Pre-Primary Education Centres.
- Although formal teaching of subjects and reading and writing skills are clearly prohibited at this stage, almost everywhere that is being done in these preparatory classes. This puts unhealthy and harmful load on children whose neuro-muscular capacities are not yet developed.

Pre-Primary Education (2 Years)

Although formal teaching of Subjects and reading and writing skills are clearly prohibited at this stage, almost everywhere that is being done in these preparatory classes. This puts unhealthy and harmful load on children whose neuro-muscular capacities are not yet developed. (2.4.1, P. 35)

[*Observations.* It is not clear which authority has prohibited this. If it has been prohibited, why is this practice being allowed to continue? Who would enforce it?]

- In view of these two points we must think afresh whether it would be advisable to continue with the current discriminatory and stressful system of Pre-Primary schooling.

- In case it has to stay, we must also find out how it can be made uniformly available to all the children of the country and how its real objectives can be ensured.

[*observation*: What is the use of posing these questions, when it is crystal clear that no consensus can be reached here! The objective of UEE is still elusive? Will the government burn its own figures by involving itself at the pre-primary stage? On the one hand the Discussion Paper talks of flexibility at every stage and on the other hand of uniformity. Both elements cannot be reconciled.]

Elementary Education (8 Years)

Primary Stage (*5 Years*)

A. *Classes I and II*

(a) One language—the home language/the regional language
(b) Mathematics

These two areas will have centrally developed curriculum and curricula materials for classroom use.

(c) Environmental Studies
(d) The three areas of Work Education, Arts (Fine and Performing), and Health activities may be put together and a suitable name may be given to them. This gets support in Mahatma Gandhi's observation that

> *Music should form part of the syllabus of primary education. The modulation of the voice is as necessary as the training of the hand. Physical drill, handicrafts, drawing and music should go hand in hand in order to draw the best out of the boys and girls and create in them a real interest in their tuition.*
>
> (*Harijan,* 11 September 1937)

Schools should be given full autonomy to use locally developed curriculum and locally available resources for covering areas under (c) and (d).

B. *Classes III-V*

(a) One language-the home language/the regional language
(b) English
(c) Mathematics
(d) Environmental Studies
(e) The three areas of Work Education, Arts (Fine and Performing), and Health activities may be put together and a suitable name may be given to them.

At this stage also schools should be given full autonomy as mentioned earlier for Classes I and II.

[*Observations*: Perhaps for the first time in the history of literature of education, the term 'home language' has been used. It is subject to several interpretations. Its meaning must be made clear so as to bring about clarity in the use of 'home language' and mother-tongue.

It is very simplistic to talk of auton0omy but very difficult to translate this concept in practice at all places. This puts very heavy demands on the teachers of Local Bodies and government schools. Altogether a new type of training/ education is needed. Of course, in several Public Schools, this concept has already been accepted and is being followed.]

In the changed socio-economic scenario and individual and national requirement generated by the process of globalisation and information technology, introduction of English at this stage seems to have been necessitated. It still should not be introduced earlier because: (i) before it can be introduced the learners' first language should be strong enough to be used as a resource for learning the second language, and (ii) the first two years, in very large number of cases, are to be devoted to a smooth transition from the home language of the learners to their school language or regional language.

[*Observations.* Here again, contradictory statements are made. The Document blows hot and cold in the same 'breath'.]

Upper Primary Stage (3 years)

(a) Three languages
(b) Mathematics
(c) Science and Technology
(d) Social Sciences
(e) Work Education, Art Education (Fine and Performing), and Health, and Physical Education (including NCC, Scouts and Guides)

- These three areas may be clubbed together and a suitable name may be given to it.

[*Observations*: It may be difficult to club all the areas together. Work Education has a distinct identity. It is totally at variance with the recommendations of the Secondary Education Commission (1952-53), Education Commission (1964-66), Ishwarbhai Patel Review Committee (1977), National Review Committee (1987-88), NPE (1986), NCERT National Curriculum for Elementary and Secondary Education (1988), Ramamurti Committee (1990) and Janardhana Reddy Committee (1992). The rationale of clubbing is not made clear. It is likely to involve several administrative problems which have been ignored by the framers of the Discussion Paper.]

Secondary Stage (2 years)

(a) Three Languages
(b) Mathematics
(c) Science and Technology
(d) Social Sciences
(e) Work Education/Pre-Vocational skills, Art Education (Fine and Performing), and Health and Physical Education (including NCC, Scouts and Guides)
    - These three areas may be clubbed together and a suitable name may be given to it.
    - We may also consider here whether Computer Literacy could also be added as one of the subjects (10%) at this stage.

[*Observations:* For clubbing as above. As regards terminology, the Zakir

Hussain Committee Report used craft, the Secondary Education Commission listed Art and Music, Craft and Physical Education as separate subjects with their separate identities, Education Commission used Work Experience and Social Service, Ishwarbhai Committee used Socially Useful Productive Work and Community Service, NPE used Work Experience, NCERT Work Experience and now new terminology of Work Education. Why to create confusion unnecessarily when the essence is the same. Change in nomenclature without proper justification is open to confusion.]

Languages and Language Formula

The three-language formula was formulated with the best of intentions and academic considerations. Under this formula, the first language had invariably to be the home language/mother tongue or the regional language. In a number of states/organisations/boards, however, the spirit of the formula has not been followed, and the mother tongue of the people has been denied the status of the first language. Moreover, because of the changed socio-economic scenario, the difference between the second and the third languages has dwindled. Thus, in reality there may be two second languages for all purposes and functions. Some states follow only a two-language formula whereas in some other classical languages like Sanskrit and Arabic are being studied in lieu of a modern Indian language. Some boards/institutions permit even European languages like French and German in the place of Hindi. In this scenario, the three language formula exists only in our curriculum documents and other policy statements.

What, then, should be our 'language formula' for the school stage? Can the following be acceptable?

Every child's home language/mother tongue or regional language should be his/her first language to be learnt right from the first standard. English as a subject may be introduced in Class III and Hindi in non-Hindi speaking states and any other modern Indian language may be taught from Class VI. All these languages must continue upto the end of the secondary stage. No doubt, flexibility in choosing the exact grade/class for the introduction of the second and the third languages is desirable.

Could the classical languages be taught as part of a composite course with mother tongue/regional languages originating from them?

Normally when children come to school for the first time they are already fluent in their home language but their language skills are often ignored in bi-lingual or multi-lingual situations. Since the languages used at home and at school are mostly different, even in supposedly monolingual societies, the crucial issue that emerges is how to help children in reconciling these two languages, their home language and the medium of instruction. This situation becomes much more complicated when a child is introduced to a third language, national or international. In such a situation the home language of the children may be used mostly, say about 80 per cent and the school language or the regional language may be slowly introduced in the oral form covering about 20 per cent of the educational activity in the first two classes. This will initiate and smoother the desired transition from the home language to the medium of instruction at school. By the end of the primary stage, the standard regional language would become the sole medium of instruction.

As stated earlier, the home language, not the second or third language, national or international, would serve as the medium of child's perception and socialisation and his/her mental, moral and emotional development. Formal teaching of language skills of reading and writing must be discouraged at this stage. Story telling, recitation of rhymes, singing of songs, playing games involving active language use may be profitably used. Free conversation with the teacher and classmates and participation in lively discussion should also be encouraged. Taking the children to outdoor trips and excursions, observation of the surroundings would involve new experience and add to the children's vocabulary. Dramatisation, picture reading, puppet play etc. which give opportunity to use orally or listen to language should also be provided for language learning at the pre-primary stage of education.

At the time of entering the primary stage, whether a child has been to a pre-primary school or not, he/she has already mastered the basic structures of his/her home language/mother tongue in the oral mode and can freely use it for day to day communication needs. It is assumed that initially children possess, on an average, about 1500 words of their own language and a fairly large number of words from English which have been freely borrowed in their language. This total vocabulary increases very fast at the primary stage. Children have to be specially helped to acquire the basic skills of speaking (pronunciation), reading and writing in the first two years of the primary stage (Classes I & II). Special attention should be paid to the process of standardisation of pronunciation according to the norms in the regional language at this level. Similarly, the skill of good handwriting, correct spelling and right habit of silent reading with comprehension are also to be developed. Children's ability for creative self expression is to be properly developed.

It is generally thought that by the end of the primary stage, a child should acquire about 5000 words of his/her mother tongue. However, with additional recommended reading this number of words perhaps could be higher.

Despite all the constitutional provisions and policy statements, Hindi or any other Indian language has not yet been raised, in practice, to the position of the most popularly used language in administration, judiciary, business, industry and information technology, science and technology. English has increasingly been recognised as a tool for access, success, prosperity, prestige and upward mobility. Even the rural first generation learners aspire for learning English to secure for themselves a place in the successful and respected social class. Hence, there has been a continuous pressure for initiating the teaching of English in the very pre-primary stage or latest by the first standard. However, formal learning of a second language at that early stage is not desirable and it results in avoidable learning load. Modern researchers have also proved wrong the popularly bold view that the earlier a second language is taught, the better it is count. In view of these contradictions, it is now considered both advisable and advantageous to introduce the formal learning of English in Class III. If some organisations/ institutions still insist on starting English in Class I, it may be done only informally, mostly in the preparatory oral mode, in Classes I and II.

At the upper primary stage, pupils' competence in both the languages has to be strengthened further to enable them acquire real life skills to be used in their future day-to-day life. In their first language, they should be introduced to various forms of literature. They should be able to react in speech and in writing to whatever they read and listen to. Balanced stress on both the applied side and the metaphorical aspect of the language should be laid. Creative expression and the ability to think on one's own should be encouraged and nurtured through language teaching with oral form of language finding important place in language curriculum. It is here at this stage that children should be exposed to applied or practical grammar in order to enable them to develop additional insight into the nature, structure and functions of the languages.

Learners are also to be introduced to the third language (or the second language). However, teaching of this language is to be planned keeping in view the reality that the exposure of the pupils to this language and the need for using it in real life situations would be comparatively restricted, pretty simple and not too frequent. As such, it should be quite satisfactory if the pupils learn to operate successfully, in speech and in writing, within the limits of a controlled vocabulary and graded structure and read with comprehension simple texts of description, narration, information, instructions, processes etc.

At the secondary stage (Classes IX and X) in the first language full mastery over the applied form of language and good acquaintance with literary language should be aimed at. Learners should achieve maturity in oral and written expression and respond to what they listen to or read. Literary texts in prose and poetry of appropriate level should be provided to them so that they may start understanding and appreciating the depth and diversities of human mind. Teaching of grammar should be systematically strengthened so that the subtle usages of language are understood and suitably used. Creativity in language use should be encouraged. More importantly, selection of the teaching material must reflect an attempt, implicit or explicit, of inculcating desirable attitudes, appreciation of and dedication to the values related to the core components of the curriculum. High order communication skill in the first language, with grammatical accuracy and appropriateness of style should be the main objectives of first language learning at the secondary stage.

In English and modern Indian languages used as second/second second/third language at this stage, the most important objective should be to make the learners capable of using the language in speech and writing whenever needed in life and read with reasonable speed for information and pleasure. A well balanced development of all the language skills at this stage is aimed at, but still, more and more reading materials of a suitable standard and literary value should be provided to the learners which will also create and nourish right attitudes and human and citizenship values. Grammar should not be taught as a theoretical subject per se. but it should be taught as practical or functional grammar in context with the minimum of theory. Similarly, too complicated or subtle literary aspects should be avoided.

Thus, more and more aural-oral skills of language are to be emphasised in language education at the primary stage, all the four skills are to be aimed at in a balanced manner at the upper primary stage and slightly more attention is to be paid to the skills of reading and writing at the secondary stage. However, despite this marginal difference in the matter of importance to the different skills at different stages of school education, the most crucial and ultimate task of language education at all these levels remains to enable the pupils to use the languages effectively in either mode whenever and wherever required in their day-to-day life situations of all sorts.

[*Observations*: The use of terms like home language, mother tongue, own language, regional language, standard language etc. tends to create a lot of confusion.

The views contained in the Discussion Paper do not conform to the language policy enunciated in the NPE 1986: "The Education Policy of 1968 had examined the question of the development of languages in great detail; its essential provisions can hardly be improved upon and are as relevant today as before. The implementation of this part of the 1968 Policy has, however, been uneven. The policy will be implemented more energetically and purposefully" (8.7). Why to open pandora's box'. Let sleeping dogs lie'.

The Ramamurti Report (Review Committee) of 1990 also observed, "Whatever be the difficulties or unevenness in the implementation of the three-language formula, it has stood the test of time. It is not desirable or prudent to reopen the formula."]

Mathematics

Mathematics has played a pre-dominant role not only in the advancement of civilisation in general but also in the development of physical sciences, and has now far wider application in other branches as well. Mathematics has been an inseparable part of school curriculum ever since the beginning of formal education and it continues to be so. The Mathematics curriculum has undergone various changes from time to time in accordance with the changing needs of the society. Realising the need of the social necessities. Education Commission set up in 1964 recommended that Mathematics should be taught as a compulsory subject of general education upto Class X. Provision of differential courses and additional or elective courses, defeats the philosophy and purposes of general education and there could be just one course in Mathematics for all. Only international numerals (Hindu-Arabic numerals) symbols, conventions should be used right from Class I onwards. Since general education envisages Mathematics for all, the selection of content should be relevant to the practical needs of every day life. The load of Mathematics curriculum should be realistic. While designing the curriculum for the primary level, the existence of a large number of single teacher schools, high dropout rate, unfavourable socio-existence conditions of a major segment of society etc. should be kept in view.

[*Observations*: The above mentioned recommendations are full of contradictions.

Coming to the last paragraph, are we going to have several types of curriculums? Every child is a unique individual. Every area has its own problems. Theoretically speaking this recommendation has a great force but from the practical point of view, its implementation is questionable. The word 'realistic' is very subjective. It connotes everything as well as nothing.]

Issues Pertaining to Teaching of Mathematics

...What should be the structure of Mathematics upto 10 years of general education? What type of Mathematics should be taught?

...As such the important issue is what sort of Mathematical skills and competency are required upto ten years of Mathematics education.

...The basic question that we need to address ourselves for any futuristic concern is whether Mathematics education can be left to the charge of non-mathematics persons, knowing well that maximum failures take place in Mathematics.

[*Observations*: If past experience is any guide, whenever changes in the mathematics are introduced, there are protests from some quarters and they are bound to occur in future also. No fool-proof curriculum can be envisaged. Experts differ on several counts.

The basic question raised here is a figment of imagination. May be at some places and that too for a brief period in the absence of a Mathematic teacher, the work is assigned to a non-mathematics person. But this is not the rule but an exception. It need not be raised as a basic issue. It is an issue to be solved at the local level whenever it occurs.]

Science and Technology

...The basic philosophy of science is shifting from scientific literacy to 'Scientific and technological literacy'.

The most important purpose of science teaching in general education (Class I to Class X) should be to fulfil the following seven dimensions of scientific literacy.

- Understanding the nature of science
- Ability to use the process of science
- Ability to properly apply appropriate science concepts
- Ability to understand values that underline science
- Ability to understand and appreciate the joint enterprise of science, technology and society.
- Ability to develop rich and more satisfied view of the universe and to continue science education throughout life.
- Development of certain manipulative skills which are required in day-to-day life situations.

[*Observations*: Change in the nomenclature of the subject science to science and technology is in consonance with the scientific and technological revolution.]

Secondary Stage

The Secondary Stage (Classes IX and X) is the terminal stage of general education after which a large number of students would not go for higher education in science. Therefore, there is little justification in teaching contents that are required for higher studies in science.

[*Observations*: The recommendation envisages different course content for students who would pursue higher education and different one for those whom class X would be the terminal stage. In the case of Mathematics, the Document has observed at page 42: "Provision of differential' courses and additional or elective courses, defeats the philosophy and purposes of general education and there could be just one course in Mathematics for all." Why change of policy in the case of Science?]

Science and Technology at School Level: Some Issues

As regards the curriculum transaction, there are normally two teachers in every school who handle the science curriculum. One teacher for 'physical sciences' (physics and chemistry) and one for 'biological science' (biology). In some of the schools there are even three teachers—teaching portions relating to biology, physics and chemistry separately. As such in classroom transaction the teachers are following both the disciplinary, and the integrated approaches. The issue before us is which approach should be followed by one and all?

[*Observations*: This is an old issue raised again and again. It is very clear that no approach can be followed by one and all. It all depends upon the resources of the educational institutions. No hard and fast rule can be laid down. Administrative and financial issues cannot be disregarded.]

Science, Technology and Values

Could the content and processes of classroom instruction in science transcend the drab act of passing information and become an effective tool of ensuring internal transformation of the learners by sowing in them the seeds of the essential values like respect for dissention, humility, honesty, truthfulness and perseverance?

[*Observations*: Inculcating of values is a joint enterprise. Teaching of science is one of the instruments for the realization of the objective of development of values. Overall environment of the institution matters.]

Social Sciences

Issues

- What should comprise social science curriculum as part of general education and why?
- What should be the nomenclature—integrated form (social studies), or composite (Social Sciences) or independent?

[*Observations*: At present these are non-issues. By posing these questions we are reverting to the 1960s controversies. Almost all the Private Publishers review their social studies textbooks from time to time rather with every reprint/ edition, and incorporate current socioeconomic issues. Due emphasis is laid on the economic, political and social aspects of human environment especially the contemporary world that too with focus on India.]

Our Past

The content may include specific contributions of India to the world civilization—in the field of science, astronomy, methodology, mathematics, medicine, surgery, creative arts, thought and philosophy, architecture, public administration etc., in the ancient, medieval and modern periods.

[*Observations*: This is an area which needs special attention of the NCERT. Graded small booklets for classes VI to XII may be prepared by it.]

Primary Stage: Schools should be given full autonomy at this stage to use locally developed curriculum and locally available resources for teaching of Environmental Sciences.

[*Observations*: The word autonomy has been used recklessly. Teachers may find it difficult to prepare locally developed or locally available material.]

Upper Primary Stage: At the upper primary stage the issues/themes identified earlier and drawn from History, Geography, Economics, Civics and Sociology should comprise the study of social sciences.

Secondary Stage: At the Secondary Stage, the same themes/issues may be expanded suitably with a focus on the contemporary India.

Economic and political literacy should be promoted.

[*Observations*. The recommendations are very revolutionary. Such a system may be tried in one or two states of India. In case, results are rewarding, the scheme may be expanded.

The term economic and political literacy needs to be illustrated.]

Value Education

In today's world different communities do not care to know the fundamentals of religions of their own or of others. This unfortunate ignorance of other faiths has bred prejudices and disunity. Therefore, an objective, and sympathetic study of all the major religions of India without their myth, dogma and rituals should be provided for.

At the secondary stage: (i) the morning assembly should observe two minutes' silence followed by readings from books of wisdom of different religions or great literature of the world or an appropriate address; (ii) the essential teachings of major world religions should be studied.

[*Observations*: On this issue, constitutional provisions may be taken note of:

"Article 28. Freedom as. to attendance at religious instruction or religious worship in certain educational institutions (1) No religious instruction shall be provided in any educational institution wholly maintained out of state funds.

(2) Nothing in clause(l) shall apply to an educational institution which is administered by the state but has been established under any endowment or trust which requires that religious instruction shall be imparted in such an institution.

(3) No person attending any educational institution recognised by the state or receiving aid out of State funds shall be required to take part in any religious instruction that may be imparted in such institution or to attend any religious worship that may be conducted in such institution or in any premises attached thereto unless such person or, if such a person is minor, his guardian has given his consent thereto.]

Medium of Instruction

Medium of instruction is a very crucial factor in determining the quality of curriculum transaction and the level of achievement. Only that language can be effectively used as the medium which the learners understand and in which they can comfortably interact. As such, it is widely recognised that the first language is the learner's most natural medium of communication, and, therefore, of instruction. In the case of learners whose first language is also the standard school language/regional language, the medium of instruction at least up to the elementary stage should be the regional language. Thereafter, wherever thought more helpful and therefore necessary, the second language, which incidentally happens to be English in the present national scenario, could be accepted as the medium because by the end of the elementary stage the learners are expected to have acquired fairly satisfactory level of receptive and expressive skills in this language. In exceptional cases, in the institutions where the general level of pupils' receptiveness and expressive skills in English is very good at the end of the primary stage, the use of English may be permitted from the first year of the upper primary stage. But this should not be made the norm.

However, in the case of those pupils whose home language/first language is different from the regional language, the regional language may be adopted as a medium only from the third standard onward. In the first two years the pupils' home language/first language should be used as the medium in such a manner that a smooth transition from the pupils' operations in the home language to those in the school/regional language takes place naturally.

The current practice of imposing a new language as the medium on the learner right from the pre-school stage and the primary classes is highly detrimental to pupils' growth, results in unproductive mugging up of text materials which is a heavy load of non-comprehensibility and seriously hampers any attempt at self-learning or self-directed learning. Besides, it also does a serious damage to pupils' progress in and command of their first language which arrests the development of their overall personality. Mahatma Gandhi's observation in the matter needs serious consideration.

> *"The foreign medium has caused brain fag, put an undue strain upon the nerves of our children, made them crammers and imitators, unfitted them for original work and thought and disabled them for filtrating their learning to the family or the masses".* (*Young India,* 1 September, 1921)

Therefore, till the end of the primary stage, no other language except the pupils' first language should be permitted as the medium of instruction.

[*Observations.* Almost all committees and commissions starting from the Wood's Despatch (1854) and the Kothari Commission (1964-66) and thereafter also have strongly recommended the use of mother tongue as the medium of instruction at the primary and upper primary (middle) stages. Considered opinion of the educators and psychologists also favour this. But in the present scenario, the tide in favour of English as the medium instruction even at the pre-primary stage can hardly be checked. It is doubtful if in this regard any legislation could be passed. Overwhelming opinion of the elitist class is definitely in favour of English. So no useful purpose would be served to have a country-wide debate on this issue.]

Instructional Time

All possible efforts should be made to ensure that the stipulated number of working days are ACTUALLY available to schools for instructional activities. Loss of instructional time due to unspecified reasons should be prevented or minimised through better educational management. After taking into account the number of days required for organising evaluation activities/tests/ examinations, school functions, etc. a minimum of 180 days in a year should be available for effective instruction.

It should be impressed upon schools that every subject should be given the recommended number of hours/periods, and time allocated for one subject area/activity should not be encroached upon as per the individual or institutional perception of the relative 'importance' of different subjects.

An early childhood centre/pre-school centre should function for three hours a day. A primary school should function for five hours a day out of which four hours may be set aside for instruction. For the upper primary and secondary schools, the duration of a school day should be six hours out of which five hours should be kept for instruction and the rest for the other routine activities. The duration of a class period may be around 40 minutes.

The actual time allocation for different curricular areas at different stages may be worked out at the time of finalising the document in the light of the suggestions/comments regarding the subjects of study.

[*Observations.* The Education Commission recommended about 234 days (39 weeks) for instructional purposes for schools and 216 (or 36 weeks) for colleges (and pre-primary schools) (2.35).

The Commission recommended that the working hours per day should vary from four hours at the primary stage to about 6 hours at the higher secondary stage. The total period does not include the time for co-curricular activities. In an academic year, the hours at the primary stage should be about 900, and at the higher primary and secondary stages, they should be not less than 1,000 and preferably raised to 1,100 or even 1,200 if conditions are favourable. (2.41)]

Organisation of Curriculum at Higher Secondary Stage

Curricular Perspectives: Context and Concerns

National Policy on Education (NPE) 1968 recommended a common structure of 10+2+3 throughout the country and stressed the need for diversification after ten years of general education. The NPE (1986) reiterated the need for diversification and emphasised a national curriculum framework and minimum learning outcome as essential ingredients of the national system of education. 10+2+3 structure is now a reality but national system of education which envisaged some elements of curricular uniformity throughout the country is yet to be achieved. Due to country's vastness and diversities, perhaps this is not going to be an easy task although desirable. In today's world where many countries (developed and developing) are talking of their National Standards in education, we cannot afford to ignore country's national standards which should be comparable to any international standards. The standard to seek at

+2 stage is of greater significance since it is at this stage that from general education of secondary stage, students gradually move towards diversification and offer specialised academic courses (of academic stream) on the one hand and job oriented or productivity oriented courses (of vocational stream) on the other. It is this stage when a student is in at a position to exercise a choice of stream/course in keeping with his/her own needs, interest, capability and aptitude while preparing to cope with the future.

For majority of the students the higher secondary stage may prove terminal. For them it would serve as a doorway to life and more importantly, to the world of work. For others it would be bridge to the tertiary stage of education, professional courses (engineering, technology and medical etc.) or academic courses, as the case may be.

Observations: A correct picture of the concerns in the context of the present scenario is presented in the above write-up.

Higher Secondary Stage as a Stage of Maximum Competition/ Challenge

It is an accepted fact that those who can afford to send their wards to private coaching institutes are probably in position to stand in the present days' competition. This has shaken the very foundations and philosophy of school education and has thrown a challenge before all of us. Therefore, this is the high time when we should look in totality and strengthen foundation of school education and provide all those necessary quantum of learning experiences as are needed for providing 'diversity' and 'flexibility' in school system and promote appropriate linkage between higher secondary and tertiary levels.

[*Observations*: Very laudable statements. While criticising the prevailing system of education, we sometimes forget that apart from it, several other discriminatory factors are also at work. It is doubtful if the present situation offers any hope to end this cleavage and especially through education. Of course, efforts can be made.]

Quality Improvement

The teacher will have to play a catalytic role, entirely different from what he or she is used to at the moment. A teacher will have to plan learning opportunities more meaningfully and imaginatively in which students are encouraged to learn individually, in small groups, from one another and from the society and environment at large.

[*Observations*: The educations and the administrators will have to provide necessary facilities in the educational institutions so that the teachers could play their role in the manner as visualized in the above description. Bare advice is not going to make any headway. Concrete and positive action is needed on the part of administrative and advisory bodies.]

Curriculum Organisation

After going through a common programme of studies, primarily of scientific literacy, basic mathematical skills, cultural heritage of the nation, issues relating to political, economic and social life and environment etc., the stage is ripe for exposing the students to differentiated and specialised in-depth courses in humanities, social sciences, commerce and the like on the one hand, and a variety of vocational courses on the other. Thus, the curriculum at this stage is organised under two streams, namely, academic stream and vocational stream. However, there is need to ensure that appropriate linkages between the two streams are not only maintained but systematically strengthened.

Academic Stream

Objectives of academic courses at this stage should be as follows:

(i) To expose learners to higher levels of knowledge in different disciplines.

(ii) To introduce students to different ways of collecting and processing data and information under specific disciplines, and help them in arriving at conclusions and generating new insights and knowledge in the process.

(iii) To promote problem solving and creative thinking abilities in the citizens of tomorrow to cope with changing demands of a society committed to use science, technology and informatics to alleviate poverty and to raise quality of life of general masses.

(iv) To assist students to explore their interests and aptitudes in order to choose appropriate careers in shaping their future.

Scheme of Studies

As stated earlier, diversification is the major characteristic of higher secondary school curriculum. But the movement from general education to diversification has to be gradual. Therefore, some amount of general education will continue to be imparted alongwith diversified courses at the higher secondary stage. Thus, the curriculum at this stage, will comprise, (i) Common foundation courses (ii) Elective courses.

Common Foundation Courses

Every student entering Class XI has a fair amount of acquaintance and facility with language (generally three), social sciences, science and mathematics, work experience, health and physical education and art education. At +2 stage the element of general education is to be kept to its minimum by incorporating in curriculum only a few but highly significant elements.

The common component of curriculum at this stage would consist of: (i) language and literature, (ii) general studies, (iii) work education, and (iv) health and physical education.

[*Observations*: In the common curriculum upto Class X, it is envisaged that students have already developed reasonable competency in the areas of the common Foundation Courses. At the Senior Secondary Stage, students are keen to devote their full attention to their preparation for the competitive examinations and annual examinations. They become career conscious. Field experience indicates that the majority of the students are averse to paying any attention to work other than competitive examinations and internal as well as external examinations. Therefore, it is not prudent to make Common Foundation Courses compulsory.]

Academic Electives

A student would be required to offer three elective courses out of the subjects prescribed by the Board of Secondary Education.

It is a common practice with the Boards of Secondary Education to put elective courses under groups like science, commerce, humanities, etc. But it would be more appropriate to put all the academic and applied courses in a single list without dividing them into watertight or exclusive groups which may at times run contrary to the spirit of real diversification and functional utility. This will help in promoting inter-disciplinarilty.

[*Observations*: The CBSE has already adopted this. Likewise several other Boards. However, in spite of this provision, on account of financial constraints, choice of subjects in general remains very restricted, especially in schools where the strength of students is relatively small.]

Languages Under Elective Courses

(i) *Modern Indian Languages*: Advanced courses with balanced components of the elements of language, grammar stylistic features, elementary literary theory and some samples of the main literary forms may be provided for those learners who would go in for the study of the language/literature at the university level. Even for those who would not go to the university, the course would be self-contained.

(ii) *Classical Languages*: Courses in classical like Sanskrit and Arabic would also contain balanced components of the elements of language and philology, grammar, stylistic and compositional features, basic history of literature in the language and some representative samples of the prominent literary masters. These would provide the learners understanding of traditional wisdom and classical literature that would smoothly lead one on to advanced study of these languages/literature at the university level or through the non-formal mode.

(iii) *English*: Two different kinds of courses in English may be offered at this stage:

- Academic English Course: At this stage the Academic English Course may aim at enabling learners to be fully equipped for studying English language and/or literature at the university level or even teaching English at the elementary stage after undergoing a teacher training course. The course should consist of some basic formal grammar, the elements of English language including basic phonology, advanced level writing and reading skills, introduction of the main literary forms and detailed study of some selected samples of these of an appropriate level.
- Specialised English Courses: Some of the learners may not pursue academic studies after class XII. They may either enter the world of work or join some professional course like the medical, engineering, architecture or management course. These learners will require specialised vocabulary and structures relevant to their work or field of specialisation. For them specialised English courses like 'Business English', 'English for Science and Technology', 'English for

Communication' etc. may be prepared which may contain a reasonable amount of literature and the specific linguistic content including vocabulary and structures in a balanced manner. Learners may be free to select the course as per their personal needs

Weightage for Different Curricular Areas

Assigning a suitable weightage to different curricular areas in terms of allotment of school time is very essential to plan and design a balanced curriculum. Assuming that the school time in a Higher Secondary School is divided into 40 class periods per week, allocation of time for different areas of study may be as under:

Areas of Study	*Time Allocation*		*Credits*
	Percentage	Period	
1. Language (One language)	12	5	20
2. General Studies	10	4	16
3. Work Education	8	3	12
4. Health and Physical Education	10	4	16
5. Elective Courses–(3) (Second language may be offered as an elective)	60	24	96
		40	160

The above mentioned distribution of time is just suggestive and may be suitably adjusted by Boards/Schools, if necessary. Regarding credits, one credit has been arbitrarily assigned to a course taught for one period per week in a semester. An alternative system may be evolved by the Boards of Secondary Stage.

[*Observations*: As already observed there is no need for general studies and Work Education at this stage. Therefore, time allocation may be readjusted.]

Attainment of Minimum Level of Learning (MLLs)

There seems to have been a major problem of communication gap with regard to the meanings derived differently by different set of people about the concept and strategy of MLLs. What is desirable is that a clear-cut explanation in terms of consensus version should be evolved and widely circulated throughout the length and breadth of the system.

[*Observations*: It appears the concept of MLLs has eluded consensus. In fact, NCERT and SCERTs are solely responsible for this confusion. It is a matter of concern that even after 14 years, we have not been able to sort out such matters. Perhaps this concept needs to be discarded!]

Examination Reform and Management of External Examinations

The earlier recommendation of decentralisation of Boards to district level is worth considering. Care would need to be taken for better management and ensuring comparability through public examinations.

Since there exist the Boards of Examinations with ever expanding wings in the country, these cannot be abandoned by a stroke of pen. It is not to say that they have lost their value and significance. Only it is the question of change in the roles. The Boards of Examinations can do a great service if they come forward to help teachers in conducting school based evaluations by undertaking the role of trainers and developers of test materials.

There is need to have reliable and valid variety of test materials for achievement and diagnostic testing for each grade of school education. Energies of organisations like NCERT, SCERTs and Boards of School Education should be utilised in this venture.

There is great need for conducting National and Regional level Surveys of students achievements at different grades of school education which should be conducted by the agencies referred to above. These efforts can be undertaken at regular intervals of time in a cyclic manner.

Major emphasis should be given to deformalising the examination system as far as possible. Fear of examination and anxiety amongst students needs to be totally removed from the system. This can be achieved through effectively implementing the school based evaluation and reducing the public examinations in a phased manner. Evaluation should be such that students should like to get themselves assessed time and again so that they could plan their learning and become life long learners.

[*Observations*: Statements are full of platitudes. In fact they are redundant in the existing scenario. All Utopian proposals! Of course, there is no harm in trying these elements in a few districts or states if the conditions permit.]

Vocational Stream

...Universalisation of vocational education thus becomes an essentiality. It would not be out of context to mention that 'vocational education for all' has become the central focus of the world today.

[*Observations*: The target of UEE which was supposed to have been achieved by 1990 is envisaged to be achieved by about 2010. It is common knowledge that vocational education is far more expensive. Therefore, it is not comprehended why to talk of universalisation of vocational education.]

Objectives of Vocational Education at the +2 stage

(i) To meet the need for middle level skilled manpower for the growing and newly emerging domains of the economy, in both the organised and unorganised sectors.

(ii) To contribute to socio-economic development in general and national productivity in particular.

(iii) To help reduce growing pressure on tertiary education by diverting a sizeable portion of student population to this more productive mode of education.

(iv) To promote national development by enhancing dignity of labour promoting healthy work ethic and reducing unemployment particularly among the educated.

(v) To develop a spirit of self help, self-reliance, enterprise and entrepreneurship by preparing the youth for self-employment, in addition to wage employment.

Foundation Courses

Common curriculum for all students would be as much part of vocational stream as in the case with the academic stream. It would include

(i) Study of one language,
(ii) General foundational courses,
(iii) Health and physical education.

The reason for formal exclusion of work experience is obvious since in practice it would receive much more emphasis in the elective vocational courses and in the specific provision for on-the-spot training.

The study of languages would take care of communication skills which in no way are less important for students pursuing vocational courses. The only, but highly significant, difference would be in organizing the language courses in such a way that they would take care of additional vocabulary peculiar to trade or vocation, of each student. In addition there would be units on culture and literature to cater to the emotional and intellectual growth of the learner and harmonious growth of his personality.

In this stream two alternative courses should be provided in General Foundation Courses. One would be the same as in the academic stream. Alternatively a student should be free to opt for another course in foundation courses comprising units from rural development, entrepreneurship, environmental education, career development, economic, finance and the like. The students of the academic stream should also be allowed the option to choose the alternate course specifically designed for vocational stream students, if they so desire. Generic vocational skills will be quite appropriate for academic students.

Vocational Electives

Before identifying a vocational course and outlining its details, it would be desirable to ascertain its need, relevance and potential.

The weightage to be given to various components of the vocational courses may be as suggested below:

Areas of Study	*Time Allocation*		*Credits*
	Percentage	*Period*	
1. Language	15	6-8	24-32
2. General Foundation Courses	8	3-4	12-16
3. Health and Physical Education	7	2	8
4. Vocational Electives	70	27-28	108-11
	100		100

Concerns

The vocationalisation of education at the senior secondary stage of schooling has achieved only partial success. The students have preferences for general courses—science, arts or commerce streams at the +2 level, and thereafter they move into general courses at tertiary sector of education. They constitute the bulk of the 60 million educated unemployed youth in the country. The school and college population constitutes 20 per cent of the population. For a large majority of this population sector, school and college education has become irrelevant to the needs of the society. About 85 per cent of the unemployed in the live register of the Employment Exchange are constituted by the secondary and the higher secondary level pass and not-pass youth. They include school dropouts from all the streams of arts, science and commerce.

The NPE 1986 put the target of 10 per cent diversion of students to vocational streams by 1990 and 25 per cent by 1995. Against this, the Centrally Sponsored Scheme of the VEP has sanctioned enrolment of 0.9 million in over 6000 institutions making the coverage of less than 10 per cent, but the actual enrolment is further lower at 4.8 per cent as per the ORG evaluation report of the scheme. Compare this with the developed countries where 65-90 per cent students join one or the other kind of vocational and technical courses right from the secondary education.

[*Observations.* It is very shocking that in spite of huge paraphernalia of all sort of institutions, personal and equipment, enrolment is less than 10 percent, even in 2000, of the target fixed for 1995. It indicates that either the approach or the implementation or both are faulty. No practical measures are offered in the Discussion Paper.]

Grading Vs Marking System

In India the whole system of assessment and evaluation is geared towards assigning of marks on 101 point scale which has its own merits and demerits. While it provides numerical description about achievement of learner on particular attributes, it provides scope for multiple interpretation of the same. Undue comparisons with others turn the whole teaching learning exercise into a cut throat competition. Sometimes the anxiety levels are so increased that youngsters are found to resort to extreme steps.

In fact learners should be encouraged to achieve the best which they can. Meaning thereby the learners should compete in achievement with their own potential or the targets set for them in accordance with their potential by the teachers/system. This calls for a very systematic grooming of learners from the very early stages i.e. the system has to prove itself helping the learners rather than detracting them from education. An obvious implication of this points towards improvement in teacher training, availability of variety of tests, their friendly administration and appropriate guidance at all levels of education.

One of the alternatives to marking system in terms of percentages is grading. The Indian psyche is that the first thing that comes to mind is marks and than these are converted into grades which is contrary to the very spirit of grading system. While grading the learners the idea of marking in terms of percentages will need to be abandoned in early stages if for proper classification in terms of grades is to be achieved and the learners may be facilitated to learn more in the environment of cooperation rather than competition. Again this can be achieved through proper awareness, teacher training and systematic monitoring at the implementation stage.

In a recent development the CBSE has announced the scheme of assigning grades in place of marks at Class X examination which is a welcome development. The conversion of grades to marks as envisaged can be done in two ways:

(a) Using percentile system which refers to norm referred approach and assume the attribute to be normally distributed. It may put examinees to undue advantage or loss if the distribution is positively or negatively skewed,

(b) Certain ranges of marks may be associated with grades as achievement distribution are not always normal and tend to be skewed.

Now the issue that emerges is that which of the above two be put to use.

Again providing marks for grades on demand will not allow this reform to take roots and the purpose may get defeated. At best the ranges as proposed in second alternative above may be published for use.

[*Observations*: There is nothing new in the scheme of grading. The Secondary Education Commission (1952-53) recommended this. The CBSE's scheme has been withheld in the teeth of opposition.]

Educational Testing Service (ETS)

Establishment of Education Testing Service (ETS) as per the recommendation of NPE, 1986 was considered as an important aspect of educational measurement and evaluation in the country. It could not come into existence although it was significantly mentioned in the National Curriculum for Elementary and Secondary Education Framework (1988). Given the situation with regard to the performance of learners, schools and boards of secondary education which have ever increasing problems and which are accepted for want of better option being available in the system. It is high time that the need for establishing educational testing service is re-iterated. A suggestion was made in the NPE, 1986 that ETS should be technically assisting the school administration to compare the achievement levels of different institutions and to provide academic inputs to schools for introduction of more innovative internal assessment procedures by the schools on their initiative. The ETS could also help selection of learners for entry to educational/ professional institutions at various levels and for grading of learners wherever necessary. It could also help various employing agencies for assigning specific jobs for persons suitable for them. There is need for re-looking into the possibilities of establishing Educational Testing Service with properly delineated objectives and purposes.

Conclusions

The above descriptions may be summarised to state the following:

(i) Proper testing materials may be developed for each stage of learning and provided to the teachers for use.

(ii) National testing surveys may become a regular feature.
(iii) continuous, periodical and comprehensive evaluation needs to be institutionalized.
(iv) Teacher education curricula need to be modified to make room for certain relevant suggestions.
(v) Orientation of teachers should lay emphasis on construction and use of evaluation devices.
(vi) Grading system may be introduced and school-based evaluation strengthened.
(vii) Public examinations may be phased out except at Class XII level.
(viii) Non-cognitive areas of learning should be given equal weightage.
(ix) Parental/community support may be sought and awareness built up.
(x) National Testing Service needs to be established.

[*Observations*: It has become our creed in the national life (including education) not to make the optimum use of our existing resources. There seems to be no end to our parrot-like talk knowing full well that what we are saying is totally divorced of the realities of the situation. The Document is silent as to whose responsibility is to create ETS. What are the circumstances which stood in its way. It must be admitted that ETS is intimately related to the evaluation and other aspects of teaching-learning.]

In-service Training Programmes

...print may be developed in a simple, jargon-free language for teachers by agencies such as NCERT in collaboration with other agencies. Experience in the past have shown that in the absence of such materials there has been a lot of confusion among the teachers regarding various emerging and new concepts.

[*Observations*: Above observations truly reflect the picture. NCERT and SCERTs and allied organisations prepare in-service training programmes. They are, therefore, responsible for all the 'jargon'.

The present Discussion Document may also be placed in this category.]

Education for Value Development

Policies of the School

Curriculum is an expression of the school philosophy, therefore, it may contain components that communicate essential values relating to physical environment, organisational health, human relations, such as discipline, cleanliness, punctuality, democratic functioning/commitment, responsibility for maintaining order, decorum, environment protection, respect for others' religion, caste, creed and community.

These may be attained by stating clearly the school goals, evolving discipline through participation of staff and students, wherever necessary, ensuring two-way communication for redressal, welfare services, providing freeship and help to needy students, remediation, re-evaluation and non-rejection of poor-achievers, rules ensuring participation of each student in the games, activities and programmes relevant to their interest.

Teaching-Learning Process

The total approach to teaching-learning may be geared to:

- highlighting the values inherent in the different subject areas
- providing children with opportunities for questioning, sharing, and respecting each other
- providing opportunities of learning democratic principles in the classroom transactions.
- learning of equality of gender, social caste, class and religions
- learning of human rights particularly children's rights, environmental protection and healthy living, etc.
- the classroom atmosphere itself needs to be made tension-free and democratic to enhance values.

The teaching process may involve use of discussions, displays, exhibitions, value clarification/exercises, open sessions, teaching of the content, etc. for ensuring the development of values. Even the counsellors/physical education teachers/special teachers may be used for value inculcation.

[*Observation*: educational institutions in varying degrees. The crux of the problem is that environment outside school is so vicious that it tends to negate the work of educational institutions. There is a general feeling among the students that leaders of all shades hardly present ideals. They laugh at them (behind them) who preach values.

Unfortunately after independence, the value system that Gandhiji and his devoted followers had so laboriously built started crumbling gradually. The emphasis shifted from simple to ostentatious living. No wonder several of our leaders started appropriating for themselves out of the social and national wealth as much as they could through means, mostly unfair.

There is a world of difference in what we say and what we do. We seem to follow the motto 'precept is better than practice' for it pays dividends. There is no dearth of instances to show that very often law-makers and value-preachers themselves are the biggest defaulters.

It was said about a Principal of a college in the 1940s that he was so particular regarding public morality that he never used his office pen for writing a personal letter. This was honesty, observed scrupulously.]

Textbooks and Supplementary Reading

There are lots of universal human values inherent in the various subject areas which could be inculcated through the textbooks. The textbook content has to be developed in such a manner that these values get represented in an explicit manner and not remain as hidden agenda. The textbooks, therefore, have to be written carefully and also reviewed frequently to assess what values they are communicating. For instance, the textbooks in history and civics may communicate to students the diversity of culture, tradition and democratic functioning, etc. Language texts may communicate the values relating to politeness, universal brotherhood.

[*Observations*: Even a cursory glance of textbooks and supplementary reading material would indicate that this is already being done. Overdosing is likely to defeat the very purpose.]

Evaluation

Elementary Stage

Evaluation of children's progress from Class I to VIII should be systematically organised within the school and the headmaster should coordinate the activity. Teachers should be trained in keen observation of children while at work or play and should be able to record judiciously. These observations must be shared with the headmaster before being communicated to the children and their parents. Support may also be drawn from the society in finding solution to the problems of children which hamper their progress in school. Children's profiles should be developed and utilised for further improvement of the quality of learning.

Block Resource Centres and Cluster Resource Centres should be established and energised to support school-based assessment up to elementary stage. DIETs may coordinate the activity at the district level by helping the personnel at the level of BRCs and CRCs. Due emphasis should be given to organisation of diagnostic and remedial teaching from the initial stages. To make it effective, teachers should be sensitised about its need and relevance and be provided with necessary training and support. Children should be motivated to move towards mastery learning, self-learning styles and acquiring necessary social skills and values along with academic achievement. Oral and practical skills should also be given due emphasis. Development of desirable habits, skills, attitudes and values along with specified competencies in curricular areas should be ensured.

Secondary Stage

From Class IX onwards disciplinary approach of teaching can come into force. The system of continuous and comprehensive evaluation needs to be extended to secondary classes. Here the idea of school complex may be put to practice. Boards of Secondary Education and Directorates of Education may provide necessary support to the teachers and headmasters in evaluating the children's progress and evolving cumulative record-cards. These agencies may interact with the school complexes (the resource centres) through their district level functionaries.

The corrected answer books should be shown to the students, discussed with them to make them aware of the mistakes committed by them and showing them how they could do better. Chances for improving performance/ achievement must be provided. There should be subject-wise committee of teachers for each class to review the cases of discrepancies and to sort out differences in a convincing logical manner. Non-scholastic aspects should be assessed on a regular basis for which ample opportunities should be provided to the learners to exhibit their best. The public examination system should be abolished in due course of time. Emphasis should be laid on acquiring competencies, developing critical thinking, creativity and evaluative judgement. Rote memorization/cramming should be discouraged at all costs.

Higher/Senior Secondary Stage

Senior Secondary stage is characterised by diversification of studies. The students prepare themselves for higher education/professional education and ultimately for life. Vocational education also finds a place at this stage. The semesterisation of the scheme of studies as advocated in the earlier document needs to be operationalised at the earliest. The Boards of Secondary Education have to play an important role in this direction. Needless to mention that the organisations like NCERT, SCERTs, and Departments of Education in the states will have to work in a cohesive manner to bring about this educational reform.

[*Observations*: There is no harm in aspiring for high ideals whether they are achievable or not. A good exercise for self-satisfaction!

If wishes were horses, beggars would certainly ride over them.]

Implementing Semesterisation

Despite +2 stage being accepted by many boards, the semesterisation; the assessment and testing, as suggested in the earlier document of 1988 has not been implemented anywhere. The whole idea of providing flexibility and dynamism in the curriculum is defeated, if the suggestions/recommendations are not implemented. Several suggestions were made with regard to the semesterisation earlier, and they are reaffirmed because any change in teaching-learning can take place only when they are implemented seriously.

- Semestrisation could be introduced in a phased manner as follows:
- To plan curriculum under each area of study in self-contained four broad themes. While respecting the logic, structure and spirit of the discipline there is ample scope to give a functional slant to these courses by making them problem oriented. This could go a long way in establishing relationship between theoretical knowledge on one hand and day-to-day problems on the other. This would enliven the process of education by enabling the students to participate in discussion and allied field work. Each theme should be good enough to be covered in one semester.
- To divide each semester course in units which would be problem oriented or thematic in nature. They should provide ample scope for interactive and participatory technique and enable students to learn on their own not only from books alone but from what goes on around them in everyday life. Students will have to be given more opportunities to learn in groups, share their findings with others and in the process cover larger ground than what is possible when they study everything individually.
- To work out the details concerning certification requirements and modalities of assessment to be conducted at the end of each semester.
- To decide the norms for credit accumulation. The teaching of a subject for one period per week during the whole semester may be allotted a credit of one point.

[*Observation*: Why put the blame on the Boards'? The NCERT and SCERTS etc. should mould public opinion in favour of semestrisation. They must find out the reasons of non-implementation and play an effective role. Mere advising and critising would not solve matters. There must be some valid reasons for not taking up this programme.]

Establishing of National Testing Service

There was a major recommendation in the National Curriculum Framework 1988 to establish National Testing Service which could not materalise up till now. There is need to take necessary steps to establish National Testing Service at the earliest. It can begin operating from the NCERT before it gets fully operationalised. It may have its regional outfits to be established in the Regional Institute of Education in the beginning. District level counterparts of Education Testing Service may be located in the DIETs. The National Testing Service may have the twin objectives of conducting national/regional/district level surveys of educational attainment and assisting various professional institutions in conducting the entrance examinations for professional courses and also assisting employing agencies in recruiting their employees.

[*Observations*: The NCERT must follow up this recommendation vigorously. Perhaps NTS may assist in solving several knotty problems relating to evaluation. Alternately its Evaluation Division can take up this work. Why wait for the setting up of a new institution.]

Research Base for Evaluation

Various educational reforms do not find a place in the system if they are not research-based. This is true with evaluation as well. Serious and systematic research has to be undertaken at the level of NCERT, SCERTs and Boards of Secondary Education so as to answer various evaluation issues faced by the system. Teachers may also be encouraged to undertake action researches. Besides that some researches may be commissioned by national/state level organisations.

[*Observations*: As its name implies, the NCERT's important function is to conduct and strengthen, research in all areas of education including evaluation. It appears its contribution in this area has not been substantial. Thus, it is a matter to be looked into.]

Guidance and Counselling

Diversification in terms of streams and sub-streams offers a wide range of options for students at the higher secondary stage. Likewise semester-length self-contained courses further add to the range and variety of choices open to a student. This calls for effective counselling and guidance services for the benefit of the adolescent. Every student is to be helped to select streams, sub-streams, courses and units in such a way that they conform to his/her psychological needs, attitude, abilities and aptitudes. To discharge this duty, the school shall have to provide specialised guidance and counselling services to the students at this crucial stage of education.

Till such time as we may be able to provide a qualified counsellor in each higher secondary school it is desirable to provide one visiting school counsellor for a cluster of three to four secondary/higher secondary schools. In course of time a career teacher for each secondary school will have to be provided.

A guidance cell needs to be set up in the SCERT to provide technical support to schools. Its functions would be two fold, namely, development of materials and provision of training facilities.

The minimum that a school can do right now is to familiarise its teachers in preparing students profiles in terms of their personality traits, interests and capabilities on the basis of school record of internal assessment and semester course grades. They should also be familiar with employment opportunities available for different vocational courses provided in the school.

[*Observations*: There are no two opinions on this issue. Guidance programmes have been undertaken in Delhi Schools for more than three decades. Perhaps very few studies have been conducted to find out its impact.]

Networking of Institution/Organisation

For bringing qualitative improvement in school education, stronger intra- and inter-sectoral lines need to be established among the institution and organisations responsible for the Human Resource Development at different levels—nation, state, district and local (village/city). A mechanism needs to be evolved for the smooth and effective functioning of the education system through this network. Delegation of responsibilities with accountability at all levels and setting clear-cut goals may help in minimising beaurocratic procedures. It would however mean training and orientation of the personnel involved in this process at all levels for clarity in ideas and action.

Task-forces may be set up at the state, district and local levels having co-ordination among themselves with regard to their objectives and working modalities. These task-forces may comprise the representatives of the government, the schools and the community having some autonomy with regard to their functioning. Though they may have a fixed tenure of 3 to 5 years, there should be some continuity in the formation of the groups so that at a given point of time all members are not replaced simultaneously.

These task-forces should be responsible for (i) identifying/assessing the basic infrastructural needs of the schools in the area in a periodic manner; (ii) making plans and strategies for augmenting the essential resources both physical and human as well as optimum utilisation of the resource both for equity and quality, and collecting and distributing used textbooks and reading materials for those who cannot buy them on their own, and procuring voluntary contribution from the community—money and professional service; (iii) suggesting suitable intervention strategies for handling problems of special nature; (iv) supervising and monitoring the implementation process; (v) evaluating the changes and reformulating strategies, if required in view of the experiences gained; and (vi) acting as an interface between the government and the community.

[*Observations*: The defects and limitations of the educational institutions are well-known. Multiplicity of task forces is likely to create more difficulties. Existing financial resources should be utilised on providing facilities which the schools lack. It is not the lack of resources that has hindered educational reforms and improvement. It is the lack of direction and clarity in determining priorities. Advisory bodies tend to create confusion.]

Growing numbers of private schools have increased the disparity between the facilities enjoyed by different sets of schools—government and private. Serious thinking is required to generate resources for the augmentation of facilities in the government schools in general and those located in rural areas in particular.

[*Observations*: The Discussion Paper should have gone into the financial aspects of the proposals contained in it. Serious thinking on this most crucial issue is awfully wanting in the paper]

Implementation of Evaluation Strategies

Evaluation plays an important role in the total reform package for education. It provides reliable and concrete evidence of attainment of learners in both cognitive and non-cognitive areas of learning. The nature of feedback received from such evaluations depends mainly on two things:

- The type of testing procedures employed; and
- The nature of feedback derived for undertaking suitable action for further improvements

If it is followed regularly in the system the quality of education can be improved on a continuous basis. It is a fact that it has not happened in the past and we have been moving on a beaten track. Although there have been systematic guidelines in the two earlier curriculum frameworks (1975 and 1988), the spirit of suggestions has not been reflected in the later developments. The main problem arises with the implementation where neither the prerequisites are met nor the suggestions are followed. It seems that the focus on the child has got lost in the haste of following evaluation rituals as a matter of compliance. This has obstructed the growth of system of education and helped in erosion of faith about such reforms.

There have been suggestions in the previous curriculum documents with regard to the continuous and comprehensive evaluation, semesterisation at the +2 stage and establishment of National Testing Service. These were thought to be important landmark developments in the field of educational evaluation which could not become a reality. Major hurdles in this regard could be on account of proper training of the personnel, non-availability of materials, absence of follow-up mechanism, inertia to change their roles by the Boards of Secondary Education and above all lack of will to implement the suggestions in right earnest. These problems need to be tackled on priority basis if the goals envisaged in the present curriculum framework are to be realised.

[*Observations*: Description is self-explanatory. It is not fair to put a lot of blame on the Boards of Secondary Education. Under the existing circumstances, they are doing their best. They follow pragmatic approaches, keeping in view their resources-assets and liabilities.]

Development of Evaluation Materials

A variety of evaluation materials may be developed by the organisations like NCERT, SCERTs and DIETs for the use of teachers, teacher-educators and parents; major items are mentioned below:

(a) With a view to avoiding communication gap, some brochures need to be developed on certain new concepts/strategies recommended for school education and be disseminated to all teachers and educational functionaries in the regional languages along with English. The major concepts may include continuous and comprehensive evaluation, using tests as feedback devices for qualitative improvement, interpreting and reporting test results, assessment of non-cognitive development in various aspects including values, maintaining cumulative records, oral testing, observations, etc.

(b) Achievement tests in all curricular areas from Classes I to XII need to be developed which could be used for ascertaining regional/national attainment levels of learners. These may also be used to improve the quality of institutions as their outcomes may act as good indicators of quality of schools. The same agencies which construct these tests may undertake programmes for assessing the learners' achievement at regular intervals of time so that inputs could be derived for educational policy making and research.

(c) Material needs to be developed for the consumption of teachers as to how to assess the participation of learners in co-curricular activities and the other non-scholastic qualities. Necessary proforma for recording of observations and assessments of learners need to be developed and provided to the teachers. Mechanism for interpreting and communicating these may also be developed and disseminated.

(d) Since evaluation is to be conducted by teachers in schools and, therefore, proper grooming of teachers through pre-service and in-service education is essential, materials will, therefore, be required for training of teachers in development of test materials, use of test materials, and deriving feedback for improvement of learners involving diagnostic and remedial teaching on the one hand and arranging the enrichment programmes on the other. These materials should be used for sensitisation of teachers about evaluation issues, practising evaluation and properly utilising the results of evaluation. Various performance for tabulating the results of evaluation to be used in the context of continuous and comprehensive evaluation should also be developed and provided to the teachers before the follow-up exercises are undertaken. Teacher education materials may also be modified accordingly.

(e) There is need to make parents and community aware of the procedures of evaluation being used by school and boards and how do they help in improving the attainment of learners. Such materials may be developed and disseminated to parents and the community and the ideas could be shared in the meetings of teachers with them. Participatory monitoring and evaluation may be encouraged with regard to school programmes. This will help generate a cooperative environment and acceptability of the testing procedures in the society.

[*Observations*: There is no dearth of such material. It already exists in abundance. It is common knowledge that the material is not being used. It remains locked up in almirahs.

Production of new material is likely to cost huge sums of money. Who would foot the bill?]

Role of the Boards of Secondary Education

It has been suggested in the previous curriculum frameworks that as the internal assessment system (school-based evaluation) takes roots, the external public examinations at the end of Class X should be abolished. The recommendation needs reiteration so that the Boards evolve a phased programme of accomplishing this. Another recommendation which needs reiteration is that of implementing letter grades, i.e. A, B, C, D, E for providing the assessment of learners' progress in scholastic and non-scholastic areas. No aggregate should be indicated. Thus, there should be no pass or fail in the final school leaving certificate and the student should have opportunities for improving their grades in individual subjects.

The Boards of Secondary Education may gradually shift their focus from merely conducting the examinations to upgrading the quality of school education and strengthening school-based evaluation. The CBSE and the academic wings of Boards of Secondary Education may undertake responsibilities of orienting teachers on various modes of evaluation, deriving feedback and implementing diagnostic and remedial teaching and the enrichment programmes. They should have to develop suitable instructional materials and training strategies in this regard. The Boards need to decentralise their functioning if these goals are to be achieved. In fact the Boards should act as facilitator of evaluation exercises besides monitoring them for the larger good of the community. The Boards may have due linkages with agencies such as NCERT, SCERTs and DIETs. The extreme idea of abolition of Boards would then become redundant.

The Boards have their unique contribution to make towards semesterisation at the +2 stage. They may attempt awareness generation among teachers and community, development of necessary testing material, orientation of teachers in developing of implementation strategies.

[*Observations*: The Boards are doing a fairly good job under the parameters of their role. They may have due linkages with agencies such as NCERT, SCERTs and DIETSs, but should constantly, keep in view that these agencies are, by and large, not accountable. Moreover, the entire wisdom is not the monopoly of these agencies. Their approach to educational issues, is, usually approach of an armed chair academician and is non-workable most of the times in the field.]

Provision of the Minimum Essential Facilities

The government alone may not be able to provide all that is required by schools and hence we may have to look for partnership in improving the school environment for enhancing quality of education.

Mechanism should be devised in consultation with the community (including professional) to extend sectorial cooperation in augmenting the resources of the schools.

[*Observations*: Since independence, role of philanthropists in the field of education has been, by and large, declining. Private enterprise is engaged in running public schools. There is very little hope of getting substantial degree of partnership as envisaged.]

10

National Curriculum Framework (NCF) 2005 and Its Evaluation

Introduction

Curriculum is considered as an important element in bringing about educational reforms and it therefore, must respond to the changing needs. It is always in a state of influx all over the world as observed by the Education Commission (1964-66). Thus curriculum framing with its implications is an ongoing process.

The National Council of Educational Research and Training (NCERT), an apex organisation of the Ministry of Human Resource Development, Government of India advises and assists in formulating and implementing policies and programmes in the field of education, particularly school education.

There are more than 40 Boards of School Education in India and each of these Boards is an autonomous body. Each Board prepares its own curriculum. Of course it does keep in view the NCF. The central Board of Secondary Education is usually considered as the pace setting Board in the country. It, in general, adopts/adapts the curriculum prepared by the NCERT.

Out of nearly 1,40,000 Higher Secondary/Senior Secondary Schools in the country, only about 6 per cent are affiliated to the Central Board of Secondary Education. The CBSE is very dynamic and progressive. It does not wait for NCERT and keeps on constantly introducing modifications.

The curriculum prepared by NCERT has no legal sanction behind it.

It may be recalled that the Central Advisory Board of Education is an advisory board. Its decisions may not be binding on all Boards which are autonomous.

All Boards of Education in the country are expected to include contents in accordance with the changing requirements.

In response to the National Policy on Education (NPE) 1986, the NCERT developed the "*National Curriculum for Elementary and Secondary Education: A Framework*" in 1988. In 2000, it prepared the '*National Curriculum Framework for School Education*'. This curriculum was prepared by the Government formed by the National Democratic Alliance (NDA) led by the B.J.P. Syllabi and Textbooks were prepared in the light of this curriculum. The curriculum came into operation with the academic session 2002-2003.

In May 2004, the NDA Government was replaced by the United Progressive Alliance (UPA) led by the Indian National Congress. Immediately taking charge of the Ministry of Human Resource Development, the Minister appointed a Committee to Screen History and Social Studies textbooks,. The textbooks introduced earlier during the NDA Government were replaced. It was stated that these did not respond to the value of secularism. The Ministry of HRD asked the NCERT to review the National Curriculum Framework for School Education (NCFSE) 2000 in the light of the Report '*Learning without Burden*' (1993). A 35-member National Steering Committee was constituted under the chairmanship of Prof. Yash Pal, former Chairman University Grants Commission. Out of 35 members, 15 were drawn from NCERT/Colleges of Education.

A Draft National Curriculum was prepared and circulated across different sections.

The Draft National Curriculum was placed before the Central Advisory of Education for its approval in June 2005. Some members suggested a few changes. The DNC underwent certain changes and came up for approval of the C.A.B.E. Discussions took place on September 6 and 7, 2005.

The BJP/State Governments raised several objections to the curriculum and also staged a walkout.

A few members of the CABE wanted some classification on a number of observations contained in the NCF.

The Human Resource Development Minister assured the members that a monitoring committee would be set up while preparing the syllabi and textbooks and the committee would give due consideration to the views expressed by some members. Thereupon the National Curriculum was approved by the CABE on September 7, 2005.

Major Observations and Recommendations

Chapter 1: Perspective

- Knowledge should be connected to life outside the school.
- Learning should be shifted away from rote methods.
- Curriculum should be enriched to provide overall development of children rather than remaining textbook centric.
- The national system of education in a pluralistic society should be strengthened.
- The curriculum load should be reduced.
- Curriculur practices should be based on the values enshrined in the Constitution, such as social justice and equality, and secularism.
- Quality education for all children should be ensured.
- A citizenry committed to democratic practices, values, sensitivity towards gender justice, problems faced by the Scheduled Castes and the Scheduled Tribes, needs of the disabled, and capacities to participate in economic and political process should be built.

Chapter 2: Learning and Knowledge

- Our perception of learners and learning should be reoriented.

- Holistic approach in the treatment of learners' development and learning should be adopted.
- Inclusive environment in the classroom for all students should be created.
- The learners should be engaged in construction of knowledge and creativity.
- Learning should be made active through experiential mode.
- Adequate room for voicing children's thinking, curiosity questions in curriculum practices should be provided.
- Knowledge across disciplinary boundaries to provide broader frame for insightful construction of knowledge should be connected.
- Forms of learner engagement—observing, exploring, discovering, analyzing, critical reflection, etc should be considered as important as the content of knowledge.
- Activities for developing critical perspectives on socio–cultural realities need to find space in curricular practices.
- Local knowledge and children's experiences are essential components of textbooks and pedagogic practices.
- Children engaged in undertaking environment related projects may contribute to generation of knowledge that could help create a transparent, public database on India's environment.
- School years are a period of rapid development with changes and shifts in capabilities, attitudes and interests that have implications for choosing and organizing the content and process of knowledge.

Chapter 3: Curriculum Areas, School and Assessment

Language

- Language skills—speech and listening, reading and writing—cut across school subjects and disciplines. Their foundational role in children's construction of knowledge right from elementary classes through senior secondary classes needs to be recognised.
- A renewed effort should be made to implement the three-language formula, emphasizing recognition of children's mother tongue(s) as the best medium of instruction. These include tribal languages.
- English needs to find its place alongwith other Indian languages.
- The multilingual character of Indian society should be seen as a resource for enrichment of school life.

Mathematics

- Mathematization (ability to think logically, formulate and handle abstractions) rather than 'knowledge' of mathematics (formula and mechanical procedures) is the main goal of teaching mathematics.
- The teaching of mathematics should enhance the child's ability to think and reason, to visualize and handle abstractions, to formulate and solve problems. Access to quality mathematics education is the right of every child.

Science

- Content, process and language of science teaching must be commensurate with learner's age-range and cognitive reach.
- Science teaching should engage the learner in acquiring methods and processes that will nurture their curiosity and creativity, particularly in relation to the environment.
- Science teaching should be placed in the wider context of children's environment to equip them with the requisite knowledge and skills to enter the world of work.
- Awareness of environmental concerns must permeate the entire school curriculum.

Social Sciences

- Social sciences content needs to focus on conceptual understanding rather than lining up facts to be memorized for examination and equip children with the ability to think independently and reflect.

Chapter 4: School and Classroom Environment

- Availability of minimum infrastructure and material facilities, and support for planning a flexible daily schedule are critical for improved teacher performance.
- A school culture that nurtures children's identities as 'learners' enhances the potential and interests of each child.
- Specific activities ensuring participation of all children – able and disabled – are essential conditions for learning by all.
- The value of self-discipline among learners through democratic functioning is as relevant as ever.
- Participation of community members in sharing knowledge and experience in a subject area helps in forging a partnership between school and community.
- Reconceptualization of learning resources in terms of:
  - Textbooks focussed on elaboration of concepts, activities, problems and exercises encouraging reflective thinking and group work
  - Supplementary books, workbooks, teachers' handbooks, etc. based on fresh thinking and new perspectives
  - Multimedia and ICT as sources for two-way interaction rather than one-way reception.
  - School library as an intellectual space for teachers, learners and members of the community to deepen their knowledge and connect with the wider world.
- Decentralized planning of school calendar and daily schedule and autonomy for teacher professionalism practices are basic to creating a learning environment.

Chapter 5: Systemic Reforms

- Quality concern, a key feature of systemic reform, implies the system's capacity to reform itself by enhancing its ability to remedy its own weaknesses and to develop new capabilities.

- It is desirable to evolve a common school system to ensure comparable quality in different region of the country and also ensure that when children of different background study together it improves the overall quality of learning and enrich the school ethos.
- A broad framework for planning upwards, beginning with schools for identifying focus areas and subsequent consolidation at the cluster and block levels could form a decentralized planning strategy at the district level.
- Meaningful academic planning has to be done in a participatory manner by headmasters and teachers.
- Monitoring quality must be seen as a process of sustaining interaction with individual schools in terms of teaching-learning processes.
- Teacher education programmes need to be reformulated and strengthened so that the teacher would play the roles of being an:
  - Encouraging, supportive and humane facilitator in teaching-learning situations to enable learners (students) to discover their talents, realize their physical and intellectual potentialities to the fullest, to develop character and desirable social and human values to function as responsible citizens; and
  - Active member of a group of persons who make conscious effort for curricular renewal so that it is relevant to changing social needs and personal needs of learners.
- Reformulated teacher education programmes place thrust on active involvement of learner in the process of knowledge construction, shared context of learning, teacher as a facilitator of knowledge construction, multidisciplinary nature of knowledge of teacher education, integration theory and practice dimensions, and engagement with issues and concerns of contemporary Indian society from a critical perspective.
- Centrality of language proficiency in teacher education and integrated model of teacher education for strengthening professionalisation of teachers as well assume significance.
- In-service education needs to become a catalyst for change in school practices.
- Panchayati Raj system should be strengthened by evolving a mechanism to regulate the functioning of parallel bodies at the village level so that democratic participation in development can be realized.
- Reducing stress and enhancing success in examination necessitate:
  - shift from content-based testing to problem-solving and understanding. For this to happen the present typology of the question paper must change.
  - shift toward shorter examinations.
  - examination with a 'flexible time limit' can be considered as a positive move.

  - setting up of a single nodal agency for coordinating the design and conduct of entrance examinations.
- Institutionalisation of work centered education as an integrated part of the school curriculum from pre-primary to +2 stage is expected to lay the necessary foundation for reconceptualising and restructuring vocational education to meet challenges of globalised economy.
- Vocational Education and Training (VET) need to be conceived and implemented in a mission mode involving the establishment of separate VET centres and institutions from the level of village clusters and blocks to sub-divisional/district towns and metropolitan areas in collaboration with the nation-wide spectrum of facilities already existing in this sector.
- Availability of multiple textbooks to widen teachers' choices and provide for the diversity in children's needs and interests.
- Sharing of teaching experiences and diverse classroom practices to generate new ideas and facilitate innovation and experimentation.
- Development of syllabi, textbooks and teaching learning resources could be carried out in a decentralized and participatory manner involving teachers, experts from universities, NGOs and teachers' organizations.

Evaluation of the NCF 2005

In the evaluation of the NCF, an attempt is made to give in brief the views of some of its supporters and critics.

Supporters of the NCF

1. *Learning Lessons*

The NCF creates room for a curriculum that talks to children rather than talks at them

The National curriculum Framework (2005) should be commended for its forward looking interventions in education. Designing a curriculum framework for India is not easy. But this document has broken new ground by adhering to some sound basic principles. It foregrounds the fact that curriculum reform must be about pedagogy as much as it is about content. It recommends a range of pedagogical innovations that should be applauded. It emphasizes creativity and critical abilities at the expense of rote learning. It creates room for a curriculum that talks to children rather than talk at them. And it recognizes that the rich work knowledge base of students from marginalized communities can be turned into a source of learning and dignity. Second, the framework allows for a nuanced appreciation of pluralism and diversity. But it does this not by wielding some ideological shibboleth called "diversity". Instead it allows for the curriculum to be adapted and modified in the light of diverse needs of many different kinds. Third, while allowing for pluralism and diversity, it sets down some basic norms that the curriculum will have to comply with. Striking a balance between pluralism and standardization, autonomy and adequate monitoring, local variations and global requirements, is not an easy task. But this framework has the foresight to acknowledge these tensions and suggest a constructive balance.

The framework has been criticized largely by those who are used to looking upon the state as a vehicle for simple-minded ideological indoctrination. The state has an important role in ensuring that all schools meet certain standards. The state also has a role in promulgating our basic constitutional values among future citizens. But it does not follow from these aspirations that the state should exercise monopoly control over textbooks, or confuse maintaining standards with complete standardisation.

The debate over textbooks, especially in the social sciences and humanities, has been reduced to a one-dimensional debate over the meaning of secularism. The NCF, while displaying fidelity to our constitutional aspirations, moves the debate considerably beyond conventional parameters. It seeks to produce self-reliant, confident, creative students. And, more importantly, it reposes trust in their abilities. The NCF should be, broadly, endorsed. (*Indian Express*, September 8, 2005)

2. *Take the Option*

Phase out Class X Board Exams. The approval, by the Central Advisory Board of Education of the proposal to make the Class X board examinations optional should be commended. This move will ensure that there is less stress on school children, who have to take two Board examinations in the last three years of schooling. However, since education is a state subject, the implementation of this decision is likely to be diluted. Already, Delhi, Maharashtra, West Bengal and Uttar Pradesh have protested against the idea of making the Class X examinations optional for students who wish to continue studying for Class XII. Students who opt for professional or vocational courses after Class X will, however, have to take the board examinations, as will the students who would want to change school after Class X.

For all practical purposes, today, it is necessary to have passed the Class XII examinations.

The Council of the Board of School Education had, on May 1, also exhorted all State Boards to adopt a standardized evaluation system and make examinations stress-free. Towards this, the National Curriculum Framework had also suggested a shorter duration of examinations and papers that comprised well-designed multiple questions and short-answer queries. The NCERT had suggested that English be made the second language and learning it should be mandatory for all classes in all streams of education. These suggestions have merit and should be implemented.

Hundreds of thousands of students all over India take the Board examinations primarily because it is the critical benchmark for entry to higher education. It is up to the Boards to ensure that what should be an important milestone in every child's development does not become a nightmare. (*Tribune*, September 9, 2005)

3. *Stick to the Text*

The big challenge to education has only just begun. The Draft National

Curriculum Framework (NCF), approved by the Central Advisory Board of Education is a document with the potential to bring about a radical shift in the approach towards school education in India. Yet, the worry lies in its implementation. It's best not to forget the fiasco that followed the adoption of the last NCF that was drawn up by the NCERT in 2000. Both the latest document as well the NCF 2000 had their foundation in the 1993 Yash Pal report, '*Learning without Burden*'. Unfortunately, the then HRD Ministry led by Murli Manohar Joshi translated the document's suggestions into action by deleting 'objectionable' portions of history textbooks and rewriting them to create new nationalistic paradigms.

The strength of the new NCF lies in the fact that it sees the classroom as part of the larger secular, pluralistic society envisaged in the Constitution. It seeks to address the socio-economic distortions that have created an imbalance in the transfer of knowledge. Its vision is to make learning a participative process, where knowledge is gained and enriched by connecting it to the experiences of child's life and his social and cultural reality.

The NCF has outlined the aims of education in India. The major task at hand is to develop concrete strategies to implement its recommendations at the ground level. There are many aspects to creating this systemic change—from changing the mindset and improving the skills of school teachers, to making examinations more flexible. The focus should not remain concentrated on revising school textbooks (they are, after all, merely facilitative tools), as has been the disturbing trend. The HRD Ministry must make sure that the reforms aren't allowed to disintegrate into yet another shallow exercise driven by political compulsions. (*Hindustan Times*, September 10, 2005)

Note: While supporting the NCF, the editorial sounds a note of caution in the last lines.

4. *How They Know What They Know*

A primary guiding principle in the NCF is to connect knowledge to life outside school. It speaks of "the need to recognise the child as a natural learner, and knowledge as the outcome of the child's own activity." Accordingly great emphasis is placed on incorporating local knowledge, on encouraging "intelligent guessing"—that zone between what an idea a child knows and what he almost knows—and on making the child pose questions.

"These are forward-looking reforms to make education more relevant and more joyful," says Ramachandara Guha, member of the National Steering Committee (NCM) for preparing the Framework. (*Indian Express*, September 18, 2005)

Critics of the National Curriculum Framework

1. *Pastoral Fantasy or Pedagogic Responsiveness*

The duly approved and still heatedly debated National Curriculum Framework 2005 comes laden with many gotcha illustrations where the world outside is ushered into the child's classroom. For instance: "On a winter morning, teacher asked children to draw a 'morning scene'.

One child completed the drawing and then darkened the background, almost hiding the sun. 'I asked for a morning scene! The sun should be bright!' teacher exclaimed. She didn't notice the child's eyes darting to the window: it was still dark, the sun was behind heavy wintry grey clouds."

There is, also, young Janabai who lives in a small hamlet in the Sahyadri hills. She assists her parents with chores related to rice and tuar farming and her brother in taking the goats to graze. Secondary school is an 8 km walk away, a daily stretch redolent with the diversity of local flora and fauna. This spurs the drafters of the NCF to ask: "Can we help Janabai translate her rich understanding into formal concepts of biology? Can we convince her that school biology is not about some abstract world coded in long texts and difficult language: it is about the farm she works on, the animals she knows and takes care of, the woods that she walks through every day? Only then will she truly learn science."

And, in another example of teaching innovativeness, the NCF teaching shows how to combat standardization and rote. Here's how teachers could frame questions, it suggests: "if the answer is '5' what might be the questions? If the answer is 'it was red' what might be the questions?"

Pastoral fantasy or pedagogic responsiveness? An attempt to construct knowledge through the student's experience or abdication of responsibility for setting universal standards for accomplishment" As a document, the National Curriculum Framework is lavish in its resolve to place the child at the centre of all learning, to abandon the sole emphasis on textbooks in instruction and on examinations in evaluation. It has, however, invited questions about how this educational reform will actually be effected. (Mini Kapoor, *Indian Express*, September 18, 2005)

2. *Stress on Local Knowledge Traditions*

Stress on local knowledge traditions could serve as an umbrella for all kinds of obscurantism and be an impediment to rationality. There are no local variations of rationality. Systematisation of knowledge must be universal.

The current emphasis on fact, says NSC chairperson Yash Pal, prioritises memorizing, not learning. "To nurture thinking children," he says, "the syllabus will have to be lightened."

Habib, however, asks: "If your classroom teaching is not based on prescribed textbooks, how do you monitor teaching? This denigrates one major instrument of transmission of knowledge." It also, he reckons, covers in advance possible criticism of the textbooks that are to be written. (Historian Ifran Habib, Prof. Aligarh Muslim University September 18, 2005)

3. *Educators Should Stick to Basics*

Secularism Not Given Adequate Emphasis. Secularism or the separation of religion and education needs to be vigorously foregrounded throughout the document. Exclusion of religion from education and school instruction must be given greater prominence than has been done in the revised draft, because the need to shift from religious value-laden education provides an important justification for NCF 2005.

Sidestepping this issue in the interest of avoiding the blame game will not help in producing progressive education, no matter how radical the teaching methods are.

Undue Emphasis on Pluralism and Diversity. The NCF has attached enormous weight to pedagogy through the introduction of child-centred knowledge. But a large number of academics and educationists have expressed concern that the strong emphasis on pedagogy may erode the content of disciplines. This erosion of perspective can be seen in the social sciences, which appears to be so pluralist in its approach as to have no framework or social philosophy at all. Is society composed of structures and webs of social relationships, or is it a basket of discrete and separate identities that require accommodation?

The NCF 2005 opts for the second view and places enormous emphasis on pluralism and diversity, as against national and developmental issues.

Time not Ripe for Shifting from Development to Post Development Approach. The NCF makes a bold statement that we need to shift from development to normative concerns such as equality, justice and dignity. But have we reached a level of economic and social development in our country where we can afford to shift from development to a post-development approach? Arguing for a normative post-development approach at this juncture amounts to avoiding the questions of why poverty, social privilege, and inequalities of all kinds persist. These issues require social explanation, which derive from social theories, and cannot be explained by local forms of knowledge.

We should not be content with accommodation and respect for diversities, pluralities, and cultures when all identities, cultures and communities do not get equal treatment from state or society.

Abuse of Plurality of Books. The NCF favours plurality of textbooks. The CABE Committee on Regulatory Mechanisms for Textbooks in Schools Outside the Government system, which I chaired, clearly demonstrates that such a plurality already exists and perhaps in excess of the demands of pluralism. The free space and plurality permitted by the system is abused and misused to inculcate prejudice and divisiveness and shoddy quality. The key issue is lack of monitoring and scrutiny of textbooks, and not lack of freedom or choice.

We must remember that educational materials under whatever pedagogic approach must be produced within the framework of the Constitution.

Needs for Wider Discussion. We need a wider discussion on the syllabus before embarking on textbook writing. State-level discussions on the syllabus are particularly important given the new approach to learning with its emphasis on local knowledge.

Hasty Approach. From all accounts the three components—curriculum framework, syllabus preparation and textbook writing—are taking place simultaneously and in just one year. Progressive and good quality books cannot be prepared in a hurry.

Need for the Constitution of Syllabus Preparation. The problems arising out of the NCF 2005 can be resolved by broad-basing the process for syllabus preparation. It is imperative to institute a CABE Standing Committee to monitor the process of syllabus preparation. (Zoya Hasan, a member of CABE, *Times of India*, September 9, 2005)

4. *Marxist Dominated NCF*

The UPA government have allowed the Marxist to make firm in-roads into the process. And allowed them to show disrespect to national leaders, like, Swami Vivekananda, Rishi Aurobindo and Netaji, by removing their references from the document.

"Besides they ignored and exiled the value education as established during the Congress rule in 1986." The BJP-ruled State Education Ministers vehemently pleaded for a discussion on the document again. "The NCF 2005 should not be allowed to be politically used, like we see it was used under the pressure from Pradeep Yadav, Chhattisgarh School Education Minister. (*The Pioneer*' September 7, 2005

5. *Emphasis on Sanskrit, India's Heritage and Spiritual Values Ignored*

Emphasisis not given to Sanskrit, which is *devvani* (language of the Gods), and yoga is only been discussed as part of physical training. Yoga should be taught as a separate stream with much more importance," he said.

On history, the BJP Minister said, "It does not appreciate India's heritage adequately." The framework, he said, was "materialistic in its approach, neglecting the spiritual aspects of life...We cannot accept the NCF in its existing form." (Vasudev Devnani, Education Minister, Rajasthan at the CABE meeting: '*Indian Express*' September 7, 2005.)

6. *Existing Pupil Teacher Ratios Ignored*

The NCF addresses the challenge posed by multigrade schools in delivering child-centred learning. Over 75 per cent of schools in rural areas, the document notes, are multigrade. It accordingly seeks reform in instruction in multigrade classrooms and "a shift away from textbooks designed for monograde classrooms."

For one asks Sadgopal, with teacher-pupil ratios deteriorating, how can a teacher take five classes simultaneously, and help students construct knowledge? He also questions this legitimization of multigrade schools and the NCF's reluctance to demand better teacher-pupil ratios. "This document," he says, "talks of some very advanced ideas in pedagogic research. But these ideas must be situated in the reality of Indian school conditions." He questions the negligible value placed on acquisition of productive skills. (Anil Sadgopal, Prof. of Education, Delhi University, *Indian Express*. September 18, 2005)

7. *Value Education Ignored*

NEP 1986, which, to repeat is binding on organs of government, is categorical on value based education. The National Curriculum for Elementary and Secondary Education based on NEP-1986 was designed to enable the learner to acquire knowledge to develop concepts and inculcate values commensurate with the social, cultural, economic and environmental realities at the national and international level.

This was followed by the Parliamentary Committee headed by S.B. Chavan which submitted its 81st Report on Value-based Education to the Rajya Sabha on February 26, 1999. An extract of the report is self explanatory. (It is quoted by the Supreme Court with approval):

Truth (*Satya*), Righteous Conduct (*Dharma*), Peace (*Shanti*), Love (*Prema*) and Non-violence (*Ahinsa*) are the core universal values which can be identified as the foundation stone on which the value-based education programme can be built up. These five are indeed universal values and respectively represent the five domains of human personality—intellectual, physical, emotional, psychological and spiritual. They also are correspondingly co-related with the five major objectives of education.

Primary school stage is the period in the child's life when the seed of value-education can be implanted in his/her impressionable mind in a very subtle way. If this seed is nurtured by the capable hands of dedicated teachers in school, if they insert values at appropriate intervals during a child's life, it can easily be said that half the battle in building up national character has been won.

It is very essential that at the school level, right from the primary stage, deliberate, planned and sustained efforts are made to inculcate basic human values among the students. Values are best initiated by a mother to her small child under her tender care in the secure atmosphere of home. However, nowadays, children are enrolled in school as early as at the age of four. At this impressionable stage, values like respect for parents, elders and teachers, truth, punctuality, cleanliness and courtesy can be easily inculcated by small children.

Apart from personal values, there are certain social values which ought to be imbibed by the young mind. These are the values which concern the whole community, concern for the aged and the handicapped, for the deprived sections of the society, etc. Sincere belief in the dignity of labour is generally found to be lacking in our young generation. The value of self-dependence and dignity of manual labour are thus required to be impressed upon small children.

The National Curriculum Framework ignores several accepted truths and reduces education to one more aspect of minority appeasement to an exercise in dehumanization. (Prof. Bal Apte, BJP Rajya Sabha, CABE Meeting, *The Pioneer*, September 10, 2005).

8. We oppose the NCF for being soft on communalism and plurality of textbooks. (Kanti Biswas, West Bengal Education Minister. *The Hindustan Times*, September 7, 2004).

9. *Document Sponsored by the Left*

It is a document sponsored by the left and the government is trying to get their agenda passed. The document should include: Sanskrit as the main language and not a classical language, draft the NCF on the principles of 1986 Education Policy make religion an intrinsic part of the curriculum and not to make class X exam optional. (Pradeep Yadav, Education Minister, Jharkhand, *The Hindustan Times*, September 7, 2005).

10. The recommendations on construction of knowledge are based on theoretical research. When a child first learns to conceptualise things, she says, the most important exercise is to enable her to reframe them in her own language, to be able to articulate what she has understood.

Rampal feels that interlinking the syllabus with the world around the student can lead to critical pedagogy, whereby he learns to question and to critique. The present environmental studies syllabus makes a conscious attempt to locate science within social studies at the primary level. (Anita Rampal, Prof. Delhi University and Chairperson of NCERT's Writing Team for Primary Schools Textbooks. '*Indian Express*' September 18, 2005).

Official Assurance on the Implementation of the Curriculum

In view of the reservations expressed about the NCF—not only by the BJP members but by others also—the HRD Minister announced that a monitoring committee would be set up to look into every aspect of preparing the syllabus and textbooks. This committee would include representatives of CABE, NCERT and State Governments.

NCERT Director Krishna Kumar sought to underline the fact at the start of the CABE session that the NCF was a "prescriptive document" and its contents were just suggestions, not decisions.

Highlighting the changes that had been made in the revised document since objections were raised at the first CABE meeting on the NCF in June, he said: "complete unanimity is not expected nor is it possible in a federal polity." (*The Hindu*, September 7, 2005)

Overall Observations on the NCF

The formulators of the curriculum have completely overlooked the words of wisdom said by the Education Commission (1964-66) on the construction of the curriculum, "The first is the need for systematic curricular research so that the revision of the curriculum may be worked out as a well coordinated programme on the findings of experts instead of being rushed through haphazardly and in a piecemeal fashion."

It is also to be remembered that while drawing out plans, their financial implications must be worked out.

The NCF falls short of these basic elements.

11

Grading System

Introduction

It is of interest to note that even after five decades, the grading system has been accepted only partially. It was the Secondary Education Commission (1952-53) appointed by the Government of India that mooted the idea of grading system.

Secondary Education Commission on the Grading System

The Secondary Education Commission 1952-53, discussed the issue of examination and evaluation in Chapter XI of its report. It observed, "The present system of evaluating by percentiles *i.e.*, numerical marks, out of a hundred, may have certain advantages but the disadvantages seem to outweigh the advantages." The Commission pointed out the following demerits of the system of numerical marking system:

First, it introduces too many sub-divisions which are not only useless but cumbersome.

Secondly, it is indeed difficult to distinguish between two pupils one of whom obtains, say, 45 marks and another 46 to 47.

The Commission recommended the following grading system:

'A' to indicate 'Distinction'.

'B' to indicate 'Credit'.

'C' to indicate 'Pass'.

'D' and 'E' to indicate 'Failure' or 'Cases Referred Back'.

The Commission observed that the values of the categories in terms of percentile marks may be determined by the examining authority. Individual examiners in different subjects may even use percentile system and then convert the percentile scores in terms of categories.

The Commission was emphatic that this system would work in all cases except where the distinctions are to be made for the award of scholarships and prizes.

It appears the Commission was not very clear on this issue. Its recommendations do not seem to provide the appropriate solution.

'A monograph on Grading in Universities' (1976)

The Monograph published by the UGC gives the following demerits of numerical marking:

1. The standards of examiners differ very widely. There is a standard error of marking ranging from 5 to 20 marks in different subject.

2. Examiners have a tendency to give an unusually great number of 35 marks (when 35 is passing mark).

3. Examiners in different subjects use different ranges. In some the full scale of 0 to 100 is used, while in many other subjects, scales used are all different.

4. Marks given by examiners are not scaled.

5. Marks in different subjects are added up when they should not be.

Objectives of the Grading System

According to the '*Monograph*', grading system fulfills the following objectives:

(a) Evaluation which is mainly judgement based on measurement is uniform if all the universities agree to adopt the 7 point scale grading system.

(b) Comparability amongst various disciplines and within various subjects in a particular discipline is possible with the grading system.

(c) In case of grading system in all universities and boards, students can move from one university or board to another.

(d) Grading system takes the emphasis away from marks.

Grades Recommended

Following grades were recommended for all subjects:

O	Outstanding	3%
A	Very Good	7%
B	Good	22%
C	Average	36%
D	Below Average	22%
E	Poor	7%
F	Very Poor	3%

Demerits of the Grading System

Prof. Atma Ram in '*Shikshak Salhi*' (May 2000) finds fault with the grading system on account of the following:

(i) It does not suit a selection situation. In view of the prevailing corruption, it can create chaotic conditions.

(ii) As the grading system does not allow ranking of the candidates, medals and prizes cannot be awarded to the deserving students.

(iii) The various appointing authorities want grades to be translated into percentage of marks.

(iv) Some education institutions are superior to others, in which case, grading of their students will not be comparable with those of others.

(v) In the grading system, there is little zeal or competition among students to strive for higher percentage of marks.

(vi) The Federation of Parents' Association, Delhi and the Delhi School Education Advisory Board, have stoutly opposed the move. They have termed it as a ploy of the NCERT to hide inefficiency. "When it (CBSE) should have worked on the revaluation system, it has embarked on a scheme to get away with its sloppy evaluation system", said Mr. Vijender Kumar, President, Delhi Abhibhavak Maha Sangh.

(vii) Some view it as a method to raise the pass percentage of government schools, to equate them with those of public schools.

He has further observed, "In terms of pure theory and academic considerations, the grading system may sound effective and desirable, but it does not suit the socio-economic conditions prevalent in the country. That it works well in several advanced countries in the world is no reason to believe that it will succeed here as well. In India, the realities of life, at the grass-roots level particularly, are different. It is not for nothing that in decades, out of 242 universities in India, only a few have opted for the grade system. We do not stress adequately the areas where revamping should be done and only hit upon short cuts and cosmetic, measures to improve the system of education or examination. At the evaluation stage, the examining body has broad-based interaction with the society. It should, therefore, take into confidence various constituents of society—students, teachers, parents, NGOs and general public. What we essentially need in education is due stress on effective teaching—220 teaching days in schools."

CBSE to Introduce Grading System

CBSE Chairman Ashok Ganguli made the following announcements on September 21, 2005

1. From the academic session 2007-2008, the term 'pass' or 'fail' will not be mentioned in the certificate of class X.
2. The report card will mention the GPA (Grade Point Average) score
3. The topmost grade will have a numerical value of 9.
4. The system will start for class IX in the 2006-2007 academic session.
5. The question papers for science, mathematics and social sciences in the class X examination and those for physics, chemistry, mathematics, biology, accountancy, business studies and accountancy, in class XII will be so designed that an average student is able to complete the paper in two and half hours.
6. The examination time will remain three hours plus the 15 minutes "cooling off" time the board had earlier announced.
7. The relative weightage of the subjects will be determined as per local needs.
8. From 2007, students would be required to answer a 60-mark theory paper instead of the 75-mark paper.
9. The remaining 40 marks will be divided between internal assessment, viva voce, practical project and a 20-mark objective-type written paper based on practicals.
10. Students will be required to get qualifying grades in four subjects out of five in order to be promoted to class XI.

(*Source*: *Times of India*, September 22, 2005)

The Council of Boards of School Examination (COBSE) in India on Examination Reforms

The Council of Boards of School Education in India (COBSE), an apex body of 41 educational boards from across the country, has rejected the suggestion to do away with the Class X board examination stating that any dilution of the "existing system is uncalled for".

Officials belonging to 31 boards participated in a deliberative session to discuss the NCF 2005. Six states—J&K, Himachal Pradesh, Maharashtra, Karnataka, Tamil Nadu, Tripura—did not participate in the discussion. The body came up with a slew of suggestions, foremost among which are exam reforms:

- Paper duration between 2½ and 3 hours. 15 minutes cool-off time
- Question paper should contain long, short, very short answers and multiple choice questions to reduce length, but at the same time maintain quality
- Results be declared in grades, marks also allowed in transitional phase
- 20 per cent marks in board exams be set apart for school based assessment of scholastic and co-scholastic areas
- Career guidance, counselling units in all schools. Teachers be trained to do counselling
- No to two levels of courses and curricular level—said students need basic grounding in all subjects. Subjects like higher mathematics can be offered as additional subjects
- Compulsory math laboratory in all schools
- Science be taught as part of environmental studies from Class I to V.
- Class VI to VIII be taught as a separate subject
- For Class XI and X introduce single science syllabus including physics, chemistry, biology etc.

Mixed Reaction to Proposals

The changes will reduce stress among school children. For bright students, the extra 15 minutes will not mean much. But for the average performer, it time will be crucial.

Jyoti Bose, principal, Springdales, Dhaula Kuan

Each school wants to improve its results and teachers and the management will try to manipulate results of internal assessments. There will definitely be a decline in the standard of education.

P. Soni, principal, Kendriya Vidyalaya, R.K. Puram

The extra 15 minutes is good. But stress cannot be relieved completely by only these measures. Schools need to do away with pre-boards. Boards shouldn't be hyped, too

Vithika Rahul, counsellor Birla Vidya Niketan
(*Source*: *Hindustan Times*, September 22, 2005)

12

Ninth Five Year Plan on Education (1997-2002)

Introduction

It is generally accepted that education is the key to all processes of development and on account of its catalytic action in this complex and dynamic growth process, it needs to be planned meticulously and executed with great sensitivity. Accordingly it has been given its due priority in the ninth plan. In the education sector, primary education and eradication of illiteracy are the major thrust areas.

Extracts from Chapter 3 of the Ninth Five Year Plan (Planning Commission, New Delhi)

In view of its significance for human resource development and economic and social transformation, education needs to be given a high priority in the allocation of resources. Considering that the present share of education in GDP is around 3.9 per cent; raising it to any substantially higher level would require a substantial enhancement of expenditures on education. The system's capacity to absorb financial resources of a large magnitude and use them productively and efficiently would also require careful consideration. As regards the convergence of Basic Minimum Services for contributing to educational development, emphasis will be laid on providing all primary schools with clean drinking water, sanitary facilities, better nutrition for the pupils through midday meals, health check-up and primary health-care facilities and a network of roads for making the schools easily accessible.

Early Childhood Education

Early Childhood Education (ECE) in the Ninth Plan requires attention for the following issues:

(a) Strengthening the educational component of Integrated Child Development Services (ICDS).
(b) Its linkage, as pre-school education, with universalisation of primary education and consequential steps in that connection.
(c) The promotion and management of ECE under the decentralised

system of Panchayati Raj Institutions (PRIs) and Urban Local Bodies (ULBs).

(d) The role of private sector and NGOs in ECE

(e) Convergence of health education and other services at the local level in the interest of ECE.

(f) Social mobilisation for ECE, through mass media and other activities.

The issues that will be addressed in the Ninth Plan are as follows :

(a) Combining pre-school and primary level methodologies, along with health and nutritional concerns, in teacher-training programmes, pre-service as well as in-service.

(b) Encouraging the adaptation of ECE to the environment and home-conditions of the children through innovative alternatives.

(c) Orienting PRIs and ULBs to provision of community-supported creches and day-care centres attached to Anganwadis/Primary schools.

(d) Mobilisation of local women's groups to set up and manage ECE centres.

(e) Production of inexpensive play materials for children by using local materials and talents of local artisans and school children engaged in socially useful productive work and social service activities according to their curriculum.

(f) Strengthening resource groups of ECE at the NCERT and SCERTs as also research institutes, NGOs and other such organisations to conduct research, training, materials production and extension activities for ECE.

Primary/Elementary Education

The Indian Constitution attaches high priority to education. Article 45 declares "The State shall endeavour to provide, within a period of 10 years from the commencement of the Constitution, for free and compulsory education of all children until they complete the age of 14 years. The Constitution also guarantees educational rights for minorities and calls for the educational development of weaker sections of society. Through the 42nd Amendment of the Constitution, the subject of education has been brought to the Concurrent List in the Constitution for fulfillment of nationally accepted goals. The 73rd and 74th Constitutional Amendments further empowered the Panchayati Raj Institutions (PRIs) to render their distribution to the development of education at the grass-root level. The Judgement of the Supreme Court in *Unnikrishnan J.P. vs Andhra Pradesh* (1993) States: "The citizens of the country have a fundamental right to education. The said right flows from Article 21 of the Constitution. This right is, however, not an absolute right. Its contents and parameters have to be determined in the light of Articles 45 and 41. In other words, every child/citizen of this country has a right to free education until he completes the age of 14 years. Thereafter his right to education is subject to the limits of economic capacity and development of the State."

Critical Issues at Primary/Elementary Stage

(i) *Drop-outs* : The problem is further accentuated by high drop-out rates. Among those who are enrolled, it is estimated that large number of children in Classes I-V drop out in between, before completing their class V. The latest available data on drop-out rates for Classes I-V for the year 1996-97 reveal that the drop-out rate for the country as a whole was 38.95 per cent. It was 39.37 per cent among boys and 38.35 per cent among girls. Further, there were wide inter-State disparities. The major problem of drop-outs as well as access to schooling is in the educationally backward States of Andhra Pradesh, Arunachal Pradesh, Assam, Bihar, J&K, Madhya Pradesh, Orissa, Rajasthan, UP. and West Bengal.

(ii) *Unserved Habitations with Primary/Upper Primary Schools/Sections* : According to the Sixth All India Educational Survey (excluding J&K where survey was not done) out of 10.60 lakh rural habitations, 8.84 lakhs (83.4%) were served within the national norms of one-km distance. Thus, about 16.6 per cent of habitations were not served by primary schools within a distance of 1 km. The survey results also revealed that about 41,198 primary schools were being run in thatched huts, tents and open space. In case of upper primary schools, about 23.85 per cent habitations were not served within the official distance norm of 3 km. 5,638 upper primary schools were being run in thatched huts, tents and open space.

(iii) *Lack of other Physical Infrastructure* : Apart from availability of access to primary school within a walking distance of habitations there are other problems which have to be addressed on an urgent basis. These relate to lack of physical infrastructure like toilet facilities for girls, drinking water facilities in schools, teaching-learning equipment etc.

(iv) *Availability of Teachers* : With regard to availability of teachers, the Survey further pointed out that about 4000 schools were without teachers and 1.15 lakh primary schools were being run by single teachers. However, the position has improved since then, as additional teachers have been provided under Operation Blackboard (OB).

(v) *Equity and Regional Disparities* : Then, there are regional disparities. Some States (like Kerala, Maharashtra, Gujarat, Tamil Nadu) have done well in providing physical access to schooling facilities as well as in improving quality of education. Some others (like Uttar Pradesh, Bihar, Madhya Pradesh, Orissa & Rajasthan) has still a long way to go. There are equity concerns like low enrolment of girls, educational requirements of special need groups, like SCs/STs, OBCs, minorities, disabled children, working children, children from disadvantaged locations like deserts, hilly, coastal and deep forest areas, children from migratory families etc.

Primary education will be a major thrust area during the 9th Plan. There will be an additional enrolment of 250 lakhs children at the lower primary stage and 160 lakhs children at the upper primary level. 75,000 additional rooms/buildings will be constructed at the elementary stage. 2,36,000 teachers will be appointed additionally at the lower primary level and 1,75,000 teachers at the upper primary level.

Action Plan

(i) *Broad Approach* : The action plan needed to address the critical issues and achieve the desired objective will be based upon ground realities. It will resort to a multi-pronged strategy which is both imaginative and innovative and also carries with it the attributes of flexibility, decentralisation, improvement of quality, cost-effectiveness result-oriented and time-bound commitment. This can be achieved through micro-planning with a focus on 'area approach' and 'target population'. It will also mean community involvement, monitoring, supervision and academic support at all levels. The existing schemes will be examined with respect to these parameters and those found suitable will be promoted.

(ii) *Phasing* : Under the Constitutional obligation, Government is to provide free and compulsory education upto Class VIII. Greater emphasis will naturally have to be laid on achieving UPE at the lower primary stage, in the first phase.

(iii) *Mobilisation of Community Support for School Improvement Programme* : The 73rd and 74th Constitutional amendments have further empowered the Panchayati Raj Institutions (PRIs) to make a positive contribution for development of education at the grass-root level. Village Education Committees (VECs) will be actively involved in School Improvement Programme (SIP).

Training will be imparted to VEC members wherever such committees have been constituted. Arrangements for this will be made through District Institutes of Education and Training (DIETs) Block and Cluster Resource Centres and through the Distance Mode. Area of concern of VECs in the development of SIP will be

(a) door-to-door survey of children of school-going age and help in enrolment particularly of girls;
(b) planning oplanning and execution of civil works of school buildings;
(c) mobilisation of physical and financial resources;
(d) provision of free accommodation to teachers, wherever possible;
(e) improvement in children's attendance;
(f) institutional capacity building for sustainability of schools;
(g) community ownership of the School Improvement Programme;
(h) to help in implementation of the Scheme of National Nutritional Support to Primary School Children;
(i) Other functions delegated by the State Governments.

(iv) *Strengthening Teacher Education Programme*

(a) *Curriculum Development:* The draft curriculum framework developed by the National Council for Teacher Education (NCTE) will be finalized and made the basis for curriculum change in institutions for teacher education. This will help to improve the quality of Teacher Education Programme.

(b) *Initiative for North-Eastern States* : The North-Eastern States, which have a larger percentage of untrained teachers in elementary schools will launch programmes to cover this gap by adopting the following measures:

- A Diploma Programme for Primary Education developed by Indira Gandhi National Open University (1GNOU) will be launched in collaboration with the State Governments.
- NCTE will establish a Regional Committee for North-Eastern States to provide the necessary fillip to the teacher training institutions.
- Induction programmes of 4 to 6 weeks duration of DIETs will enrich the capabilities of freshly appointed teachers.

(c) *Upgradation of Infrastructure* : The process of strengthening Teacher Education Programme will be given a further impetus by upgrading the physical and academic infrastructure of:

- State Councils of Educational Research & Training (SCERTs)
- Colleges of Teacher Education (CTEs)
- Institutes of Advanced Studies in Education (lASEs)
- District Institutes of Education and Training (DIETs)
- Block Resource Centres/Cluster Resource Centres (on a pilot basis)
- National Council for Teacher Education (NCTE)
- Departments of Education in Universities.

(d) *Reaching out of Primary School Teachers in Remote Areas* : To supplement the efforts to improve school effectiveness, an institutional mechanism will be put in place to provide on-the-spot counselling the guidance to teachers located in remote areas. This will be in thc form of Mobile Teams of Resource Persons (MTRPs). Logistic arrangements will be location-specific, based upon felt needs and environment.

(v) *Alternative Education* : In order to provide access to drop-outs, working children, girls, migratory population and other similar categories, alternative education will be provided through institutional arrangements.

Non-formal Education centres for such categories of children as are unable to avail themselves of the formal system of schooling in hilly, desert and forest areas, or due to the migratory nature of the population will be expanded. The expansion will be based upon a cluster approach, so as to make the scheme cost-effective.

It has been found by experience that NFE centres achieve more meaningful results when these are run by NGOs. Accordingly, the number of centres run by NGOs will be enhanced significantly. Where NGO participation is not forthcoming, State-run NFE centre will be established.

The scope of the National and State Open Schools will be expanded by bringing elementary education within their fold for the purpose of providing a lateral entry to NFE children as well as to neo-literates for certification.

Private initiative will be tapped in industrial project sites to run "project schools". Incentives like allotment of land on a subsidised basis and other concessions under the Companies Act or the Income Tax will be provided.

(vi) *Education of Working Children* : According to the 1991 census, there were 11.28 million working children in the country. More than 90 per cent of them were engaged in agricultural labour, rearing of livestock, forestry and fisheries.

Ministry of Labour has a direct responsibility at the Centre for the following:

(a) to lay down policies and programmes for elimination of child labour, particularly in hazardous trades,

(b) to monitor the progress of implementation of programmes, projects and schemes for elimination of child labour; and

(c) to coordinate implementation of child labour-related projects of the various sister Ministries of the Government of India in order to ensure convergence of services for the benefit of the families which have child labour. Ministry of HRD will extend all support to the Ministry of Labour in the setting up of education-related projects*. These will be "area specific* and focussed particularly in State of Andhra Pradesh, Madhya Pradesh, Maharashtra and Uttar Pradesh, where there is a large concentration of child labour.

Adult Education

Literacy, the key to most of India's development programmes, is the catalyst to accelerate initiatives in health care, agriculture, primary education and in all critical areas of development.

In the light of the 73rd and 74th constitutional amendments, literacy has assumed even greater significance. If power for local self-governance is to devolve to the panchayats and nagar palikas, literacy is an essential prerequisite for these institutions to be effective.

Critical issues in Adult Education

Despite this key role, much still needs to be done. India has the largest number of non-literate people in the world—about a third of the world's total of around 900 million. Although literacy levels have increased from 16.67 per cent to 52.21 per cent since independence, unrestrained population growth has proved to be a serious impediment.

The literacy levels of women are low—32.29 per cent as compared to 64.13 per cent for men. The fact that female literacy is acknowledged as being one of the most significant indicators of development makes this all the more alarming. With one-third of the seats in panchayats and nagar palikas reserved for women, the need for them to become literate is vital.

There are large regional disparities in literacy rates - between urban and rural areas, as well as between states. While about three quarters of the urban population is literate, the literacy rate in rural areas is less than 45 per cent. The literacy rate of women in rural areas is even lower at 31 per cent.

Seven States—Uttar Pradesh, Bihar, Madhya Pradesh, Rajasthan, Andhra Pradesh, West Bengal and Maharashtra—account for around 70 per cent of India's non-literate population. The first four of these States alone, are home to around half of India's non-literate people.

In its endeavour to achieve the goals it has set for itself in adult education, India faces several challenges. Studies by expert groups and the constant evaluation of the programme, indicate several principal challenges.

The four Hindi speaking states—Uttar Pradesh, Bihar, Madhya Pradesh and Rajasthan—account for half of India's non-literate population. The large number of non-literate people, and therefore the relatively small number of educated people from whom volunteers can be drawn, as well as the overall socio-economic backwardness of these states, combine to make the achievement of literacy particularly difficult in these areas.

There are large regional disparities—between States, between districts in a State, between males and females and between tribal and non-tribal areas.

Campaigns have sometimes been launched without adequate planning and quality has suffered in certain places in the pre-occupation with total literacy. The pre-occupation has also sometimes led to overestimation of achievements, with some districts being prematurely declared totally literate.

The vital importance of post-literacy efforts to prevent a relapse into illiteracy has already been mentioned. Post Literacy Campaigns have not been implemented adequately or in time, even in districts where TLCs have been successful. There have often been unnecessarily long time gaps between the completion of a TLC and the beginning of a PLC in a district. To ensure that the gains of TLCs are realized, post literacy needs for greater attention and emphasis, to sustain the interest of the neo-literates, and to make them "functionally literate" in the true sense.

Greater community involvement is required to convert literacy into a people's movement.

Action Plan

(i) Literacy campaigns have already covered 447 districts, of which 215 are in Total Literacy Campaigns, 173 are in Post Literacy Campaigns and 59 are in Continuing Education Phase. In addition, 38 districts have been covered under Rural Functional Literacy Projects. Hence, the total coverage comes to 485 districts. Efforts would be made to bring the remaining 40 odd districts under the coverage of literacy.

(ii) Gradually, all districts will be brought under the Continuing Education programme which will be further strengthened as well as linked to other socio-economic programmes such as health and hygiene, nutrition and sanitation, skill upgradation and capacity building, culture, sports, etc.

(iii) For such neo-literates who wish to pursue further education, an equivalency programme is being developed to enable neo-literates to enroll in courses at the national/State open schools.

(iv) Efforts have been set in motion to decentralise and devolve administrative and financial powers to State Literacy Mission Authorities. The sanctioning of projects will largely be done by these authorities.

(v) Sensitistion and orientation workshops are proposed to be conducted for functionaries of Panchayati Raj Institutions so as to involve local government bodies in the literacy programme.

(vi) It is proposed to further strengthen and revitalise State Resource Centres and Shramik Vidyapeeths (proposed to be renamed as Jana Shiksha Sansthans). This will provide additional fillip in the areas of training, skill upgradation, capacity building and preparation of materials.

(vii) The stress of awareness generation among women and their empowerment is proposed to be continued as one of the major planks of the programme.

Secondary Education

Conceptually, secondary education is meant to prepare young persons both for the world of work and entry into higher education. But traditionally, it has come to be looked upon a bridge between the elementary and higher education stages. This process has to be reversed.

Critical Issues in Secondary Education

(i) *Revision of Curricula*: After the formulation of the New Policy on Education in 1986 (revised in 1992) the need for change of curriculum has arisen. The change will take into account the areas of scientific development, environmental education, computer education and social issues in the context of economic liberalisation.

(ii) *Vocationalisation of Education*: The scheme of Vocationalisation of Education at 10+2 stage was introduced to regulate admissions at College level. The purpose was to divert at least 25 per cent students of 10+2 stage to self-employment or wage-employment, while providing them with vocational competence in a field of their choice. However, the scheme has not taken off due to logistic and academic constraints which require streamlining and strong industry-institution linkages. At present, only 4.8 per cent students are opting for vocational stream, against a target of 25 per cent.

(iii) *Distance Education*: Distance Education is an alternative approach for providing secondary education. With the tremendous expansion of elementary education in the country, the demand for secondary education is likely to grow enormously in the next decade. This challenge has to be met by providing distance mode of education through the Open Learning System (OLS) in the country.

(iv) *Quality Improvement of Teaching in Mathematics, Science and Computer Education* : The quality of teaching in Science and Mathematics has deteriorated so much that it has started having adverse effects at under-graduate and post-graduate levels. Further, with the fast development of Information Technology, the need for quality education in computers at school stage has become imperative.

(v) *Hostel Facilities for Girls* : In remote and tribal areas, secondary schools do not have adequate hostel facilities for girls, and this results in failure to attract girls to them.

(vi) *Minority Education* : In spite of adequate facilities at secondary stage, children from minority groups are not taking full advantage of these.

(vii) *Integrated Education for the Disabled :* After the enactment of the Disabled Act, 1995, the education of the disabled upto age 18 has become a legal obligation. Though efforts have been made to provide educational facilities to this special group, these are not commensurate with the tremendous needs.

Action Plan

(i) *Revision of Curricula*

(a) National Council of Educational Research & Training (NCERT) in collaboration with State Councils of Educational Research & Training (SCERTs) will revise curricula and a National Draft will be prepared for discussion and adoption. New areas of concern will be included in the curriculum. After the draft is adopted, the same organisations will upgrade the text-books so as to keep pace with international standards.

(b) Simultaneously, NCERT and SCERTs will review the training needs of in-service teacher and take steps to meet the new challenges.

(c) National Council for Teacher Education will prepare a framework for pre-service teacher education, so that the standards are upgraded.

(ii) *Vocationalisation of Education (VE)* : The Scheme of vocationalisation of Education at 10+2 stage will be restructured so as to provide employability to the target group. An Empowered Committee representing the Government, industry and trade will be constituted to promote a meaningful partnership and better inter-departmental coordination. Vocational courses with strong linkages with industrial units will be encouraged.

(iii) *Distance Education* : Distance Education will be broad-based by providing wider responsibilities to National Open School (NOS) and the State Open Schools (SOSs). These will be in the areas of elementary education, vocationalisation of education for neo-literates, drop-outs, secondary students and adult population, including working women. Special initiatives will be taken to derive full advantages from the state-of-art Information Technology (IT).

(iv) *Teaching of Mathematics, Science and Computer Education*

(a) Special measures will be taken to promote teaching of Mathematics and Science at the secondary stage by devising new popular source-books. A Science Talent Research Scheme will be promoted.

(b) Science & Mathematics will be linked to the immediate environment of the child. Efforts will be made to avoid the unnecessary load of a crowded curriculum.

(c) The recommendations made the Task Force on Computer Education will be implemented in a time-bound manner.

(v) *Hostel Facilities for Girls :* Additional hostel facilities for girls will be provided, particularly in tribal and remote areas, so that the attendance rate of girls improves. MHRD will coordinate its programmes with those of the Ministry of Welfare.

(vi) *Minority Education*

(a) The scheme of Modernisation of Madarasas will receive all possible attention, so as to cover more Madarasas and improve the access of Muslim children to education.

(b) Area Intensive Programme for Educationally Backward Minorities will be strengthened by allocating a higher outlay. A vigourous publicity drive will be undertaken to generate necessary awareness among the minority communities so that they come forward to take full advantages of the scheme. The cooperation of the leaders of the minority communities will be elicited for the fulfillment of the same objective.

(vii) *Integrated Education for the Disabled :* A composite area approach will be adopted and additional blocks covered under the programme. Training of teachers for these special groups will be ogranised in universities.

Technical Education

Despite efforts in the past, only a few technical institutions have managed to achieve high academic standards. Major qualitative reforms are necessary to upgrade the Regional Engineering Colleges (RECs). While the Indian Institutes of Technology (IITs) have enjoyed autonomy, flexibility, and responsive governance, there is an urgent need to enhance their output and quality.

Critical Issues in Technical Education

(i) *Quality Improvement :* The areas which need specific attention are adequacy and quality of faculty, modernisation of institutional resources, upgradation of educational technology, relevance and flexibility of curricula, interaction with industry etc.

(ii) *Infrastructure Development and Innovations :* Over the years, regional imbalances have emerged in respect of infrastructure development. Further, paradigm shifts are needed across the board from knowledge-based education to skill and competence development and from classroom learning to work-place learning.

(iii) *Flexibility, Mobility and Curricula :* Economic liberalisation and industrial expansion have brought in new institutions and programmes. Hi-tech programmes, curriculum development, flexibility and mobility assume special significance in this rapidly changing scenario.

(iv) *Governance of Institutions :* Governing and management structures at the Central and State levels need to be strengthened, so as to manage the manifold changes described above.

(v) *Excellence in Polytechnic Education :* Technical Staff produced through polytechnics form the backbone of middle level management and technical manpower and demand of them is steadily growing. There is need for greater flexibility autonomy to these institutions, which have also to forge linkages with technical institutions of higher level on the one hand and industry on the other.

Action Plan

(i) *Quality Improvement*

(a) To meet the growing manpower needs as well as improve the quality of technical education, the intake capacity of Indian Institutes of Technology (IITs) and other reputed institutions will be doubled, particularly in high-demand areas like software engineering.

(b) There will be an attempt at quality improvement in RECs and other technical institutions. They will be given greater functional autonomy and their performance would be closely watched. RECs will be integrated into the academic and faculty improvement programmes of IITs.

(ii) *Infrastructure Development and Innovations*

(a) To promote innovations and help meet gaps in infrastructure, institutions of technical education will be encouraged to create a corpus of funds by suitable remodelling and restructuring their tutition fees and development charges. Necessary autonomy will be allowed to these institutions so that they can adopt innovative practices for institution building. Training of staff will be paid more attention.

(iii) *Flexibility, Mobility and Curricula*

(a) To cope with the globalisation of the economy and rapid industrial expansion in the country, hi-tech and new technology programmes will be promoted. All possible steps will be taken to device in-built flexibility in course structure, credit transfer and upward vertical mobility through modular design of the curriculum.

(b) To meet the shortage of faculty for post-graduate teaching, special incentive schemes for M.tech., M.Phil, and Ph.D. programmes will be devised.

(iv) *Governance of Institutions*

(a) Autonomy and deemed university status will be granted to identified technical institutions. The style of management will be more responsive and accountable through induction of eminent academicians, technologists, industrialists and other men of stature. These bodies will focus on vision, goals, objectives and policies for the institutions and not meddle with issues of micro-management.

(v) *Excellence in Polytechnic Education*

(a) The implementation of the Technician Education Project during the Eighth Plan attempted to bring Polytechnics close to industrial establishments, other technical institutions of higher education and industrial training institutes. This process will be further facilitated in the times to come.

(b) The scheme of Community Polytechnics will be brought closer to target groups requirements by transfer of appropriate technology to the community and training in such technology to rural folk.

University & Higher Education

The country is going through major economic and technological changes. The system of higher education has to prepare its products for participation in the emerging social, economic and cultural environment. Universities are witnessing sea changes in their outlook and perspective. Information technology is leading to fundamental changes in the structure, management and mode of delivery of the entire educational system.

Critical Issues

(i) *Relevance and Quality* : Today, the relevance and quality of education is the most critical issue in higher education. The delivery system is under tremendous pressure.

(ii) *Use of Media and Educational Technology* : Information technology has changed the educational systems throughout the world. India at the cross-roads can easily use this opportunity, as she has a major potential for supplying software to the world.

(iii) *Structure of Curriculum* : It is widely argued that the structural arrangement of the curriculum is rigid and fails to respond to the emerging needs of the student community.

(iv) *Access and Equity* : Although there has been massive development and expansion of University and higher education in the country, we are faced with the issue of regional imbalances. There are numerous institutions without adequate physical infrastructure and academic climate. The representation of women is also much lower than that of men.

(v) *Management of Education* : Management of education is being done on traditional lines with right structures, high wastage and low efficiency.

(vi) *Resource Utilization* : There is a problem of under-utilisation of the existing physical infrastructure due to proliferation of institutions of higher education.

Action Plan

(i) *Relevance & Quality*

- (a) *Vocational Education* : At the under-graduate level, vocational education will be expanded in disciplines which have strong linkages with industry and improve employability, UGC, in collaboration with the universities, will re-structure the under-graduate courses and actively involve industrial houses in the development of curriculum, on-the-job training etc.
- (b) *Higher Education:* Teaching in post-graduate and doctoral programmes and research will be oriented towards applied fields so as to establish relevance, need-based specialisation and market-driven skill generation.
- (c) *Faculty Improvement* : Faculty improvement scheme will be strengthened through incentives, self-development, sponsored research, in-service training through distance mode etc. Academic staff colleges will be restructured accordingly.
- (d) *Faculty Exchange* : Faculty exchange between industrial houses and universities will be promoted in technical disciplines so as to enrich the content of Education.

(ii) *Use of Media and Educational Technology* : A purposeful action plan will be formulated in consultation with the field agencies in order to impart a multi-media approach to teaching. Quality will be ensured through Internal Quality Assessment Cells and accreditation through the National Assessment and Accreditation Council.

(iii) *Structural Arrangement of Curriculum* : Universities will be asked to develop a system of credit and credit transfers. This will help in shifting from rigid, structured, undisciplinary programmes to the credit-based cafeteria system with core, optional and extra-developmental courses at under-graduate and postgraduate levels.

(iv) *Access and Equity*

(a) *Unserved Areas* : Unserved areas will be brought into the fold by providing additional educational facilities. College mapping will be done on an area based approach so that there is optimal utilisation of existing resources and regional imbalances are removed.

(b) *Distance Education* : Since resources for expanding physical facilities are limited. Distance Education in conventional as well as open universities will be strengthened and promoted.

(v) *Linkage Changes* : Necessary changes will be made in the legislation pertaining to the UGC and the Universities so as to cope with newly emerging requirements and challenges.

(vi) *Resource Utilisation*

(a) *Fiscal Discipline* : Fiscal discipline will be strongly enforced in institutions of higher education.

(b) *Resources Sharing* : Adoption of a cluster approach to sharing of resources by neighbouring institutions and setting up of inter-university centres will help in achieving economies of scale.

(vii) *Resource Mobilisation* : Additional Resources will be mobilised by:

(a) *Fee Restructuring* '. Restructuring of fees based upon the criteria of Unit Cost and the socio-economic background of the student.

(b) *Public Funding* : Widening the public funding resource-base by attracting contributions from various departments of the Government and the community, in order to support basic infrastructure such as laboratories, libraries and new courses.

(c) *Industrial Funding* : Encouraging contributions from industrial establishments for sponsored research projects.

(viii) *Performance and Accountability* : UGC will work out a concrete programme of action for ensuring better accountability. This will be done by:

(a) *Leveraging UGC Funds* : Using UGC's plan and non-plan financial assistance as a leverage to encourage better performance.

(b) *Evaluation* : Utilising the UGC's evaluation machinery much more vigorously to rank universities and publishing evaluation *reports as* widely as possible.

(c) *Model Code :* Developing a model code of governance which would minimize political interference and improve standards.

(ix) *Extension Education*

(a) *Continuing Education :* Adult and continuing education programmes will be targetted for those who have had the benefit of university education but need to return, for updating or acquiring knowledge or skills.

(b) *Skill-based Courses :* Extension education programmes will be aimed at the needs of specific groups who would not otherwise be entrants to the university system. Such courses could be based on skills for income generation, entrepreneurship, para-legal work, etc.

(c) *Community Education :* Community education programmes will be focused on transfer of skills which require upgradation due to technological progress.

Women's Empowerment

The National Agenda for Governance also states, "We will institute plans for providing free education for girls up to college level, *i.e.* under-graduate level including professional courses would be made free". An adequate provision will be made for the scheme for this purpose during the 9th Five Year Plan. On a long-term basis and in close collaboration with State and local governments, the financial implications of making education free for girls upto the graduation level will be worked out, in so far as these relate to the Department of Education.

Critical Issues

Free Education for Girls

The concept of free education has to be defined explicitly in terms of its coverage. The components could be :

(a) tuition fees;
(b) basic text books;
(c) maintenance expenditures in hostels; and
(d) library books

Action Plan

Free Education for Girls

(a) *Financial Requirements :* The financial requirements for implementation of the concept of free education to girls upto college level will be worked out by Ministry of Human Resources Development (MHRD).

(b) *New Scheme :* A new scheme called "Free Education for Girls" will be devised and implemented in a time-bound manner.

Physical Targets: IX Plan (1997-98 to 2001-2002)

	Items	1997-98	1998-99	1999-2000	2000-2001	2001-2002	Total
1.	Additional Enrolment at Lower Primary Stage (in lakhs)	45	48	50	52	55	250
2.	Additional Enrolment at Upper Primary Stage (in lakhs)	25	28	32	35	40	160
3.	Civil works Elementary Stage (in thousand units)	15	15	15	15	15	75
4.	Supply of Teaching Learning Equipment (TLE)						
	(a) Lower Primary Schools (in thousand units)	8	9	10	11	12	50
	(b) Upper Primary Schools (in thousand units)	67	8	9	10	40	
5.	Sanctioning of Post of Teachers/NFE Instructors						
	(a) Lower Primary Stage (in thousands)	43	45	4850 50	236		
	(b) Upper Primary Stage (in thousands)	30	32	35	38	40	175
6.	Strengthening of Teacher Education Programme						
	(a) Upgradation of Colleges of Teacher Education (CTEs)/Institute of Advance Studies in Education (IASEs) (Nos)	55	55	5	25		
	(b) District Institutes of Education and Training (DIETS)	2020 20	20	20	100		
	(c) Block Resource Centres	-	5	10	15	20	50
	(d) Cluster Resource Centres	-	10	20	300	40	100
7.	Adult Education Programmes						
	(a) Coverage of addl. Districts Under literacy and post-literacy campaigns (incl. Operation Restoration)	45	50	40	40	40	215
	(b) Covering of addl. Districts Under cont. Edn. Programme	15	40	40	40	40	175
	(c) Opening of Shramik Vidyapeeths (Jan Sikshan Sansthans)	5	5	10	15	15 50	
	(d) Making Adult Literate (millions)	10	10	10	10	10	50

Physical Targets : X Plan (2002-03 to 2006-07)

Items	2002-2003	2003-2004	2004-2005	2005-2006	2006-2007	Total
1. Additional Enrolment at Lower Primary Stage (in lakhs)	55	58	60	62	65	300
2. Additional Enrolment at Upper Primary Stage (in lakhs)	40	45	50	55	60	250
3. Civil works Elementary Stage (in thousand units)	25	25	25	25	25	125
4. Supply of Teaching Learning Equipment (TLE)						
(a) Lower Primary Schools (in thousand units)	10	15	20	25	30	100
(b) Upper Primary Schools (in thousand units)	10	10	15	20	25	80
5. Sanctioning of Post of Teachers/NFE Instructors						
(a) Lower Primary Stage (in thousands)	50	52	55	58	60	275
(b) Upper Primary Stage (in thousands)	40	45	50	55	60	250
6. Strengthening of Teacher Education Programme						
(a) Upgradation of Colleges of Teacher Education (CTEs)/Institute of Advance Studies in Education (IASEs) (Nos)	10	10	10	10	10	50
(b) District Institutes of Education and Training (DIETs)	10	10	10	10	10	50
(c) Block Resource Centres	25	25	25	25	25	125
(d) Cluster Resource Centres	50	50	50	50	50	250
7. Adult Education Programmes						
(a) Coverage of addl. Districts Under literacy and to post-literacy campaigns (inci Operation Restoration)	45	50	40	40	40	215
(b) Covering of addl. Districts Under cont. Edn. Programme	15	40	40	40	40	175
(c) Opening of Shramik Vidyapeeths (Jan Sikshan Sansthans)	5	-	5	10	15	35
(d) Making Adult Literate (millions)	10	10	10	10	10	50

13

Tenth Five Year Plan on Education (2002-2007)

Extracts from the Plan Document

Volume II Chapter 1

Social Development and Quality of Life

Education, Health and Family Welfare

Most of the monitorable targets of the Tenth Plan relate to significant improvements in social indicators, particularly in the areas of education, health and family welfare. These are not only important in themselves, but they also have an important bearing on the achievement of the growth and employment targets. These sectors are highly employment intensive and are also perceived to be particularly suitable for providing employment to women. In most of these areas, public investment will continue to be critical for some time to come, but efforts have to be made to improve the quality of the services

Decentralised Management

There has been less than adequate decentralisation of the functions of Government, to the detriment of the delivery of a number of key services. The spirit of the 73rd and 74th Constitutional Amendments has not been observed in many of the states. It is believed that little improvement will be possible until such decentralisation becomes effective, both in terms of functions and resources. But decentralisation cannot stop at the level of Panchayati Raj Institutions (PRIs) and urban local bodies (ULBs). The potential of civil society organisations, such as health and education committees to name only a few, to improve delivery of services is vast, and advantage must be taken of these possibilities through appropriate devolution of functions and authority.

Education for All

Performance in the field of education is one of the most disappointing aspects of India's developmental strategy. Out of approximately 200 million children in the age group of 6-14 years, only 120 million are in schools and net attendance in the primary level is only 66 per cent of enrolment. This is completely unacceptable and the Tenth Plan aims at a radical transformation in this situation. Education for all is one of the primary objectives of the Tenth Plan. The principal vehicle for this is the *Sarva Shiksha Abhiyan*, which is being launched in cooperation with State Governments, and which aims at providing universal elementary education by the end of the Plan.

Encouragement to Private Enterprise

It is also important to ensure that provision is made for the eventual out-turn from the elementary stream so that the transition from the school to the work place can be made with the least disruption. For this, it is necessary to expand the secondary stream with particular emphasis on vocational training. Since most of the resources during the Tenth Plan period will be devoted to elementary education, encouragement must be given to private sector, charitable trusts and religious bodies to step into this area. Plans must, however, be made for expanding the secondary stream in public schools for the Eleventh Plan period.

Role of Local Bodies

Mere establishment of schools and hiring of teachers will not lead to an improvement in education if teachers remain absent as happens in many parts of the country, especially, in rural areas. It is therefore essential that control over schools and teachers should be transferred to local bodies which have a direct interest in teacher performance.

Elementary Education (Chapter 2.2)

Education is a critical input in human resource development and is essential for the country's economic growth. Though the major indicators of socio-economic development *viz.*, the growth rate of the economy, birth rate, death rate, infant mortality rate (IMR) and literacy rate, are all interconnected, the literacy rate has been the major determinant of the rise or fall in the other indicators. There is enough evidence even in India to show that a high literacy rate, especially in the case of women, correlates with low birth rate, low IMR and increase in the rate of life expectancy. The recognition of this fact has created awareness on the need to focus upon literacy and elementary education programme, not simply as a matter of social justice but more to foster economic growth, social well-being and social stability.

Sarva Shiksha Abhiyan

The *Sarva Shiksha Abhiyan* was launched towards the end of the Ninth Plan to achieve the goal of UEE through a time-bound integrated approach, in partnership with states. The medium-term goals for the scheme are given in Box. The programme, which aims to provide elementary education to all children in the 6-14 age group by 2010, is an effort to improve the performance of the school system and provide community-owned quality elementary education in the mission mode. It also envisages bridging of gender and social disparities at the elementary level. The *Sarva Shiksha Abhiyan* has a special focus on the educational needs of girls, SCs and STs and other children in difficult circumstances.

Box 14.1: Objectives of Sarva Shiksha Abhiyan

— All children to be in schools, Education Guarantee Scheme centres, alternate schools, back-to-school camps by 2003;
— All children to complete five years of primary schooling by 2007;
— All children to complete eight years of schooling by 2010;
— Focus on elementary education of satisfactory quality with emphasis on education for life;
— Bridge all gender and social disparities at the primary stage by 2007 and at the upper primary level by 2010; and
— universal retention by 2010.

Under the programme, habitation plans, prepared after micro-planning, household surveys, school mapping and diagnostic studies, form the basis for the District Elementary Education Plans (DEEP). Funds released to states would be channelised to registered societies at the State level. The *Sarva Shiksha Abhiyan* is expected to accord the highest priority to community monitoring, transparency in programme planning and implementation of capacity building at all levels as also to the adoption of a mission approach by the mainstream Education Department functionaries. A National Mission for *Sarva Shiksha Abhiyan* was constituted in November 2000 with the Prime Minister as the Chairman and the Minister for Human Resource Development as Vice-Chairman.

The scheme is expected to absorb most of the existing programmes, including externally–aided programmes, within its overall framework with the district as the unit of programme implementation. To make the approach totally holistic and convergent, efforts would be made to dovetail programme implementation at the district level with all other departments. This would include programmes of children in the 0-6 age group under the Department of Women and Child Development, sports-related interventions of the Ministry of Sports and Youth Affairs, establishment of public library under the Department of Culture and nutrition and health programmes of the Ministry of Health.

Goals, Targets and Strategies for the Tenth Plan

Goals and Targets

In the elementary education sector, the *Sarva Shiksha Abhiyan* is in place with clear focus and medium-term goals as specified in Box 14.1. The Tenth Plan targets in respect to elementary education are:

Universal Access

- All children in the 6-14 age group should have access to primary schools, upper primary schools or their alternatives within a walking distance of one km and three km respectively.
- All children in the 3-6 age group must have universal access to ealy childhood care and education centres.
- Need-based expansion of upper primary education facilities, particularly for the disadvantaged sections. There should be one upper

primary school for every two primary schools.

- All schools should have buildings, toilets, drinking water, electricity, playgrounds, blackboards and other basic facilities. There must be provision of one classroom for every teacher at the elementary stage.

Universal Enrolment

- Enrolment of all children in schools or alternative arrangements by 2003.
- All children to complete five years of primary schooling by 2007.

Universal Retention

- Universal retention in the primary stage by 2007.
- Dropout rate to be reduced to less than 10 per cent for grades VI-VIII by 2007.

Universal Achievement

- Improvement in the quality of education in all respects (content and process) to ensure reasonable learning outcomes at the elementary level, especially in literacy, numerics and in life skills.

Box 13.2: Innovative Programmes in Education in Different States

Several State governments have designed innovative programmes to improve the quality of education in schools.

Head Start

The Rajiv Gandhi State Mission in Madhya Pradesh has introduced a project on a pilot basis for using computers to improve the quality of teaching in rural elementary schools through indigenous customised educational software. The idea is to integrate the use of computers with classroom activities to improve the child's comprehension of difficult parts of each subject as well as to instill computer literacy. A syllabus mapping the difficult areas of learning has been developed and educational software on this for all subjects is being prepared for use in the academic year 2002-03.

Started in November 2000, 648 Head Start centres were operationalised in middle schools that have a primary section and serve as Jan Shiksha Kendras or school cluster resource centres for primary schools in a radius of eight km. A total of 2,358 teachers have been given training in computer-enabled education.

Gyankalash

The District Primary Education Programme in Himachal Pradesh, in collaboration with All India Radio, Shimla, has started a 15-minute bio-weekly programme called Gyan Kalash to provide academic support to primary teachers.

Equity

- Bridge all gender and social gaps in enrolment, retention and learning achievement in the primary stage by 2007 and reduce the gap to 5 per cent in the upper primary stage by 2007.

- Special interventions and strategies to include girls, SC/ST children, working children, children with special needs, urban deprived children, children from minority groups, children below the poverty line, migratory children and children in the hardest-to-reach groups.

Strategies for Universalisation of Elementary Education

The strategies and interventions during the Tenth Plan will mainly be guided by three major considerations: (a) magnitude of the task; (b) present challenges; and (c) the existing administrative and policy framework and the one that will be in place during the Plan period.

Magnitude of the Task. The Working Group on Elementary and Adult Education for the Tenth Five-Year Plan has estimated that in order to achieve the goal of UEE by 2010, enrolment at the primary level needs to grow at an average annual growth rate of 1.12 per cent for boys and 4.16 per cent for girls during the Plan period. At the upper primary level, the growth rate must be 4.62 per cent for boys and 8.03 per cent for girls. The average growth rate for boys and girls taken together should be 2.51 per cent at the primary and 6.08 per cent at the upper primary levels. The year-wise-estimated additional enrolment during the Plan period are given in Table.

Present Challenges. Achieving the goal of UEE poses three main challenges: (i) access to basic education for the unreached segments and social groups; (ii) qualitative improvement in content and processes so as to raise learning achievements; and (ii) tackling high drop-out and low retention rates in primary and upper primary schools.

Administrative and Policy Framework. The administrative and policy framework needs to be guided by the following concerns:

- The national resolve to provide free and compulsory education of satisfactory quality to all children up to the age of 14 years, as stipulated in the National Policy on Education;
- The 93rd Constitutional amendment making the right to elementary education a fundamental right and enforcing it through necessary statutory measures; and
- The spirit of the 73rd and 74th Constitutional amendments setting the stage for greater decentralisation of power and a significantly enhanced role for local bodies, community organisations as well as voluntary agencies in the efforts towards UEE.

Salient Features of the Tenth Plan Strategy for Achieving UEE

Given this backdrop, the Tenth Plan strategy for achieving UEE must have the following salient features:

Holistic and Convergent Approach. As the existing policies and programmes are either for specific target groups/regions, there is need for an all-comprehensive programme covering the entire country. The *Sarva Shiksha Abhiyan* is such a programme and will be the main vehicle for achieving the goals of UEE.

Year-wise Estimated Additional Enrolment

(in million)

Year	Additional Enrolment					
	Primary (Grade I-V)			Upper Primary (Grades VI-VIII)		
	Boys	Girls	Total	Boys	Girls	Total
2002-03	0.57	2.01	2.68	1.14	1.44	2.58
2003-04	0.67	2.10	2.71	1.19	1.54	2.73
2004-05	0.67	2.18	2.85	1.25	1.67	2.92
2005-06	0.69	2.27	2.96	1.31	1.81	3.12
2006-07	0.69	2.37	3.06	1.37	1.95	3.32
Total	3.39	10.93	14.32	6.26	8.41	14.67

Community Participation in UEE Programmes. The involvement of the community will be made more systematic by involving the Panchayati Raj Institutions (PRIs) and urban local bodies. Further down the hierarchy, VECs, Mother-Teacher Associations (MTA) and Parent-Teacher Associations (PTA) would have a formal role in the management of schools in the village.

Target-Groups Oriented Strategy. The Tenth Plan will lay emphasis on identifying the problem areas and formulating a separate strategy for each area, under the overall umbrella of the *Sarva Shiksha Abhiyan.* There will be special focus on children who have never enrolled or those who have dropped out without completing eight years of elementary schooling. Specific strategies would be devised for the difficult-to-reach groups in order to ascertain the reasons for their staying away from school system and to take steps to provide them quality elementary education.

Schemes for Achieving DEE

The following schemes would be the instruments by which these strategies would be translated into action during the Tenth Plan. Scheme-wise break-up of the Tenth Plan outlay is given in the Appendix.

Sarva Shiksha Abhiyan. Out of the approximately 207.76 million children in the 6 14 age group in 2000, the number of children not attending the schools is 40 million. Those outside the school system are mostly girls, SCs/STs children, working children, urban deprived children, disabled children and children in difficult circumstances. Providing access and motivation to these difficult to reach groups, without compromising on the quality of education, would be the challenge that the *Sarva Shiksha Abhiyan* would tackle in the Tenth Plan.

The Sarva Shiksha Abhiyan will totally subsume all existing programmes, barring the Mid-day Meals scheme, and the scheme of Restructuring and Reorganisation of Teachers' Education. All legal agreements regarding externally-aided projects such as Mahila Samakhya, DEEP, Lok Jumbish, Shiksha Karmi, etc., will continue to apply unless specific modifications have been made in consultation with the funding agencies. In order to achieve a holistic and convergent approach, efforts would be made to dovetail programme implementation at the district level with all other programmes. This would include programmes for children in the 0-6 age group under the Department of Women and Child Development, sports-related interventions of the Department of Sports and Youth Affairs, establishment of public libraries under the Department of Culture, nutrition and school health programmes of the Ministry of Health and the employment generation/poverty alleviation programmes of Ministry of Rural Development. This dovetailing exercise would be undertaken while formulating the DEEPs.

Gender-Specific Programmes. The Tenth Plan would also rely on some women-centric programmes such as the existing Mahila Samakhya, and two new schemes; the Kasturba Gandhi Swantantra Vidyalaya (KGSV) and the National Programme for the Education of Girls at the Elementary Level (NPEGEL). Mahila Samakhya will be expanded both in terms of geographical reach and activities like the Mahila Shikshan Kendras. However, it will retain its objectives, identity and non-negotiable principles.

The KGSV and the NPEGEL are proposed to be taken up during the Tenth Plan, with the following features:

- focus on educationally backward areas in girls' education;
- focus on girls from the disadvantaged sections like those belonging to SC/ST, minorities, etc.;
- tackling gender-specific issues that prevent girls and women from having access to education;
- providing women and adolescent girls with the necessary support structure, and an informal learning environment to create opportunities for education;
- creating circumstances for larger participation of women and girls in formal and non-formal education programmes; and
- helping girl's to overcome socio-cultural and economic factors inhibiting their access to elementary education.

Mid-day Meal Scheme. A Supreme Court order in 2001 makes it obligatory for states to provide cooked meals instead of dry rations within the stipulated time-frame, under the Mid-day Meals scheme. Further, in order to achieve the goals set in the Sarva Shiksha Abhiyan programme, modifications would be made in the scheme in the light of feedback received from evaluation studies, the experience gained from the working of the scheme, and the opinions of experts. The modifications would include the following:

- Expanding the programme to cover the children of the EGS & AIE scheme,
- Ending the present practice of distributing food grains and providing hot cooked meals or ready-to-eat food based on sound nutritional principles.
- Allowing adequate flexibility in the management of the programme; by the local bodies/community through VECs, School Management Committees (SMCs), PTAs etc. Also, fostering stronger community participation in the implementation of the programme and encouraging the participation of credible NGOs, wherever possible.

- Decentralising the management of the programme to enable reduction in leakages and mismanagement etc.
- Providing funds in advance to the implementing agencies through their state nodal officer for the transportation of food grains
- Limiting teachers' involvement in the programme to supervision activities.
- Extensive use of the computerised MIS (CMIS) net for monitoring purposes. External agencies are to be involved in monitoring and supervision to ensure greater accountability. Elected representatives will also be involved in supervision
- Linkage with poverty alleviation programmes in rural and urban areas, adequate support of the Union Ministry of Health and the State Health Departments for a school health programme and support from the Department of Women and Child Development for nutrition education.
- A memorandum of understanding be entered into with the key stakeholders (State governments, local bodies, etc.) on the key parameters of the programme.

Strategies for Quality Improvement

While the goals of universal literacy and enrolment are laudable in themselves, the achievements in these areas would remain hollow without ensuring quality education. A qualitative improvement in the content and processes of basic education, in order to make them more responsive to the learning needs of individuals and the development needs of different socio-economic sectors, continues to be a major challenge. The challenge for providing quality education at the elementary level involves improvements in the preparation, motivation and deployment of teachers, the quality of textbooks and of infrastructural facilities. It also involves making education relevant to society's needs and strengthening the management and institutional capacity of educational institutions especially at the State, district and local levels.

Improving the quality of textbooks is crucial as they are the main instructional alies in elementary schools, and are the only reading material for most students.

The quality of infrastructural facilities (particularly toilets for girls), equipment and support services, also has a significant impact on enrolment and retention. In this context, the main challenge is to provide a classroom for every teacher in the primary and upper primary schools and a separate room for the headmaster in upper primary schools along with playground facilities and clean toilets. Although one-third of the expenditure approved under DEEP is earmarked for the construction of buildings etc., there are still a substantial number of primary schools without these facilities. The main thrust in the Tenth Plan should be to ascertain that all the primary schools have *pucca* buildings with all supporting infrastructural facilities.

Systematic Learner Evaluation

A mechanism for regular learner assessment will be designed and put in place to evaluate the impact and efficacy of measures taken for improvement in school quality.

Strategy for Drop-outs

A large number of children drop out of school because of reasons relating to the school environment. These include attitude of teachers, irrelevant curriculum, sub standard and uninteresting teaching, teacher absenteeism, corporal punishment, poor school infrastructure, inability to cope with the pace of learning, lack of parental support in the case of first generation learners, maladjustment, etc. Girls form the majority of the drop-outs in all categories. The National Family Health Survey-11 (NFHS-I1), conducted in 1998-99, also observed that the main reasons for students dropping out include their not being interested in studies, the high private cost of education and the need for them to work, whether in their own farms, business/households or outside. These reasons held true for 75 per cent of drop-outs.

The main challenge for education authorities at the central, State and district levels is to (a) improve the supply, quality and retention power of education, particularly in rural primary schools and in the unreached segments; and (b) introduce innovative methods of providing education to identified disadvantaged and difficult groups to suit their timing and interests. The focus in the Tenth Plan would, therefore, be on pedagogic improvement and adoption of child-centered methods, which have been developed in programmes like DPEP; and building a positive environment that would include more attractive classroom designs, local contextual curriculum and more friendly evaluation techniques Apart from a number of steps undertaken under the *Sarva Shiksha Abhiyan* to reduce the private cost of education, an incentive scheme linked to attendance has been suggested for girls, SCs/STs and poor children.

Where the children are dropping out because of the need to work, the emphasis would be on involving the community in motivating the parents to bring their children back to school so that they are in position to complete eight years of elementary education. For those children who have already dropped out, suitable alternative education systems such as bridge courses, remedial teaching, back to school camps, etc, would be provided so that they can be mainstreamed into the formal system.

Strategy for Early Childhood Care and Education (ECCE)

Early childhood development is globally acknowledged as a significant input for lifelong development and successful completion of primary education. The Tenth Plan acknowledges ECCE as the first step in the education ladder. The major provider of ECCE is the Integrated Child Development Services (ICDS) scheme which covers 15.8 million children (17.8 per cent of the child population of 3-6 years) through about 5,20,000 *anganwadis* in 35 States and Union Territories. Early Childhood Education or Pre-School Education is among the six components of the ICDS scheme and is one of its weakest. The *Sarva Shiksha Abhiyan* aims to support (i) strengthening the pre-school component in ICDS by need-based training of *anganwadi sevikas*, provision of learning materials, etc.; (ii) setting up *balwadis* as pre-school centres in uncovered areas; (iii) building advocacy on the importance of early child development; (iv) organising training programmes for community leaders; (v) providing for intensive planning for ECCE; (vi) development of materials; and (vii) promoting convergence between the school system and the ECCE.

Community Participation in Elementary Education

Thrust on Decentralisation

Decentralisation provides a clear correlation between the needs of people and the steps taken by the Government to meet these demands. Planning from below and contextualised resource allocation for basic services would not only be more cost effective and produce better results but will also ensure that the quality of the services is directly proportional to the degree of community control and supervision. People's participation in the provision of basic services can, as mentioned in the Mid-Term Appraisal of the Ninth Five-Year Plan, contribute to the achievement of four main objectives, *i.e.*, effectiveness, efficiency, empowerment and equity.

The thrust on decentralised planning and management came as early as in 1986, in the National Policy of Education, which had proposed decentralisation as a fundamental requirement for improving the efficiency and effectiveness of educational planning and management and for evolving a meaningful framework for accountability. The Approach Paper to the Tenth Five-Year Plan has also reiterated that the mere establishment of schools and hiring of teachers will not lead to an improvement in education if teachers remain absent, as is common, especially in the rural areas. It is, therefore, essential that control over schools and teachers should be transferred to local bodies, which have a direct interest in teacher performance. Planning, supervision and management of education would have to be through local bodies at the district, block and village levels. Efforts should also be made for the social mobilisation of local communities for adult literacy campaigns and for the promotion of primary education.

Community Participation and Creating Suitable Environment

While the decentralisation of governance, through the 73rd and 74th Constitutional amendments, has facilitated the transfer of the management of school to panchayats/local bodies, the real challenge now is to create an enabling environment for the qualitative participation of all groups. The qualitative participation should mean that the community is able to have a voice and exercise its choice. It also involves the development of human, organisational and management capacity to solve problems and sustain the improvements.

Recognising the fact that community participation is the surest way to ensure UEE and improve the quality of education, several State governments have already initiated the process of decentralising the management of elementary education by involving the community. Other States would also be encouraged to transfer the management of primary schools to panchayat/local bodies with special emphasis on:

- Encouraging community participation in promoting enrolment, retention and other aspects of education. PRIs and grassroot level organisations like VECs, PTAs, MTAs etc. should become the vehicles of community mobilisation;
- Evolving a community-based monitoring system evolved with full transparency;
- Making community mobilisation through intensive micro-planning and school mapping mandatory; and
- Participatory implementation of goals and strategies.

Change in the Outlook of Functionaries

This shift in planning and management strategy will also require a massive effort to train and continually support educational bodies set up under the PRIs/urban local bodies. There is an urgent need to reorient the outlook of government functionaries and their perception of their roles. Efforts will be made to reorient the programmes of various resource institutions at the national and State levels to meet these requirements. "Towards this end, the local level institutions in education and allied suitors will be strengthened adequately.

The National Council of Educational Research & Training (NCERT), New Delhi, conducts a National Talent Search Examination to identify talent. International Chemistry, Mathematics and Physics Olympiads are held every year to identify talent in these subjects. India has been participating regularly in these Olympiads.

Talented students from rural areas are provided scholarships at the secondary stage in order to develop their potential by providing them access to good schools. A total of 38,000 scholarships have been awarded to students.

Major Thrust in Secondary Education

Internal compulsions and international commitments are forcing the secondary education system to gear up to meet the ever-increasing demand for education. Initiatives such as the externally-aided District Primary Education Programme (DPEP), the Sarva Shiksha Abhiyan, increasing number of schools in the private sector and the drive for elimination of the gender gap in line with the Dakar Declaration on Education for All in 2000. Concerted efforts, backed by national consensus, are called for to meet these daunting challenges.

The major thrust in the Tenth Plan, thus, is to meet the increase demand for secondary education. The Government has to play a greater role to encourage opening of new secondary schools, expansion of capacity of the existing schools including double shifts, upgrading of upper primary schools in backward, unserved and under-served area, as also expansion and diversification of open schooling and distance education system. One of the many options being considered during the Tenth Plan is for the Kendriya Vidyalaya Sangathan to establish schools in partnership with voluntary agencies. It is proposed to set up 150 Kendriya Vidyalayas (fully funded by the Government) in addition to the present network of 854 schools. Another option is to provide a one-time grant/seed money to societies, trusts and not-for-profit organisations like the R.K. Mission, the Jesuits, the DAV Trust, which already run reputed schools to encourage them to set up more schools.

More Navodaya School

It is proposed to establish more Navodaya Vidyalayas to cover the districts which do not have one right now and also to strengthen these existing schools by providing them facilities for cultural activities, computers and sports facilities. It is also proposed to help the Central Tibetan School Administration (CTSA), which runs about 70 schools for children of Tibetan refugees, to set up more schools.

Secondary Education for the Under Privileged

During the Tenth Plan, the National Open School (NOS) would intensify efforts to ensure that the open school system is beneficial to the under-privileged groups. A scheme to reimburse to the NOS the fees incurred on Scheduled Castes/Scheduled Tribe (SC/ST) students, girls and physically challenged students is also on the anvil. The NOS will also be restructured to affiliate regular schools/centres, which offer NOS curriculum as an alternative to the curricula of other school Boards. The nearly 1,200 study centres are proposed to be increased by around 15 per cent per year. New admissions, which are around 200,000 students a year, is likely to increase at 20 per cent per year. The NOS proposes to implement the schemes of 'On-Demand Admissions' and 'On Demand Examinations', which give flexibility to the students to take admissions and examinations during mid-session.

Boarding and Hostel Facilities for Girls

The scheme of providing boarding and hostel facilities for girls, initiated in 1993, has already been revised in order to increase the enrolment of girls at the secondary level. The scheme provides for financial assistance to eligible voluntary organisations to improve the enrolment of adolescent girls belonging to the rural areas and weaker sections.

Role of NCERT

In order to make secondary education more relevant in the current context, the NCERT will continue to emphasise modernisation and revision of curriculum, updating of courses and vocationalisation of education. The Council would operationalise the fifth Regional Institute of Education for the North-Eastern Region at Shillong. The NCERT is starting the nation-wide Seventh All India Educational Survey in order to strengthen the database during the Plan period.

CBSE and CISCE

The Central Board of Secondary Education (CBSE) and the Council for the Indian School Certificate Examination (CISCE) conduct public examinations at the end of Classes X and XII. Both are self-financing bodies, which do not receive any assistance from the government. A total of 5,850 schools are affiliated to the CBSE as on 15 April 2001 and 1,119 schools to the CISCE as on 31 August 2001. The NOS is the third national-level body conducting equivalent examination at the secondary and senior secondary level.

Schemes of Secondary Education

As part of the zero-based budgeting exercise and in order to bring in greater effectiveness in the implementation of the central sector and the centrally sponsored schemes, the schemes of secondary sector have been grouped under following four broad heads:

Quality Improvement in Schools. This comprises the centrally sponsored schemes of Promotion of Science Laboratories, Environmental Orientation to School Education, Promotion of Yoga, as well as the central sector schemes of Population Education Project, International Mathematics/Science Olympiad. The State Governments would develop training modules for in-service training of teachers and provide infrastructure and research inputs for quality improvement in schools.

Information and Communication Technologies (ICT). This will include the reworked centrally sponsored schemes—Computer Education and Literacy in Schools (CLASS) and Educational Technology (ET)—which seek to familiarise students with IT. Keeping in view the current demand for IT, a major thrust is to be given to this scheme. State governments would prepare Computer Education Plans (CEPs) for computer literacy and education. The components of the merged scheme ICT in Schools would include (a) funding support for CEPs; (b) strengthening and reorientation of the staff of the State Institutes of Education and Training (SIETs); (c) Digitalisation of SIETs' video and audio cassettes in partnership with NGOs; (d) web/internet-based education to be managed by the SIETs.

Access and Equity. This scheme will comprise, among other components yet to be designed, the on–going scheme of Strengthening of Hostel/Boarding Facilities for Girl students.

Integrated Education for Disabled Children (IEDC). In the Tenth Plan, greater efforts will be made to expand inclusive education to cater to the needs of mentally and physically challenged students. The scheme will continue as a separate centrally sponsored scheme and will be redesigned. It will now focus on the following elements: convenience with the Integrated Child Development Services (ICDS) scheme for early interventions; with the DPEP and Sarva Shiksha Abhiyan for education of the mentally and physically challenged up to the elementary level; with the special schools under the Ministry of Social Justice and Empowerment. Other components of the scheme will include pedagogy and curriculum, training of teachers and preparation of teaching learning material; research and development (R & I)), advocacy and evaluation; and funding through the PTAs/VECs/management committees of the schools.

The Path Ahead

The impact of recent initiatives undertaken for the universalisation of elementary education is resulting in increased demand for expansion of secondary education. Unless steps are taken to expand the secondary education system, it would be difficult to accommodate the increasing number of upper primary pass-outs. While there has been an increase in the number of secondary schools, the spread has been uneven; there are regional disparities and variations in the socio-economic status of various States and Union Territories. The significant gender gap also has to be narrowed down.

Quality Improvement as the Key Theme

The key theme in the Tenth Plan is imparting quality education at all stages of education and the pursuit of excellence. The on-going efforts in revision of curricula at the secondary education level, so as to make it more relevant, would continue in the Tenth Plan. The convergence of centrally-sponsored schemes will help in imparting science, mathematics and computer education as well as environmental and value education in a more focussed manner. There is a line of thinking which believes that subsidising students through a 'voucher system', as is the practice in some of the Latin American countries, is more effective than 'subsidising' institutions. The students will enroll themselves in reputed schools, letting the market forces weed out the inefficient and poor quality institutions.

Teacher Education

Restructuring and Reorganisation of Teacher Education

The scheme of Restructuring and Reorganisation of Teacher Education started in 1987, aims to strengthen the institutional base of teacher training by taking up special programmes for training of teachers in specified areas and other non-institutional training programmes. Other objectives of the scheme are: setting up District Institutes of Education and Training (DIETs) to provide academic and resource support to elementary school teachers and non-formal and adult education instructors; and establishment of Colleges of Teacher Education (CTEs) and Institutes of Advanced Studies in Education (IASEs) for pre-service and in-service training for secondary school teachers. The scheme also envisages strengthening State Councils of Educational Research and Training (SCERT); orienting teachers in the use of Operation Black-Board material; and implementation of the Minimum Levels of Learning (MLL) strategy.

Improving the Performance of Teachers

Improving the performance of teachers is the most important challenge in elementary education as they are the principal instruments of education. Besides, teachers' salary claims the major share of the State education budget. Although a lot has already been done to improve the quality of teachers, historical deficiencies in teachers' education and training has resulted in many of them having little understanding of the material they teach, poor teaching skills and poor motivation levels.

Besides addressing the issue of quality, the Tenth Plan would also place an exclusive emphasis on teacher education. Some of the broad strategies, which would be followed, are:

Development and Strengthening of Teacher Education Institutes

The focus of teacher education would be on the development of the following institutions:

- *District Institute of Education and Training (DIETs).* Each State would be encouraged to rethink the structure of its DIETs as per needs of the district and effectiveness of the institution. Each DIET would be encouraged to draw up a development plan for itself, defining its role and setting goals for itself. Special attention will be paid to the development of libraries in DIETs, as well as providing computer facilities (including computer literacy training), exposure visits, networking and sharing among DIETs and other academic institutions on professional issues and the establishment of district resource groups. Further, new DIETs would be set up only in those States where the existing ones are functional and steps are taken to improve sub-standard DIETs.
- *Colleges of Teacher Education (CTEs)* and *Institutes of Advanced Studies in Education* (IASEs). The need for CTEs and IASEs in each State would be ascertained in terms of the needs for secondary teacher education and identified institutions would be strengthened. The identified CTEs/IASEs would need to prepare their individual plan of development, mentioning the areas in which they need to be strengthened and make a need assessment survey in the areas of their jurisdiction. They must also develop schedules and materials of in–service teacher training to cover secondary teachers and implement the National Council of Teacher Education (NCTE) project on imparting information technology (IT) literacy to the teachers. IASEs would be encouraged to play a greater role in elementary education and education of teacher educators.

Under this scheme, 171 DIETs, 86 CTEs, 38 IASEs have been sanctioned so far. More than 1.9 million teachers have been trained under the Special Orientation Programme of School Teachers in the use of Operation Blackboard material and implementation of the MLL strategy. The scheme has recently been revamped with greater thrust on improving the quality of teacher training institutions in partnership with States. The revised scheme provides for more assistance to States; memorandums of understanding (MOU) with states to improve the efficiency of key resource institutes; widening the scope of the Special Orientation Programme for school teachers; and enhancing the capacities of existing personnel for the management of teacher education programmes.

- *Strengthening of State Councils for Educational Research and Training (SCERTs).* The SCERT is identified as a key area for teacher education in the Tenth Plan. The State governments need to fulfill some essential conditions for being eligible for funds for strengthening of SCERTs, such as recruitment of appropriate faculty, linkage to DIETs; resource centres and schools, autonomy of SCERTs and proper maintenance of buildings etc. Only then would the Central government fund capacity building and training of SCERT faculty, development of infrastructure, computers and IT literacy programmes and hostels for residential/training programmes, etc. SCERTs should be equipped to plan for computer education curricula, teacher training etc. at the school even, strengthening of cells for teaching of English language at the elementary level, strengthening of pre-service education etc., pre-service as well as In-service Training of Teachers, including Para-Teachers.

Professional Development of Teachers

The focus in the Tenth Plan would be on:

- Ensuring pre-service training to all elementary school teachers so that all untrained teachers can be trained within a period of three years, including through the distance learning mode.
- Enhancing pre-service training facilities in selected districtswhere the present capacity is not adequate.
- Improving the quality of elementary teacher pre-service education.
- Extending the provision of pre-primary teacher training by strengthening existing institutions that provide, or are willing to provide, pre-service education for the pre-primary stage.
- Developing specialised correspondence courses, of two months to one year's duration, for elementary teachers in collaboration with open universities, higher education institutions, good IASEs, NGOs with experience in quality education, and other professional organistions.
- Development of courses for in-service education of teachers that will carry credits and linking these to promotions and benefits.

Strengthening of Block Resource Centres (BRCs) and Cluster Resource Centres (CRCs)

With an emphasis on providing academic support to the teachers locally, depending on context-specific needs, DIETs would have close linkage with BRCs and CRCs whose personnel get academic support from them.

Professional Development of Practitioners, i.e. Teacher Educators, Managers and Others

New courses for teacher educators and curriculum developers would be developed and tried out on a pilot basis. Innovations and pilot projects in pre–service and in-service teacher education will be supported. Another major focus area would be networking of teacher education institutions and strengthening of teacher education by excluding access to digital resources. The networked institutions would then be able to use the Information and Communication Technologies (ICT) for on–line sharing of resources and for breaking the isolation of institutions.

Vocational Education (Chapter 2.4) Centrally Sponsored Scheme: of Vocationalisation of Secondary Education

An outlay of Rs. 350 crore has been provided for the Centrally-Sponsored Scheme of Vocationalisation of secondary education in the Tenth Plan.

The Apprentice Act

The Apprentices Act serves a dual purpose—firstly, to regulate the programme of training apprentices in industry to ensure that it conforms to the syllabi, period of training etc. prescribed by the Central Apprenticeship Council; and secondly, to utilise fully the facilities available in industry for workers. As on 31 March 2001, over 17,800 public/private sector establishments were covered under the Apprenticeship Act and the number of seats allocated were 2.20 lakh, out of which about 1.58 lakh seats were utilised.

Craftsmen Training Programme

The Craftsmen Training Programme relates to theoretical training on any area of craftsmanship with little exposure to practical training. This training is being imparted in 43 engineering and 24 non-engineering trades in order to reduce unemployment among the educated youth by equipping them with suitable skills for industrial employment.

Skill Development and Employment Service for SCs/STs and Women

Skill development and employment services, as in the past, continue to be provided to vulnerable sections with special needs like women, SCs/STs, and persons with disabilities, including disabled ex-servicemen. To provide training facilities to women so as to enhance their participation in industry as skilled workers and/or to help them in acquiring skills for taking up self-employment, income-generating activities, training programmes, exclusively for women, are being provided through the National Vocational Training Institute (NVTI) and 10 Regional Vocational Training Institutes for Women (RVTI). The present training capacity of these Institutes is 2,068 seats. In the State sector, there is a network of 231 ITIs, exclusively for women, besides 534 Special Wings for Women in general ITIs with 46,750 seats, offering craftsmen training in various engineering and non-engineering trades.

In spite of the available infrastructure and facilities, skill development and training in the country is highly inadequate. Every year 5.5. million students pass out of Class X, of which 3.3 million go to Class XI, leaving 2.2 million out of the education stream. There are, besides, those who drop-out after Class VIII, who number 19 million. These are the people who look for vocational training and self-employment avenues. Therefore, attention has to be paid to this 21 million-target group. As against this, available formal training capacity of the country is only 2.3 million students, which leaves a gap of 18.7 million. The ITI system needs to be revamped to fill up this gap. Further, there is an urgent need to look into training of trainers as only 40 per cent of the 55,000 instructors have undergone a full instructor-training course.

Besides these initiatives of the Ministries of Labour and Human Resource Development, there are several other programmes and activities under the purview of different Departments/Ministries. These include Ministry of Rural Development, Department of Women and Child Development, Ministry of Industries, Khadi & Village Industry Commission, etc. All these programmes largely cater to the needs of the informal sector in a limited manner and need to be expanded to meet the emerging needs.

The Path Ahead

Measures for Recasting Vocational Education

The growing problem of unemployment among the youth requires a recasting of the entire vocational education scheme. Future policies on vocational courses must revolve around the following issues:

- There is a need to sensitise State Governments and Union Territory Administrations on the importance of skill training/vocational education in the context of the problem of unemployment.
- There is an urgent need to cater to the Class VIII pass-outs whose numbers will swell with success of the Universalisation of Elementary Education and the Sarva Shiksha Abhiyan initiatives.
- There is need for careful assessment of the stage at which the trades of Fitter, Turner, Blacksmith, as also courses like Accountancy, Typing, Book-keeping and Secretarial practices are to be introduced.
- The duration of various vocational courses also needs to be carefully assessed.
- There is also a need for vertical mobility in the vocational stream. Students who complete +2 in a particular stream should be able to specialise and obtain diplomas and degree certificates as to get value-added jobs and better employment opportunities.
- The vocational courses should be demand and need-based, keeping in mind the constantly changing requirements of technologies/ industries. Vocational courses must have an in-built flexibility to allow students to switch courses with changes in demand patterns.
- The existing scheme should be strengthened by involving industries through MoUs in the designing and certification of courses and training of students and faculty.
- At present, most of the vocational courses are in the manufacturing sector. Given the slow growth in this sector and the exploding opportunities in the services sector, vocational courses should concentrate more on the latter.
- There should be focus on convergence of schemes like the Sarva Shiksha Abhiyan Adult Education, and Vocational Education Programme at schools, *i.e.*, polytechnics, community colleges etc.
- There is a need to have a re-look at the vocational education scheme given the fact that a number of districts in Uttar Pradesh, Bihar, Haryana, Rajasthan and Madhya Pradesh have a pool industrial base.
- The syllabi of vocational subjects should be updated on a regular basis to keep pace with changes in technology. This is specially relevant in trades like food processing, dairy technology, leather and tanning technology, etc.
- Vocational institutes should also be networked with professional institutes like the Central Food and Technology Research Institute (CFTRI), Mysore. Central Leather Research Institute (CLRI), Chennai etc. to keep abreast with technological developments.
- The vocational education scheme should focus on the capacity of

the local industry to absorb students of a particular trade. Excess supply of students of a particular trade needs to be avoided. In this context, there is need for diversification even within a trade.

- Urgent attention needs to be given to training vocational education teachers.
- There should be regular exchange of ideas/skills among vocational education teachers, master craftsmen and trainees.
- The apex industry associations like the Federation of Indian Chambers of Commerce and Industry (FICC), Associated Chambers of Commerce and Industry (ASSOCHAM) and Confederation of Indian Industry (CII) need to be involved to a greater extent in the implementation of vocational education programmes and amenities of skills

Adult Education

Goals, Targets and Strategies for the Tenth Plan

The Tenth Plan Targets for adult education are:

- To achieve full literacy, *i.e.* at sustainable threshold level of 75 per cent by 2005.
- To cover all left over districts by 2003-2004.
- To remove residual illiteracy in the existing districts by 2004-05.
- To complete Post Literacy Campaigns in all districts.
- To launch Continuing Education Programmes in 100 districts by the end of the Plan period.

Higher Education

Objectives, Key Issues and Focus on Higher Education during the Tenth Plan

The main objective in the Tenth Plan is to raise the enrolment in higher education of the age-group 18-23 years from the present 6 per cent to 10 per cent by end of the Plan period.

The strategies would focus on increasing access, quality, adoption of state-specific strategies and the liberalization of the higher education system.

Emphasis would be laid on the relevance of the curriculum, vocationalisation, and net working on the use of information technology.

The Tenth Plan would focus on distance education, convergence of formal, non-formal distance and IT education institutions, increased private participation in the management of colleges and deemed to be universities; research in frontier areas of knowledge and meeting challenges in the area of internalisation of Indian education.

Technical Education

Objectives, key Issues and Focus on Technical Education during the Tenth Plan.

The key issues in technical and management education during the Tenth Plan would be a continuing focus on increasing intake; quality of education, including research in technology. Other issues include; faculty development, optimal utilisation of resources through net-working; development of information technology education, modernisation of the curriculum, international benchmarking, developing capacity in new and emerging technology areas; strategic planning and management of the technical education system and developing the informal sector.

Development of Electronic Management Information System (EMIS): Among the several initiatives for strategic planning and management of technical education mention may be made of the EMIS to be supported by the AICFE at the national level to plan the coordinated development of the technical education system and to be implemented in selected lead institutions. The information collected through the EMIS will be available on line and provide an effective real time decision support system to Central and State Government for effective planning development and monitoring.

(*Source*: *Tenth Five Year Plan*, 2002-2007, Planning Commission)

14

Sachar Committee Report (2005-06)

Major Recommendations

The Government of India, Prime Minister's Office, New Delhi constituted in March 2005, a High Level Committee to prepare a comprehensive report on the social, economic and educational status of the Muslim community of India. The Committee, popularly known as Sachar Committee after the name of its Chairperson, submitted its report in November, 2006.

The Committee consisted of the following members:

(1) Justice Rajender Sachar - Chairperson
(2) Shri Saiyid Hamid - Member
(3) Dr. T.K. Ooman - Member
(4) Shri M.A. Basith - Member
(5) Dr. Rakesh Basant - Member
(6) Dr. Akhtar Majeed - Member
(7) Dr. Abu Saleh Shariff - Member Secretary

The Terms of Reference of the above High Level Committee (HLC) were as follows:

(1) The HLC will prepare a report on the social, economic and educational status of the Muslim community of India. The HLC will finalise and present its report within fifteen months from the date of this notification.

(2) More specifically, the HLC will:

(a) Obtain relevant information from departments/agencies of the Central and State Governments and also conduct an intensive literature survey to identify published data, articles and research on relative social, economic and educational status of Muslims in India at the State, Regional and District levels, to address, inter alia, the following questions:

(i) In which States, Regions, Districts and Blocks do Muslims of India mostly live?

(ii) What is the geographical pattern of their economic activity, i.e., what do they mostly do for a living in various States, Regions and Districts?

(iii) What is their asset base and income levels relative to other groups across various States and Regions?

(iv) What is the level of their socio-economic development in terms of relevant indicators, such as, literacy rate, dropout rate, MMR, IMR etc.? How does this compare with other communities in various States?

(v) What is their relative share in public and private sector employment? Does it vary across States and what is the pattern of such variation? Is the share in employment in proportion to their population in various States? If not, what are the hurdles?

(vi) What is the proportion of Other Backward Classes (OBCs) from the Muslim community in the total OBC population in various States? Are the Muslim OBCs listed in the comprehensive list of OBCs prepared by the National and State Backward Classes Commissions and adopted by the Central and State Governments for reservation for various purposes? What is the share of Muslim OBCs in the total public sector employment for OBCs in the Centre and in various States in various years?

(vii) Does the Muslim community have adequate access to education and health services, municipal infrastructure, bank credit and other services provided by Government/public sector entities? How does this compare to access enjoyed by other communities in various States? What is the level of social infrastructure (schools, health centers, ICDS centers etc.) located in areas of Muslim concentration in comparison to the general level of such infrastructure in various States?

(b) Consolidate, collate and analyse the above information/ literature to identify areas of intervention by Government to address relevant issues relating to the social, economic and educational status of the Muslim community.

Observations and Data on the Literacy Rates

Table 14.1 reports age specific literacy rates computed from the NSSO 61st Round data (2004-05). The estimates clearly show that in recent years the literacy rates for the SC/ST population have risen more sharply than for Muslims; while persons of the older age groups in the Muslim community had much higher literacy levels, these are higher for SCs/STs in the younger age groups. Therefore, the trends observed in the Census data are also evident in the National Sample Survey Organisation (NSSO) data.

Differentials in Educational Attainment: Higher Education

In India, a significant proportion of the relevant population still remains deprived of the benefits of higher education, and the Muslims comprise an important category of the deprived communities (Table 14.2). According to Census data, while only about 7 per cent of the population aged 20 years and

Table 14.1: Literates as Proportion of Population by Age Groups – 2004-05

Age Groups	*Hindus*			*Muslims*	*Other Minorities*
	Gen.	*OBC*	*SCs/STs*		
6-13 years	90.2	80.8	74.7	74.6	88.5
14-15 years	95.7	87.5	80.0	79.5	91.9
16-17 years	95.0	85.2	78.6	75.5	91.3
18-22 years	91.4	76.9	65.0	70.5	85.8
23 years and above	74.0	50.6	36.5	46.1	67.0
Total	**80.5**	**63.4**	**52.7**	**59.9**	**75.2**

Source: Estimated from NSSO 61st Round, Sch. 10(2004-05)

Table 14.2: Graduates and Diploma Holders by SRCs (Socio-Religious Communities)

Census 2001

SRCs	*Number (in lakhs)*		*Percentage of 20 Years + Population*		*Distribution Across SRCs*	
	Graduates	*Diploma and Certificate*	*Graduates*	*Diploma and Certificate*	*Graduates*	*Diploma and Certificate*
Total	376.7	40.5	6.7	0.7	100	100
Muslim	23.9	2.7	3.6	0.4	6.3	6.8
SCs/STs	30.8	4.1	2.4	0.3	8.2	10.2
All Others	322.2	33.7	8.8	0.9	85.5	83.0

above are graduates or hold diplomas, this proportion is less than 4 percent amongst Mzuslims. Besides, those having technical education at the appropriate ages (18 years and above) are as low as one per cent and amongst Muslims, that is almost non-existent.

A comparison (Table 14.3 and 14.4) between Muslims and SCs/STs also reveals interesting results. Initially, Muslims had a marginally higher Graduation Attainment Rate (GAR) than SCs/STs. In the initial phases of planning, the SCs/STs had performed more slowly and this had led to a slight widening of the gap between them and the Muslims. In the 1970s, however, the GARs for SCs/STs grew at a faster rate than for Muslims. This led to convergence in the GAR of Muslims and SCs/STs. In fact, among urban males, the convergence process had begun in the 1950s itself, and had resulted in SCs/STs 'overtaking' Muslim males after the 1970s; it also resulted in the current significantly higher levels.

Some Concluding Observations

Relative deprivation in education of Muslims vis-à-vis other SRCs calls for a significant shift in the policy of the State, along with the creation of effective partnership with private and voluntary sectors. Given the vastness of the population to be served and the limited resources available with policy makers,

Table 14.3: Graduates as Proportion of Population by Age Groups – All India, 2004-05

Age Groups	*Hindus*			*Muslims*	*Other Minorities*
	Gen.	*OBC*	*SCs/STs*		
20-30 years	18.6	6.5	3.3	4.5	11.6
30-40 years	16.8	4.6	2.3	3.3	9.2
40-50 years	14.6	3.2	1.5	2.8	8.1
51 years and above	9.8	1.9	0.9	2.1	5.7
Total	**15.3**	**4.4**	**2.2**	**3.4**	**8.9**

Source: Estimated from NSSO (2004-05) 61st Round, Sch. 10.

Table 14.4: Children Currently Studying as a Proportion of Population by Age Groups – 2004-05

Age Groups	*Hindus*			*Muslims*	*Other Minorities*
	Gen.	*OBC*	*SCs/STs*		
6-13 years	19.1 (17.3)	36.1 (35.5)	25.7 (27.4)	14.0 (15.1)	5.1 (4.8)
14-15 years	24.3 (19.9)	36.1 (35.2)	21.4 (25.2)	12.2 (14.5)	6.0 (5.3)
16-17 years	28.9 (21.1)	33.7 (35.0)	20.2 (24.7)	10.7 (14.0)	6.3 (5.1)
18-22 years	34.0 (20.8)	30.5 (34.4)	17.7 (25.5)	10.2 (13.9)	7.6 (5.5)
23 years and above	35.6 (23.9	29.2 (35.1)	18.3 (24.1)	7.4 (10.9)	9.5 (5.9)

Source: Estimated from NSSO (2004-05) 61st Round, Sch. 10.

Note 1: Figures in parenthesis report the share of each socio-religious group in the total population of that age group.

the emphasis on provisioning of a minimum level of school education by the State seems justified. That does not mean, however, that the State can withdraw from participation in higher levels of education. The policy focus should be in those areas of education where private investment is not adequate to cover the weaker section of the population. While investment and effort from private and voluntary sectors could help in promoting convergence of educational levels of Muslims with that of other communities, the task remains essentially that of the State. Muslims have not been able to sufficiently reap the benefits of state intervention and growth in education. We first summarise the key findings of this chapter so that areas of policy focus can be delineated.

With regard to school education, the condition of Muslims is one of grave concern. The data clearly indicates that while the overall levels of education in India, measured through various indicators, is still below universally acceptable standards, the educational status of the Muslim community in particular is a matter of great concern. Though the all-India literacy levels of Muslims are somewhat satisfactory, disaggregative analysis of state data, by place of residence and by gender, presents a less flattering picture of the status of Muslims. When alternative indicators of educational achievement, more representative of the progress made in education, are considered, a significant disparity between the status of Muslims and that of other SRCs (except SCs/

STs) can be noted. For example, both the Mean Years of Schooling (MYS) and attendance levels of Muslims are low in absolute terms and in contrast to all SRCs except in some cases SCs/STs. In fact, in several context, SCs/STs are found to have overtaken Muslims.

While there is a significant rural-urban differential, it was observed that the gap between Muslims and the other SRCs is generally higher in urban areas than in rural areas. Similarly, though Muslim women have lower educational attainments than men, the gap with other SRCs is lower for women.

Analysis of time trends indicate that, despite overall improvement in educational status, the rate of progress has been the slowest for Muslims. In other words, while educational attainments of Muslims have improved over the years, it has done so at a more gradual pace than other SRCs, so that the expected convergence has not occurred. Instead, the gap between Muslims and advantaged sections has actually widened since Independence, and particularly since the 1980s. In fact, a steady divergence in the level of achievements has seen traditionally under-privileged SCs/STs catching up and overtaking Muslims in several contexts. The last point is of special importance as at the time of Independence, the socio-economic position of SCs/STs was recognised to be inferior to that of Muslims. Apparently, Muslims have not been able to reap the benefits of planning and, while progressing through the operation of trickle down or percolation effect, have gradually slipped further and further behind other SRCs.

Attainments at the graduation level and in technical education are low for all SRCs. Even at these low levels differences across SRCs exist and Muslims lag behind in both areas. That the share of Muslims is poorest in streams having brightest employment prospects is of special concern. This has serious long-term implications for the economic empowerment of the Community and consequently for economic development of the country. Differentials in the attainment levels of SRCs become more apparent when lower levels of education are considered. The differences between SRCs become significant when attainments at the matriculation level onwards. One of the key reasons for the low participation of Muslims in higher education is their significantly low achievement level in higher secondary attainment rates. Muslims seem to have significant disadvantages vis-à-vis most SRCs in school completion rates. Once this hurdle is crossed and persons from the Community become eligible for higher education, the gaps between their achievements and those of other SRCs (with similar eligibility) narrow down considerably.

Moreover, the recent trends in enrolments and other educational attainments and Committee's interactions with the Muslim Community are adequate to dispel certain misconceptions and stereotypes with respect to education of Muslims. These need to be highlighted:

- Muslim parents are not averse to modern or mainstream education and to sending their children to the affordable Government schools. They do not necessarily prefer to send children to Madarsas. Regular school education that is available to any other child in India is preferred by Muslims also. A section of Muslims also prefer education through the English medium, while some others would like the medium of instruction to be Urdu. The access to government schools for Muslim children is limited.

- There is also a common belief that Muslim parents feel that education is not important for girls and that it may instil a wrong set of values. Even if girls are enrolled, they are withdrawn at an early age to marry them off. This leads to a higher drop-out rate among Muslim girls. Our interactions indicate that the problem may lie in non-availability of schools within easy reach for girls at lower levels of education, absence of girls' hostels, absence of female teachers and availability of scholarships as they move up the education ladder.

Initiatives in School Education

Muslims have the largest percentage share of children in the age group of less than 10 years with 27 per cent falling in this range as compared to the 23 per cent for the country as a whole. However, the current enrolment and continuation rates at elementary level (though picking up in recent years) are the lowest for the Muslims. These facts make primary education particularly important for the Community and the need to ensure that all children in the age group 0-14 have access to free and high quality education more urgent. In addition, the following initiatives are desirable:

- Given the fact that a substantial proportion of households in urban settlements live in one-room accommodation, it is absolutely necessary to create local community study centres for students so that they can spend a few hours to concentrate on their studies. This is an area in which the government, NGOs and the corporate sector can cooperate.
- High quality Government schools should be set up in all areas of Muslim concentration.
- Exclusive schools for girls should be set up, particularly for the 9-12 standards. This would facilitate higher participation of Muslim girls in school education. In co-education schools more women teachers need to be appointed.
- Availability of primary education in one's mother tongue is constitutionally provided for. There is an urgent need to undertake appropriate mapping of Urdu speaking population and provide primary education in Urdu in areas where Urdu speaking population is concentrated.

Technical Education and Training for Non-matriculates

Majority of Muslim girls and boys fail in their matriculation examinations or drop-out before that. This group of children who have completed middle school but have not managed to study further needs to be incorporated in different types of technical training. The skill demands in the manufacturing and service sectors are changing continuously. And for many of these, highly educated/trained persons may not be required and youth with middle school education with adequate technical training may be appropriate for meeting these needs. However, almost all vocational training programmes run by the

ITIs and polytechnics require a matriculation certificate. The Committee recommends that:

- The pre-entry qualification for admission to ITIs should be reduced to Class VIII. The scope of ITI courses should be expanded to focus on emerging market needs including those of the retail sector.
- Skill development initiatives of ITIs and polytechnics should focus on sectors which have high growth potential and in which the Muslim population is concentrated. These training initiatives should also focus on areas where the minority population is concentrated.
- The eligibility for such programmes should also be extended to the Madarsa educated children, as they are ineligible to get training under many current formal technical education streams.

Initiatives for Higher Education

Our analysis has shown that there is a high "deficit" as far as Muslim population in the higher education is concerned. And this "deficit" is higher than for all SRCs except SCs/STs. The best long term measure to correct this deficit is to increase school completion rates among the Muslims. In the medium and short run, a two prong strategy can be employed:

Strategy No. 1: The University Grants Commission (UGC) should be encouraged to evolve a system where part of the allocation to colleges and universities is linked to the diversity in the student population. Even private colleges, including those run by the minorities and which have affiliation with universities or are recognised by state bodies can be provided additional funds if they have a diverse student population and charge reasonable fees. An appropriate diversity index will need to be developed for such purposes. It is advisable that the UGC undertakes a proactive exercise to sensitise the educational institutions with respect to the need to reflect diversity on these campuses.

The Muslims of some states like Andhra Pradesh, Karnataka, Tamil Nadu have established a number of 'minority managed professional institutions' which have opened up avenues for higher education for Muslims and other minorities. They need to get encouragement as community initiatives but even these institutions need to have diverse populations. Government financial aid to these institutions can be linked to low tuition and other fees and partly to diversity of student population. These 'minority institutions' are typically inaccessible to the poor from these communities. Low fees combined with merit-cum-means scholarships (partly funded from the additional government grants) would enhance participation of poor among the minorities.

Strategy No. 2: To facilitate admissions to the 'most backward' amongst all the SRCs in the regular universities and autonomous colleges, alternate admission criteria need to be evolved. The following example provides a rating/grading system that can potentially be used (Table 14.5):

Table 14.5

Total Points	**100**
■ Assessment of Merit to the maximum of	60
■ Assessment of Backwardness to the maximum of Backwardness to be defined as the sum of the following (Each with about one third weight)	40
(1) Household income (income criteria to be revised periodically)	13
(2) Backward district (list to be updated on annual basis)/ residence in a notified urban slum	13
(3) Backward class (assessed based on a combination of family occupation and caste)	14

This system should help the poor among all communities. As a complement to the first strategy, part of state funding can also be linked to the use of such criteria in admissions by the educational institutions.

Provision of Hostels

Providing hostel facilities at reasonable costs for students from minorities must be taken up on a priority basis. While this is required for all minority students, such facilities for girls in cities of all sizes are particularly desirable. The availability of such hostels would ensure that many girls would continue schooling (beyond secondary/college education) as they would not have to commute on a daily basis to access educational institutions located at a distance form their place of residence. Hostels are equally important in the context of boys accessing college education. High rents in cities are a deterrent for those from lower income households to access higher levels of education. Besides the high cost are other factors, like reluctance to accept Muslims as tenants, which make it difficult for them to rent accommodation. Ideally, the provision of such facilities should be made in partnership with the Community; the State can facilitate Community initiatives in this area through grants and other support. The taluka headquarters and educational centers would be the best locations for such facilities.

Another possibility is to create boarding houses for backward SRCs in taluka headquarters where large number of poor minority and other children can stay and study in local schools. This may reduce drop-out rates and ensure retention in school up to higher secondary levels. Apart from taking the children out of the ghettos, such facilities would ensure that the backlog of parental illiteracy will not negatively impact the performance of these children because of the 'learning friendly' atmosphere in these hostels. In fact, tutors can be provided for remedial classes in these boarding houses to supplement and monitor their studies.

For both these initiatives allocations can be made from the special funds earmarked by the Centre for the upliftment of the educational status of educationally backward groups. Once again, participation of the community should be encouraged. Muslim Wakfs should be encouraged to utilise their assets for this endeavour. In addition, donations from NGOs and multilateral organisations can also be utilised.

Teacher Training Programme

Teacher training should compulsorily include in its curriculum components which introduce the importance of diversity/plurality within the country and sensitise teachers towards the needs and aspirations of Muslims and other marginalised communities. The implementation of this should be monitored by the National Council of Teacher Education (NCTE). The other issue is that of dearth of Muslim school teachers, especially women. Given the current education levels, the possibility of more Muslims opting for B.Ed. course is limited. But more Muslims may be able to participate as para teachers. An effort should be made to enhance participation of Muslims in this cadre as an interim measure.

There are only a few teachers who can teach in the Urdu medium. Given the commitment to provide primary education in the child's mother tongue, the State is required to run Urdu medium schools. This in turn would require teachers capable of teaching in the Urdu medium. Preference to teachers who can instruct through Urdu medium is desirable in all teacher training departments in States where Urdu speaking population is substantial.

Interventions to Support the Urdu Language

While Urdu language is not a language of the Muslims alone, contemporary circumstances make it appear to be so. The language has been neglected. The fallout of this has been inadequate access to education in the mother tongue for many Urdu speaking children. The neglect has also resulted in poor performance of Urdu medium school students because of poor infrastructural facilities and absence of adequate number of qualified teachers. As mentioned above, given the constitutional responsibility of the State, it is imperative that Urdu language is supported to provide a regular stream of Urdu teachers. Moreover, for secondary education the distortions made in the Three Language Formula should be corrected in order to accommodate Urdu in schools of the Hindi region. In addition, three more measures are desirable:

- Often Urdu schools have teachers who have no knowledge of Urdu. This problem is partly compounded by the fact that posts of Urdu teachers are reserved for the SCs/STs and such candidates are not available. This anomaly needs to be corrected urgently.
- High quality Urdu medium schools can be opened in those parts of the country wherever there is demand for them. However, it needs to be ensured that good quality text books are available in Urdu language and the products of these schools are employable.
- Urdu should be introduced as an optional subject in all government and government-aided schools in states having a substantial Urdu speaking population.

Madarsas and Mainstream Education

Madarsas have played an important role in providing religious education to the Muslim population. They also provide 'mainstream' education in many cases and several of them are in the process of modernising their curriculum. While this is an important initiative of the Community to improve educational conditions, it is important to take note of the fact that less than 4 per cent of the Muslim children in the school going age actually attend the full time regular Madarsas. Therefore, the modernised Madarsas are unlikely to satisfy the educational demand of the Community and the State will have to make provision for mainstream schools in areas where such schools are not available. In other words, Madarsas should not be looked upon as alternatives to the regular school, but a complement. The following steps seem desirable:

- Work out mechanisms whereby Madarsas can be linked with a higher secondary school board so that students wanting to shift to a regular/ mainstream education can do so after having passed from a Madarsa.
- Provision of "equivalence" to Madarsa certificates/degrees for subsequent admissions into institutions of higher level of education. Flexibility should be introduced so as to enable Madarsa graduates to move across to regular mainstream education after graduating from these institutions, if they so wish. In other words the opportunity should be made available to them, especially in courses where admission is done through an entrance test/competitive examination.
- Recognition of the degrees from Madarsas for eligibility in competitive examinations such as the Civil Services, Banks, Defence Services and other such examinations. The idea is to facilitate a process whereby Madarsa graduates too have a choice and an incentive to participate in these employment streams. This should, however, remain within the existing framework of these competitive examinations.
- In the 1990s government introduced a scheme for modernisation of Madarsas. This was a step in the right direction but it was robbed of part of its utility because of some deficiencies relating. for example, to choice of subjects, quality of teachers, accommodation of the modern subjects in a time-table intensely packed with traditional subjects. Government will be well advised to review and revamp the scheme before embarking on its expansion.

15

National Knowledge Commission (2006)

Major Observations and Recommendations

On June 13, 2005, the Prime Minister of India, Dr. Manmohan Singh constituted the National Knowledge Commission (NKC) as a think-tank to advise the Prime Minister's Office (PMO) on policy related to education, research institutes and reforms needed to make India competitive in the knowledge economy.

The National Knowledge Commission (NKC) consists of the following seven members:

1. Sam Pitroda, Chairman
2. Ashok Ganguly, Corporate Leader
3. Nandan Nilekani, Infosys
4. Dr. Deepak Nayyar, Former Vice-Chancellor, University of Delhi
5. Dr. Jayati Ghosh, Economist at Jawaharlal Nehru University
6. Dr. Sujatha Ramadorai, TIFR
7. Dr. P. Balaram, Indian Institute of Science, Bangalore

The Terms of Reference of the NKC are:

1. "Build excellence in the educational system to meet the knowledge challenges of the 21st century and increase India's competitive advantage in fields of knowledge.
2. Promote creation of knowledge in science and technology laboratories.
3. Improve the management of institutions engaged in Intellectual Property Rights.
4. Promote knowledge applications in Agriculture and Industry.
5. Promote the use of knowledge capabilities in making government an effective, transparent and accountable service provider to the citizen and promote widespread sharing of knowledge to maximise public benefit".

The secretariat is headed by an Executive Director and consists of about 8-9 research associates. It has four advisers to advise the Commission on different issues. The Secretariat of the Commission is located at Chanakyapuri, New Delhi.

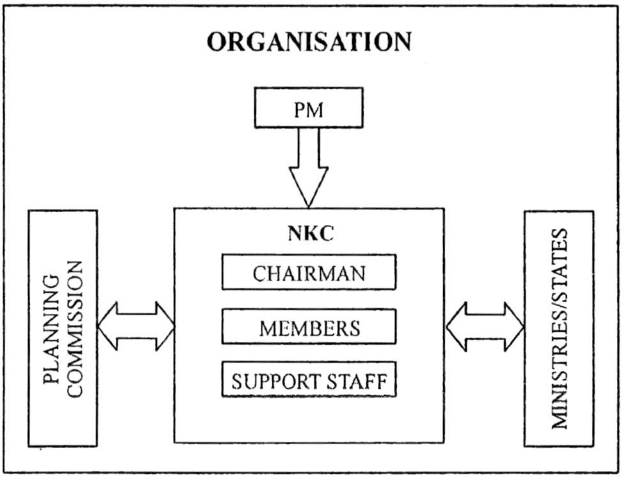

OVERSIGHT MECHANISM

- A national steering group for the NKC headed by the PM, includes Ministers of
  - Agriculture
  - HRD
  - S&T
  - Commerce
  - IT
  - Planning

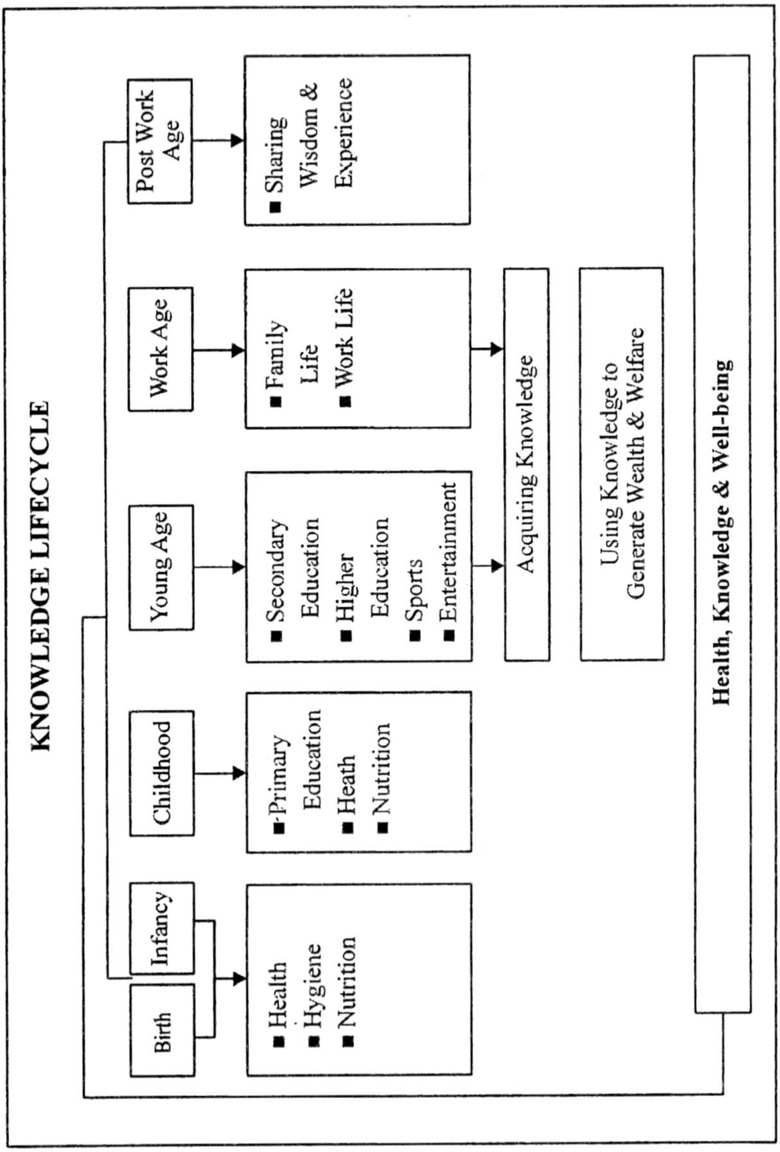
KNOWLEDGE LIFECYCLE
Birth
Infancy
Childhood
Young Age
Work Age
Post Work Age
■ Health
■ Hygiene
■ Nutrition
■ Primary Education
■ Heath
■ Nutrition
■ Secondary Education
■ Higher Education
■ Sports
■ Entertainment
■ Family Life
■ Work Life
■ Sharing Wisdom & Experience
Acquiring Knowledge
Using Knowledge to Generate Wealth & Welfare
Health, Knowledge & Well-being

KNOWLEDGE PENTAGON

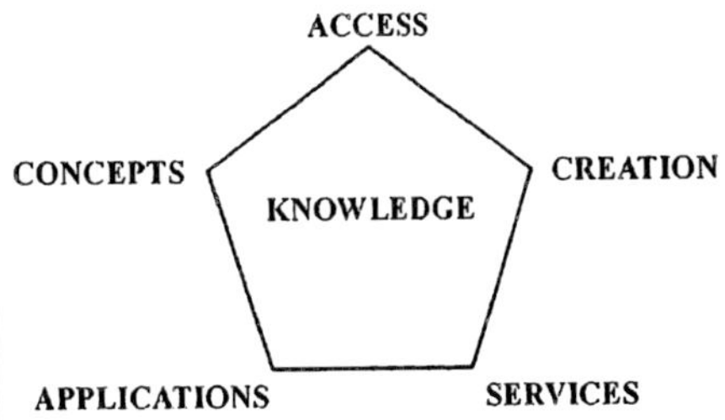

ACTIONS – GENERAL

- Link knowledge initiatives to expedite the process of meeting basic human needs
- Encourage innovations and entrepreneurship at all levels
- Use knowledge to fuel growth in agriculture, manufacturing and services
- Restructure existing institutions to respond to knowledge needs of tomorrow
- Create new institutions to respond to the needs of tomorrow
- Empower people and institutions to participate in the knowledge economy
- Encourage knowledge sharing forums and discussion groups in schools, colleges, libraries, R & D institutions, youth groups, etc.
- Institute district, state, and central awards to recognise people for
  - Innovations
  - Entrepreneurship
  - Education
  - Health
- Motivate, mobilise, support and encourage existing and new knowledge initiatives at various levels in the country
- Help build knowledge infrastructure and institutions
- Focus on knowledge for
  - Individual advancement
  - National development
  - Security
- Use knowledge to leverage new economic opportunities from globalisation

Scaling Excellence in Education and Research

- Extensive access to quality educational resources

- For faculty development
- Direct education (formal and non-formal)
- Meet hr (kw) needs in all sectors
- Quality educational and research interactions
- Global participation in research and education
  - Sharing
  - Benchmarking

Observations and Recommendations of the Commission (2006)

The observations and recommendations of the Commission are contained in the following letters addressed by the Chairman of the Commission to the Prime Minister.

1. Right to Education — Letter dated October 23, 2006
2. Higher Education — Letter dated November 29, 2006
3. Vocational Education — Letter dated December 1, 2006

RIGHT TO EDUCATION

Observations

The National Knowledge Commission has been examining a range of issues related to school education, including access, quality and other issues. We believe that providing universal access to quality school education is a cornerstone of development and a minimum necessary condition for any progress towards making India a knowledge society. We are in the process of extensive consultations and will make detailed recommendations on various issues relating to school education at a later date.

However, at this point we would like to respond specifically to the recent initiative of the central government of sending a model Right to Education Bill to the Secretaries of State Education Departments, with incentives for the state governments to enact this bill. We have perused the bill and consulted with a wide range of experts and educationists. We feel that the model bill is flawed for a number of reasons, and most importantly that such legislation must be enforced by the central government following upon the commitment made in the Constitutional Amendment Article 21A. We recognise that there may be concerns about federalism, since school education is dominantly the responsibility of the state governments at present.

Recommendations/Proposals

However, we feel that this matter can be resolved through appropriate central legislation which takes into account the following proposals:

1. *Central Legislation*: Legislation at the national level is required to affirm the Right to Education, which is a fundamental right mandated by Article 21A. Since it cannot be dependent upon which state a citizen is resident in, a model bill sent to be enacted individually by State Governments is not adequate to meet the constitutional responsibilities of the Government of India.

Therefore, a central legislation should be enacted along the lines of the Panchayati Raj (Amendment) Act, requiring the states to enact Right to Education Bills within a specified time period, and with the primary financial responsibility for this resting with the central government.

2. *Financial Commitment*: The Central Government must provide the bulk of the additional funds required to ensure the Right to Education. Therefore there must be financial provision in the central legislation, requiring the central government to share the revenues of the Prarambhik Shiksha Kosh with state governments and to provide additional resources as required to meet the requirement of ensuring the right to education for all children. Estimates for the additional resources required to achieve the goal of universal elementary education currently range from 0.8 per cent to 2.5 per cent of GDP, depending on the criteria used. However, the required financial resources are likely to be at the lower end of these estimates, since there is already close to universal provision in several states and there has been recent progress in providing more access through the Sarva Shiksha Abhiyan in other states.

3. *Time Frame*: The state-level legislation should specify the period within which universal education of reasonable quality is sought to be achieved, preferably within three years. The model bill does not provide any time frame for adoption and implementation of the provisions.

4. *Schedule of Norms and Standards*: To ensure a minimum quality of education, it is important to have a schedule of norms for all schools to follow. The model bill does not have such a schedule of norms, and there is no specification of the minimum quality of education that schools should provide. There is only a reference to 'equitable quality' without defining the parameters of quality. While ensuring quality is a complex matter, certain norms regarding infrastructure, number of teachers per school and per student, teaching methods and other facilities, etc. must be adhered to as necessary conditions.

5. *Specification for Teachers*: Since teachers are critical in ensuring the quality of education, laying down well-defined but flexible norms for the minimum qualifications of teachers is particularly important. The model bill has no specification of a teacher, or the qualifications and in-service training needed for the position. A teacher is only defined as a person who teaches in the classroom. However, here too it is necessary to specify norms for teacher qualification and training.

6. *Justifiability*: Any right, including the Right to Education, is only meaningful if it is justifiable. However, in the model bill sent to state governments, the onus is placed on parents/guardians of the child. The responsibility of the Government, at different levels, must be recognised and made justifiable. The example of the National Rural Employment Guarantee Act (NREGA) could be used in this context.

7. *Redressal Mechanism*: To ensure justifiability, a redressal mechanism should be outlined and an appropriate procedure must be set in place for students or parents in case the right is not upheld.

8. *Universal Schooling*: School education must be provided to all, which

necessarily also requires that children of the disadvantaged, landless and minority communities must also be integrated, along with children with disabilities or special needs. This requires there should be no distinction made in terms of the type of schooling provided within the government system, for children from different social, economic and cultural backgrounds. The model bill has the potential of creating a parallel and discriminatory system of schooling which can result in stratification of the education system for children from disadvantaged communities and backgrounds, because it requires only provision of non-formal education in such cases, rather than mandating the provision of regular schooling. Obviously, in all cases, the school system should be flexible enough to cater to particular needs of students.

We will be happy to provide detailed explanations on the points mentioned above. The National Knowledge Commission is continuing to consult with stakeholders and examine other issues in relation to school education. We are focussing in particular on the questions of bow to ensure better quality across the board; the institutional structures and forms of control by local communities that could contribute to improved quality of schooling; issues related to common schooling and neighbourhood schools; ensuring adequate quantity and quality of school teachers, especially in specified areas; etc. We will submit a broader set of recommendations on school education in the near future.

HIGHER EDUCATION

Observations

Higher education has made a significant contribution to economic development, social progress and political democracy in independent India. But there is serious cause for concern at this juncture. The proportion of our population, in the relevant age group, that enters the world of higher education is about 7 per cent. The opportunities for higher education in terms of the number of places in universities are simply not adequate in relation to our needs. Large segments of our population just do not have access to higher education. What is more, the quality of higher education in most of our universities leaves much to be desired.

At the outset, we would also like to stress that foundations are critical. We believe that an emphasis on expansion and reform of our school system is necessary to ensure that every child has an equal opportunity to enter the world of higher education.

The NKC has engaged in formal and informal consultations on this subject with a wide range of people in the world of higher education. In addition, we consulted concerned people in parliament, government, civil society and industry. The concerns about the higher education system are widely shared. There was a clear, almost unanimous, view that higher education needs a systematic overhaul, so that we can educate much larger numbers without diluting academic standards. Indeed, this is essential because the transformation of economy and society in the twenty-first century would depend, in significant part, on the spread and the quality of education among our people, particularly in the sphere of higher education. And it is only an inclusive society that can provide the foundations for a knowledge society.

The objectives of reform and change in our higher education system, as you have often stressed, must be expansion, excellence and inclusion. We recognise that meaningful reform of the higher education system, with a long-term perspective, is both complex and difficult. Yet, it is imperative. Our analysis, diagnosis and prescriptions are set out in a detailed note on higher education which is attached. In this letter, we simply highlight our prescriptions.

Recommendations

A. Expansion

1. *Create Many More Universities*: The higher education system needs a massive expansion of opportunities, to around 1500 universities nationwide, that would enable India to attain a gross enrolment ratio of at least 15 per cent by 2015. The focus would have to be on new universities, but some clusters of affiliated colleges could also become universities. Such expansion would require major changes in the structure of regulation.

2. *Change the System of Regulation for Higher Education*: The present regulatory system in higher education is flawed in some important respects. The barriers to entry are too high. The system of authorising entry is cumbersome. There is a multiplicity of regulatory agencies where mandates are both confusing and overlapping. The system, as a whole, is over-regulated but under-governed. We believe that there is a clear need to establish an Independent Regulatory Authority for Higher Education (IRAHE). The IRAHE must be at an arm's-length from the government and independent of all stakeholders including the concerned Ministries of the Government.

- The IRAHE would have to be established by an Act of Parliament, and would be responsible for setting the criteria and deciding on entry.
- It would be the only agency that would be authorised to accord degree granting power to higher education institutions.
- It would be responsible for monitoring standards and settling disputes.
- It would apply exactly the same norms to public and private institutions, just as it would apply the same norms to domestic and international institutions.
- It would be the authority for licensing accreditation agencies.
- The role of the UGC would be re-defined to focus on the disbursement of grants to, and maintenance of, public institutions in higher education. The entry regulatory functions of the AICTE, the MCI and the BCI would be performed by the IRAHE, so that their role would be limited to that of professional associations.

3. *Increase Public Spending and Diversify Sources of Financing*: The expansion of our system of higher education is not possible without enhanced levels of financing. This must necessarily come from both public and private sources.

- Since government financing will remain the cornerstone, government support for higher education should increase to at least 1.5 per cent of GDP, out of a total of at least 6 per cent of GDP for education.

- Even this would not suffice for the massive expansion in higher education that is an imperative. It is essential to explore other possibilities that can complement the increase in public expenditure.
- Most public universities are sitting on a large reservoir of untapped resources in the form of land. It should be possible to draw up norms and parameters for universities to use their available land as a source of finance.
- It is for universities to decide the level of fees but, as a norm, fees should meet at least 20 per cent of the total expenditure in universities. This should be subject to two conditions: first, needy students should be provided with a fee waiver plus scholarships to meet their costs; second, universities should not be penalised by the UGC for the resources raised from higher fees through matching deductions from their grants-in-aid.
- We should nurture the tradition of philanthropic contributions through changes in incentives for universities and for donors. At present, there is an implicit disincentive in both tax laws and trust laws. These laws should be changed so that universities can invest in financial instruments of their choice and use the income from their endowments to build up a corpus.
- Universities should also seek to tap other sources such as alumni contributions and licensing fees. We need to create supportive institutional mechanisms that allow universities to engage professional firms for this purpose.
- It is essential to stimulate private investment in education as a means of extending educational opportunities. It may be possible to leverage public resources, especially in the form of land grants, to attract more (not-for-profit) private investment.

4. *Establish 50 National Universities*: We recommend the creation of 50 National Universities that can provide education of the highest standard. As exemplars for the rest of the nation, these universities shall train students in a variety of disciplines, including humanities, social sciences, basic sciences, commerce and professional subjects, at both the undergraduate and post-graduate levels. The number 50 is a long term objective. In the short run, it is important to begin with at least 10 such universities in the next 3 years. National Universities can be established in two ways, by the government, or by a private sponsoring body that sets up a Society, Charitable Trust or Section 25 Company.

Since public finance is an integral constituent of universities worldwide, most of the new universities shall need significant initial financial support from the government. Each university may be endowed with a substantial allocation of public land, in excess of its spatial requirements. The excess land can be a subsequent source of income generation. Exceptions need to be made in existing income tax laws to encourage large endowments. Further, there should be no restriction on the utilisation of income in any given period or in the use of appropriate financial instruments. And these universities should have the autonomy to set student fee levels and tap other sources for generating funds.

The National Universities we propose shall admit students on an all-India basis. They shall adopt the principle of *needs-blind admissions*. This will require an extensive system of scholarships for needy students. Undergraduate degrees in the National Universities, in a three-year programme, should be granted on the basis of completing a requisite number of credits, obtained from different courses. The academic year shall therefore be semester-based and students shall be internally evaluated at the end of each course. Transfer of credits from one National University to another shall also be possible. An appropriate system of appointments and incentives is required to maximise the productivity of faculty in these National Universities. Strong linkages shall be forged between teaching and research, universities and industry, and universities and research laboratories. The National Universities shall be department-based and shall not have any affiliated colleges.

B. Excellence

5. *Reform Existing Universities*: Our endeavour to transform higher education must reform existing institutions. Some steps are listed below:

- Universities should be required to revise or restructure curricula at least once in three years.
- Annual examinations, which test memory rather than understanding, should be supplemented with continuous internal assessment which could begin with a weight of 25 per cent in the total to be raised to 50 per cent over a stipulated period.
- We propose a transition to a course credit system where degrees are granted on the basis of completing a requisite number of credits from different courses, which provides students with choices.
- Universities must become the hub of research once again to capture synergies between teaching and research that enrich each other. This requires not only policy measures but also changes in resource allocation, reward systems and mindsets.
- There must be a conscious effort to attract and retain talented faculty members through better working conditions combined with incentives for performance.
- The criteria for resource allocation to universities should seek to strike a much better balance between providing for salaries or pensions and providing for maintenance, development or investment. It should also recognise the importance of a critical minimum to ensure standards and strategic preferences to promote excellence.
- The elements of infrastructure that support the teaching-learning process, such as libraries, laboratories and connectivity, need to be monitored and upgraded on a regular basis.
- There is an acute need for reform in the structures of governance of universities that do not preserve autonomy and do not promote accountability. Much needs to be done, but two important points deserve mention. The appointments of Vice-Chancellors must be freed from direct or indirect interventions on the part of governments, for

these should be based on search processes and peer judgment alone. The size and composition of University Courts, Academic Councils and Executive Councils, which slow down decision-making processes and sometimes constitute an impediment to change, need to be reconsidered on a priority basis.

- We need, and should strive to create, smaller universities which are responsive to change and easier to manage.

6. *Restructure Undergraduate Colleges*: The system of affiliated colleges for undergraduate education, which may have been appropriate 50 years ago, is no longer adequate or appropriate and needs to be reformed. Indeed, there is an urgent need to restructure the system of undergraduate colleges affiliated to universities.

- The most obvious solution is to provide autonomy to colleges either as individual colleges or as clusters of colleges, on the basis of criteria. However, this would be able to provide a solution for a limited proportion, or number, of undergraduate colleges.
- Some of these affiliated colleges could be remodelled as community colleges, which could provide both vocational education and formal education.
- A Central Board of Undergraduate Education should be established, along with State Boards of Undergraduate Education, which would set curricula and conduct examinations for undergraduate colleges that choose to be affiliated with them. These Boards would separate the academic functions from the administrative functions and, at the same time, provide quality benchmarks.
- New undergraduate colleges could be established as community colleges, could be affiliated with the Central Board of Undergraduate Education or State Boards of Undergraduate Education, or could be affiliated with some of the new universities that are established.

7. *Promote Enhanced Quality*: The higher education system must provide for accountability to society and create accountability within. An expansion of higher education which provides students with choices and creates competition between institutions is going to be vital in enhancing accountability.

- There should be stringent information disclosure norms for all educational institutions, such as, their financial situation, physical assets, admissions criteria, faculty positions, academic curricula, as also their source and level of accreditation.
- Evaluation of courses and teachers by students as well as peer evaluation of teachers by teachers should be encouraged.
- There must be a focus on upgrading infrastructure, improving the training of teachers and continuous assessment of syllabi and examination systems.
- It is particularly important to enhance the ICT infrastructure. Websites and web-based services would improve transparency and accountability. A portal on higher education and research would increase interaction and accessibility. A knowledge network would connect all universities and colleges for online open resources.

- It may be necessary to rethink the issue of salary differentials within and between universities along with other means of attracting and retaining talented faculty members. Such salary differentials between and within universities could be effective without being large.
- It is necessary to formulate appropriate policies for the entry of foreign institutions into India and the promotion of Indian institutions abroad, while ensuring a level playing field for foreign and domestic institutions within the country.
- The system of higher education must recognise that there is bound to be diversity and pluralism in any system of higher education, and avoid a uniform one-size-fits-all approach. This sense of pluralism must recognise, rather than ignore or shy away from, such diversity and differentiation.

C. Inclusion

8. *Ensure Access for All Deserving Students*: Education is the fundamental mechanism for social inclusion through the creation of more opportunities. It is, therefore, essential to ensure that no student is denied the opportunity to participate in higher education due to financial constraints. We propose the following measures:

- Institutions of higher education should be encouraged to adopt a needs blind admissions policy. This would make it unlawful for educational institutions to take into account any financial factor while deciding whether or not to admit a student.
- There must be a well-funded and extensive National Scholarship Scheme targeting economically underprivileged students and students from historically socially disadvantaged groups.

9. *Affirmative Action*: A major aim of the higher education system must be to ensure that access to education for economically and historically socially underprivileged students is enhanced in a substantially more effective manner.

- Reservations are essential but they are only a part, and one form, of affirmative action.
- Disparities in educational attainments are related to caste and social groups, but are also strongly related to other indicators such as income, gender, region and place of residence. Therefore, we need to develop a meaningful and comprehensive framework that would account for the multi-dimensionality of differences that still persist. For example, a deprivation index could be used to provide weighted scores to students and the cumulative score could be used to supplement a student's school examination score.

The recommendations set out in our letter require action at three different levels: reforms within existing systems, changes in policies, and amendments in, or the introduction of, new statutes or legislation. The suggested changes would also be implemented at three different levels: universities, state governments and the central government. As a next step, we would like to meet with you and concerned colleagues to work out the modalities of implementation.

In conclusion, it is important for us to recognise that there is a quiet crisis in higher education in India which runs deep. And the time has come to address this crisis in a systematic, forthright manner. Our recommendations in this letter constitute an important beginning. The changes suggested by us are essential and would make a real difference. Of course, the process of reform and change is continuous. And there is more to be done. We are writing to you, separately, about vocational education. We do recognise that a comprehensive reform of the school system is necessary to ensure that every child has an equal opportunity to enter the world of higher education.

We are convinced that it is important to act here and now. At the same time, we believe that there is an opportunity in this crisis. Given the demographic reality of a young India, expansion, inclusion and excellence in higher education can drive economic development and social progress. Indeed, what we do in the sphere of higher education now can transform economy and society in India by 2025.

VOCATIONAL EDUCATION

Observations

The National Knowledge Commission (NKC) considers Vocational Education and Training (VET) as an important element of the nation's education initiative. In order for VET to play its part effectively in the changing national context and for India to enjoy the fruits of the demographic dividend, there is an urgent need to redefine the critical elements of imparting vocational education to make them flexible, contemporary, relevant, inclusive and creative. The Government is well aware of the important role of VET and has already taken a number of important initiatives.

Recommendations

Through consultations with industry groups, academics, civil society and practitioners, NKC has deliberated ways and means to strengthen these initiatives and recommends the following long and short term strategies:

1. *Place Vocational Education Entirely Under the Ministry of Human Resource Development (MHRD)*: In view of the role of VET in human resource development and importance of its linkages with other streams of education, placing all aspects of VET under MHRD may be considered by the Government. Currently, VET falls under the purview of MHRD as well as the Ministry of Labour, which leads to fragmented management of the VET framework. MHRD may consider setting up a National Institute of Vocational Education Planning and Development to formulate strategy, advise the Government, and undertake research and development in areas pertaining to technology and workforce development.

2. *Increase the flexibility of VET within the mainstream education system* through the following steps:
   (i) Aspects of general education (such as, numeracy skills, etc.) should be retained in VET as far as possible, to enable students to return to mainstream education at a later stage.

(ii) Courses in training institutes and polytechnics should have distinct tracks for students of different educational attainments.

(iii) Entry requirements for certain trades should reflect the requirement of the trade (as appropriate, for instance the entry requirement of Class X could be relaxed to Class VIII in some cases). Students should be permitted multiple entry and exit options in the vocational education stream.

(iv) Links should be established between the vocational education stream and school education as well as higher education.

(v) Courses devoted to certain skills training at the primary and secondary level should be introduced in all schools.

(vi) Vocational training should be made available in various literacy and adult education schemes.

(vii) Schemes for lifelong skill upgradation, through short training programmes, should be introduced.

(viii) There should be a provision for generating a cadre of multi-skilled persons.

3. *Quantify and Monitor the Impact of Vocational Education*: Data should be collected periodically and analysed in order to assess the impact of training on employability. Empirical evidence on wage premium or other advantages enjoyed by VET graduates; seat utilisation in training institutes; nature of employment post-training; efficacy of various schemes, etc. is essential for continuous improvement. A detailed exercise of manpower analysis is a necessary step to understand the nature and quantum of demand for VET and the mismatch between the skills of VET certificate holders and the requirements of the labour market. This exercise may be undertaken by the proposed National Institute of Vocational Education Planning.

4. *Increase Resource Allocation to Vocational Education*: In per capita terms vocational education is costlier than general education, however, public expenditure on vocational education has been extremely low, as compared to general secondary education. Given the demand for skilled manpower in manufacturing and services the Government should aim to spend at least 10-15% of its total public expenditure on education, on vocational education.

Some options that may be considered for raising additional funds to finance a modernised VET scheme are:

(i) Enhancing fees, coupled with student loan schemes. This would also make VET institutions more responsive to market needs.

(ii) Raising funds through a cess on employers (for instance 2% of salaries of all employees, as in Singapore).

(iii) Making it obligatory for companies to finance public vocational education and training programmes (as in Korea).

5. *Expand Capacity Through Innovative Delivery Models*: In order to meet the burgeoning requirements of skilled and unskilled labour, a massive increase in quantity of training is needed. The Government may explore new delivery models to increase capacity such as public private partnerships, decentralised delivery, distance learning and computerised vocational training.

At the same time, the Government must introduce certain minimum standards as a measure of quality and ensure that these are adhered to by all public and private VET institutions.

6. *Enhance the Training Options Available for the Unorganised and Informal Sector*: The greatest challenge lies in providing training for potential entrants in the unorganised/informal sector, which accounts for the largest proportion of employment. Systematic efforts need to be made to impart the skills required by the unorganised sector. These should be formally introduced in the curricula and practical training courses. This aspect of VET is critical for the success of the system as a whole.

7. *Strengthen the Current Institutional Structure*: The existing Industrial Training Institutes (ITIs) and Industrial Training Centres (ITCs) are widely recognised to face problems, such as, poor quality trainers, lack of flexibility, outdated infrastructure, etc. Measures to improve the existing institutions are as follows:

- (i) Extent of functional autonomy must be increased. ITIs should be given more power to strengthen and adapt their training programmes to better meet local market needs.
- (ii) Indicators of internal and external efficiency should be developed (by the proposed National Institute) to incentivise good performance.
- (iii) Modules on literacy, numeracy, communication skills, entrepreneurship and other general skills relevant to workplace requirements must be introduced in all courses.
- (iv) Different tracks within courses for different levels of specialisation should be introduced.
- (v) Students should be offered incentives such as tools, membership of trade associations, etc. as part of their degree/diploma.
- (vi) Industry and trade involvement should be enhanced not only at the internship stage, but also at the time of examinations and placements.
- (vii) Curricula should be constantly monitored and updated.
- (viii) The skills and courses offered should be reviewed periodically. The number of skills currently offered needs to be increased.
- (ix) Teaching should be conducted in English as well as local languages.
- (x) Infrastructure should be regularly upgraded.
- (xi) Quality of teaching should be drastically improved.

8. *Ensure a Robust Regulatory and Accreditation Framework*: In order to achieve the desired modernisation and expansion outlined above, a critical aspect will be regulating entry of new institutions and accreditation of all institutions. It is therefore recommended that an independent regulatory agency for VET be established. This body would license accreditation agencies and prescribe standards for certification. The procedures and methodologies adopted by the body would need to be simple and transparent to ensure unhindered growth in the sector.

9. *Ensure Proper Certification*: At present the process of certification is handled by the National Council for Vocational Training (NCVT), in association with State Councils for Vocational Training (SCVTs). Clear

demarcation between the roles of the NCVT, the SCVTs and the DGE&T is essential for the proper functioning of the certification process. In order to ensure recognition of certification by employers, both in India and abroad, an electronic database of certified training providers as well as electronic identification for certified workers should be introduced. Electronic identification should contain information regarding skills and qualifications (and eventually other relevant information as well) about certified individuals and can be used in order to facilitate mobility of workers, encourage bank linkages and entrepreneurial initiatives etc.

10. *Undertake a Re-branding Exercise*: It is widely recognised that a crucial problem with vocational training in India is a negative association with manual labour. In order to match the modern requirement of the skills and competitiveness of the workforce a massive re-branding exercise is of the highest priority. This could be the prime task of the recently announced National Skills Mission. Initiatives, such as, replacing the use of terms such as 'vocational education' by 'skill development' are a step in the right direction. Efforts should be made by training institutes to chart out a career path for their students and introduce entrepreneurship training modules.

In conclusion, it is essential to significantly increase public and private investment in VET. However, a detailed analysis of manpower requirements in terms of numbers, skills and competitiveness is essential before formulating a master plan and deciding the quantum of expenditure in the 11th Plan. A robust framework needs to be put in place as a visible and dedicated resource in the MHRD is a pre-requisite in order to ensure quality and facilitate significant private investment and participation. Most importantly, the quality as well as the image of VET needs to be actively promoted in order for it to be viewed as comparable, and as relevant as general secondary education.

(*Source*: National Knowledge Commission Website)

REPORT OF THE NATIONAL LEVEL DISCUSSION ON THE REPORT OF THE NATIONAL KNOWLEDGE COMMISSION

A two-day National Level Discussion Meeting of eminent experts was organised by the National University of Educational Planning and Administration, New Delhi on September 3-4, 2007 to critically review the recommendations of the National Knowledge Commission that submitted its report, *Report to the Nation 2006* to the Prime Minister a few months ago. Several distinguished experts and officials from Central and State governments have participated in it.

Among those who attended include P.M. Bhargava, former Vice Chairman of the Commission, Tapas Majumdar, M. Anandkrishnan, Amrik Singh, Amresh Bagchi, J. Veera Raghavan, A.K. Sharma, H.P. Dikshit, K.N. Chandrasekharan Pillai, Atul Sharma, D.N. Rao, Vinod Raina, Brahm Prakash, Kiran Datar, Madhu Prasad, Vijender Sharma, Arjun Dev, Chandana Chakarvarty, V.K. Tiwari, apart from the faculty from NUEPA including its Vice Chancellor Ved Prakash, Jandhyala B.G. Tilak, R. Govinda, K. Sudha Rao and Sudhanshu Bhushan. But for a brief presence of Jayati Ghosh that too for a very short period, none of the members of the National Knowledge Commission attended the meeting.

The participants discussed both the process of making the recommendations and the Report, and the recommendations along with their implications. There were remarks that the process of making the Report and submission of recommendations to the Prime Minister was not transparent enough. It did not involve public discussions and consultations with educationists the way it should have been, nor did it have even structured and formal discussions within the Commission. Since the recommendations were not even discussed within the Commission, one cannot say that there was any consensus or any compromise on the Report. Even the reports of the working groups of the Commission were not adequately considered in making the report, it was observed. Nevertheless, it was felt that since the Report was submitted to the Prime Minister, and it has some important recommendations with varied implications, it is necessary to discuss the Report.

According to a member of the Commission, NKC should not be viewed as any other normal commission or committee and the Report should not be seen as a report. The methodology adopted by the Commission was to send a series of letters to the Prime Minister as and when the Commission feels, on several issues that come under the terms of reference of the Commission, and not to make any report *per se*. Hence it should be seen as a set of communications from the Commission to the Prime Minister. If this is so, there is a danger: while one can expect a coherent set of well-reasoned proposals in a report, a series of letters or commutations may end up with making a few random proposals and piece-meal solutions, not necessarily knit together. Such an approach also does not allow the Commission to have a comprehensive and holistic approach to the education sector. It is also not clear whether these letters will be in public domain at least after they are submitted to the Prime Minister, if not before, so that meaningful public discussions would take place.

The Commission made several recommendations in the 'Report'—some new, some not so new, many controversial and perhaps very few relevant.

The three general comments made by the expert participants of the meeting on the Report are as follows:

- First, the a historical approach adopted by the NKC on many issues was indeed appalling. The Commission did not note strengths and weaknesses of the system as it developed over several decades, if not centuries. Nor did it take into account the current status of the system, the recommendations made by several committees in the recent past some of which were acted upon and many not, the federal structure and the centre-state relations in education, the dangerous implications of reduced role of the government and increased role of the private sector in education, internationalisation of education merely for economic gains, etc.
- Second, the NKC seems to have taken a fragmented outlook of the education sector, rather than looking at it in a holistic way. It makes some proposals on some sub-sectors of education — elementary

education (only on right to education), vocational education and training and some on higher education, apart from brief comments on libraries, languages, translation, knowledge network, e-governance, etc. The predominant focus of the report is on education; but it is not a report on education, nor is it of course a commission on education.

- Third, neither the rationale for the recommendations, nor the implications and the details on implementation of the proposals made are described in the Report.

Besides the very nature of the report, participants of the meeting discussed in detail many of the recommendations made by the NKC on education.

While the NKC favoured a Central legislation on the right to education, it was observed that the NKC did not grasp the whole issue, as originally articulated in the famous Unnikrishnan judgment of the Supreme Court in 1993 that highlighted the links between the right to live and the right to education, as enshrined in the Constitution of India. Nor did it go into details on the recent controversies raised during the CABE and subsequent meetings on making the Right to Education Bill. Of course the NKC promised to make a broader set of recommendations on school education in near future. But no such recommendations seem to have been made during the last several months after the report was published in January 2007. As a member of the NKC reported, much work is in progress and more letters are in the pipeline to be sent to the Prime Minister on educational issues, including specifically on school education. It appears that the NKC has expressed doubts on the data used by the Planning Commission on enrolments, teachers and students that include non-formal education systems, including EGS schools, bridge course centres and Para teachers. It is also concerned about the rigidity of the SSA norms, teacher training facilities and lack of infrastructure, and the syllabi and examination system.

The view that the country will go broke if it were to spend the required resources on making elementary education a fundamental right, was resented by many participants in the meeting. The classic Confucius dictum, also made by Alfred Marshall, is: 'no nation goes bankrupt by investing in education of its people.'

The major omissions in the Report, according to the participants, inter alia, relate to teacher education and teacher training. Teacher education is in a dismal state, while the shortages of teachers are increasingly felt at almost at all levels of education.

Several recommendations relating to higher education were found to be quite controversial. They include setting up of the Independent Regulating Authority for Higher Education (IRAHE), restructuring and reduced scope of functions of the UGC, dismantling of some national level bodies, setting up of central boards of undergraduate education, etc. Some found the setting up of the IRAHE and central board of undergraduate education desirable proposals, but many were skeptical on the efficiency of these proposed new structures that are expected to replace some of the existing structures; some also felt that it would affect the federal structure. The Commission, some members felt, did not have a fair understanding of the history, structure and functions and the functioning of some of the existing institutions. They, however, admit that there is a plenty of scope for reforming the existing institutions.

While the Commission recommended raising of student fees to at least 20 per cent of the recurring expenditure on higher education institutions, some felt that it could be the maximum and not the minimum, as any raise beyond this level will be affecting socio-economic equity dimensions in education. Some questioned even the rationale for the numbers—number of universities recommended, and the rationale for the elitist proposal of setting up 50 national universities.

There are some who appreciated and many questioned the recommendations of the Commission on privatisation, and on trade in education, though these recommendations or even the arguments made by the participants are not altogether new. Privatisation and internationalisation of (trade in) education mutually feed on each other.

In the increasingly globalised contemporary world, many view that internationalisation of higher education is an unalterable component. Even many educationists do find virtues in internationalisation of higher education; after all, universities are and should be universal in their nature and scope. Also, this has been there for several centuries. However, the new dimension of trade in education is a matter of contention in internationalisation. Few question the old mode, but many have serious reservations on the emerging modes of internationalisation. It was observed that before one thinks of internationalisation of our higher education system, it is necessary that our higher education system is raised to a level equivalent to the best systems in the world, so that competition becomes meaningful and will be between equals and not between unequals. So any move towards internationalisation will be counterproductive, if our system is not made an excellent one in terms of quality of education, quality of teachers and quality of graduates it produces. It might require huge public investments in education. But that is necessary. We have left our system severely-under invested all these years.

If there is one coherent and consistent line of thinking that underlines the whole Report that is relating to private sector in education. The NKC strongly favoured an increased role of the private sector in education under different forms—public-private partnerships, diversification of financing of higher education, stimulating private investments and setting up of private institutions. Some welcomed the role of the private sector in education as (a) the state does not have much money and (b) it may improve competition and quality. It was also felt that philanthropic private sector needs to be encouraged. Many participants highlighted the limits of privatisation and the danger of privatisation leading to commercialisation of education. Perhaps Indian higher education is more privatised than most other systems of higher education in developing and developed countries with very few exceptions, in terms of number of private institutions and enrolments in private institutions; and it is already highly commercialised, posing problems relating to access and equity. It is also crowding out the public institutions. Some of those who argue in favour of private sector also stressed the need to recognise that private sector will necessarily go for profits, and they also need to be regulated. But unfortunately in practice the difference between (non-philanthropic) privatisation and commercialisation is very thin. Privatisation is viewed as a solution to the public inadequacies; but an improved public system may be the best solution to the problems created by the private system. Perhaps this will also be a measure that checks the trends in internationalisation. Improvement in the public education system is of course very important on its own.

The participants of the meeting stressed the need to critically examine each recommendation in great detail and to look at alternatives available before it is implemented. Many participants felt that most recommendations are elitist in nature and doubted whether such proposals would help in 'better and faster inclusive growth'—the goal of the eleventh five year plan! The two-day discussion meeting coincided with media reports that the Planning Commission has accepted 'many' recommendations of the NKC. *Report by Prof. J.B.G. Tilak*

Source: University News, 45(48) November 26-December 02, 2007

16

Prof. Yash Pal Committee Report (2009)

Renovation and Rejuvenation of Higher Education

The Government of India appointed a committee on 28 February, 2008 to review the role of statutory bodies in the context of changes in higher, professional and technical education in the country and demands of a new knowledge society.

Subsequently the nomenclature of the committee was changed as Committee to '*Advise on Renovation and Rejuvenation of Higher Education*' (14 Oct. 2008). The Committee submitted its first report in August 2008 and its final report in July 2009. The Committee consisted of 20 members including the Chairman—Prof. Yash Pal.

TERMS OF REFERENCE OF THE COMMITTEE

The following were the terms of reference of the Committee:

(a) To review the functioning of the UGC/AICTE and to critically assess the role of the UGC/AICTE and their preparedness to provide institutional leadership to the emerging demands of access, equity, relevance and quality of higher education/technical education and the university system.

(b) To review the provisions of the University Grants Commission Act 1956 and the All India Council for Technical Education Act, 1987 and various suggestions for amendments to the said Acts by earlier Committees such as the Prof. Amrik Singh Committee.

(c) The role of the UGC in coordinating standards of higher education vis-à-vis the functional role of other statutory bodies such as AICTE, MCI, DCI, NCI, NCTE, DEC, etc.

(d) An assessment of the requirements of autonomy of the UGC vis-à-vis the Central Government and that of the university system vis-à-vis the UGC.

(e) The role of the UGC/AICTE in determining and enforcing standards of higher education/technical education in State Universities and the possibility of introducing a system of incentives and disincentives so that national standards of higher education/technical education are not compromised or diluted.

(f) Recommendations in regard to an effective and efficient mechanism for flow of resources from the UGC to the universities for their timely utilization including a mechanism of feedback thereto.

(g) The requirement of transparency and efficiency in the functioning of the UGC/AICTE.

(h) The role of the UGC vis-à-vis declaration of institutions to be deemed universities and recommendations for streamlining the process adopted by the UGC.

(i) Recommendations about the need to change the eligibility criteria for becoming eligible to receive grants under Section 12B of the UGC Act 1956.

(j) Any other issue arising out of or relating to the above terms of reference and, the functioning of the UGC/AICTE which the Government or the Committee on its own, may desire to look into.

AGENDA FOR RENOVATION AND REJUVENATION OF HIGHER EDUCATION: FINAL REPORT

The Committee made the following recommendations:

1. Creation of an all-encompassing National Commission for Higher Education and Research (NCHER), a Constitutional body to replace the existing regulatory bodies including the UGC, AICTE, NCTE and DEC and to follow up the Constitutional amendment with an appropriate law for the Commission's functioning;
2. Universities to be made responsible regarding the academic content of all courses and programmes of study including professional courses. Professional bodies like the AICTE, NCTE, MCI, BCI, COA, INC, PCI etc. to be divested of their academic functions, which would be restored to the universities;
3. Curricular reform to be the topmost priority of the newly created NCHER which would create a curricular framework based on the principles of mobility within a full range of curricular areas and integration of skills with academic depth;
4. It should be mandatory for all universities to have a rich undergraduate programme and undergraduate students must get opportunities to interact with the best faculty. While appointing teachers to the universities their affiliation to a particular college should also be specified to emphasize the need for their exposure to undergraduate students;
5. Undergraduate programmes to be restructured to enable students to have opportunities to access all curricular areas with fair degree of mobility. It is highly recommended that normally, no single discipline or specialized university should be created;
6. The vocational education sector is at present outside the purview of universities and colleges. Alienation of this sector can be overcome by bringing it under the purview of universities and by providing necessary accreditation to the courses available in polytechnics, industrial training institutions, and so on. Additionally the barriers to entry into universities for students going through vocational

training should be lowered to enable them to upgrade their knowledge base at any stage of their careers;

7. The NCHER should also galvanize research in the university system through the creation of a National Research Foundation;
8. New governing structures to be evolved to enable the universities to preserve their autonomy in a transparent and accountable manner;
9. Practice of according status of deemed university be stopped forthwith till the NCHER takes a considered view on it. It would be mandatory for all existing deemed universities to submit to the new accreditation norms to be framed on the lines proposed in this report within a period of three years failing which the status of university should be withdrawn. However, unique educational initiatives which have over a period of time enriched higher education by their innovations to be given recognition and supported appropriately;
10. Modern higher education system requires extension facilities, sophisticated equipment and highly specialized knowledge and competent teachers. It would not be possible for every university to possess the best of these infrastructures. Hence, one of the primary tasks of the NCHER to create several inter-university centres (IUCs) in diverse fields to create the best of these possibilities and attract the participation of several institutions of higher learning to avail them. The model already successfully demonstrated by the IUCs of the UGC like the Inter University Centre for Astronomy and Astrophysics, Inter University Accelerator Centre and others, would be a valuable guidance in their structures, governance, operation and support.
11. Institutions of excellence like the IITs and IIMs to be encouraged to diversify and expand their scope to work as full-fledged universities, while keeping intact their unique features, which shall act as pace-setting and model governance systems for all universities;
12. One of the first tasks of the NCHER should be to identify the best 1,500 colleges across India to upgrade them as universities, and create clusters of other potentially good colleges to evolve as universities.
13. Universities to establish live relationship with the real world outside and develop capacities to respond to the challenges faced by rural and urban economies and culture;
14. All levels of teacher education to be brought under the purview of higher education;
15. A national testing scheme for admission to the universities on the pattern of the GRE to be evolved which would be open to all the aspirants of University education, to be held more than once a year. Students would be permitted to send their best test score to the university of their choice.
16 Quantum of Central financial support to State-funded universities, be enhanced substantially on an incentive pattern, keeping in view the needs for their growth;

17. Expansion of the higher education system to be evaluated and assessed continuously to excel and to respond to the needs of different regions in India in order to ensure not only equity and access but also quality and opportunity of growth along the academic vertical. The NCHER too should be subject to external review once in five years.
18. Establish a National Education Tribunal with powers to adjudicate on disputes among stake-holders within institutions and between institutions so as to reduce litigation in Courts involving universities and higher education institutions; and
19. Set up a Task Force to follow up on the implementation of this Agenda for Action within a definite time-frame.

A: ROLE OF THE NATIONAL COMMISSION FOR HIGHER EDUCATION AND RESEARCH (NCHER)

- While acting as the apex regulatory body in the field of higher education in India it creates an enabling environment for universities to become self-regulatory bodies;
- Becomes the premier advisory body to the Central and State Governments on policy issues regarding higher education in India;
- Prepares and presents a Report on the State of Higher Education in India annually to Parliament;
- Serves as a think tank on higher education policy in the country: provides a vision of higher education to be reflected in a curriculum framework, benchmarks universities, compares with institutions globally, develops requirements of disciplines, proposes new education policies both for Central and the State institutions, and evaluates the costs and price of education;
- The Commission would create appropriate norms, processes and structures for ensuring quality and accrediting universities;
- Establishes transparent norms and process for entry and exist of institutions—the need is to make the process easy for good and serious proposals for setting up new institutions;
- Develops sources and mechanisms of funding for universities and other institutions, including for research;
- Initiates measures to ensure that governance in universities is done in a transparent and accountable manner;
- Provides the mechanism for a national database on higher education;
- Helps in creating an environment in academic institutions that is conducive to bring young people to take up academia as a career;
- Creates soft processes for interaction between students and teachers;
- Lightens the load of Universities, by developing a scheme to gradually free the universities of the colleges affiliated to them.

STRUCTURE OF THE NATIONAL COMMISSION FOR HIGHER EDUCATION AND RESEARCH (NCHER)

The National Commission for Higher Education and Research (NCHER) has to be a body, which would inspire confidence in the academic community of

India and serve as the voice of the academic community related to higher education and gains the serious attention of policy-makers. Its structure and composition and the process of its formation has to be such that it acquires an autonomous character of its own.

The NCHER would be an autonomous body created by making a suitable amendment to the Constitution, accountable only to the Indian parliament and drawing its budgetary resources from the Ministry of Finance. It would have a seven-member board with a full-time Chairperson. Of the seven members, one would be an eminent professional from the world of industry and one with the background of a long and consistent social engagement. All other five members would be academic people of eminence, representing broad areas of knowledge.

The structure of the National Commission for Higher Education and Research would not be top heavy and its role would be free of excessive centralization of regulation of universities and colleges. The status of the Chairperson of the commission should be analogous to that of the Chief Election Commissioner and that of the members should be comparable to the Election Commissioners.

The Process of identifying the Chairperson and members should be vested with a search committee comprising the Prime Minister, the Leader of the Opposition in Parliament and the Chief Justice of India in consultation with a Collegium consisting of eminent academics, learned academies and prestigious institutions relating to the fields of knowledge in diverse fields.

The Chairperson of the NCHER should be invited to appear before both the Houses of the Parliament or its Committees and appraise the members about the state of Higher Education in India and the directions for its growth and development. While the NCHER is expected to devise its own processes and structure for functioning, it is suggested that the Commission may initially consist of five divisions. These are suggested to be as follow:

Future Directions: Developing global benchmarks on student performance; university performance; salaries, potential programmers; new research directions; and articulation of needs of the government in terms of manpower etc.

Accreditation Management: Creating norms for accreditation and certifying multiple accreditation agencies which would be independent of the government. Institutions and universities may like to get accreditation from one or more than one agencies depending on their reputation. They would be also providing annual feedback to universities, and organizing workshops etc.

Funding and Development: Developing funding needs of universities, developing mechanisms for funding institutions, helping universities with development of corpus and good endowment management, managing the guaranteed student loan/scholarship programme, and funding the requirements of universities etc.

New Institutions and Incubation: Including training workshops for first-time VCs as well as on themes like accounting, investing the corpus, communication within and outside the university, negotiations and managing vendors, good office practices, human resource management etc.

Information and Governance: This division will focus on managing the data needs of the commission, display of information on universities, develop performance parameters on the governance of universities, support other divisions with information as well as provide students with information on each university. This division will also inform the Accreditation and Funding and Development divisions of the performance or lack thereof, for each university, each year.

An eminent academic with a tenure of five years would head each division. Each board member would be an overseer of one or two of the divisions. Each division will have an advisory board. The advisory board will comprise eminent persons from India or abroad.

The Chairperson and the five heads of the above-mentioned divisions would form the executive body of the commission, which would oversee all its functions.

The Commission will be independent of all ministries of the Government of India. It will have the autonomy to hire talent at various levels within and outside the government. It will also have the autonomy to define the compensation of its employees.

It is also crucial that NCHER develops a talented group of professionals who understand the proposed philosophy and see the difference between the existing and proposed processes.

It is important to keep in mind that the transition from the present regulatory system to the proposed one would not be easy. A smooth transition would require availing the expertise already available with the present apex bodies. Transition to the new organizational frame should enhance the people working in the present structures. Maximum care needs to be taken to ensure that the creation of the new apex body does not affect these people adversely. However, this need not be a constraint while deciding the structure of the new body. All this needs very careful analysis of the potential requirements. It is proposed that the job to provide operational frame should be assigned as a project on a consultancy basis to a competent professional organization. A task force would need to be constituted by the Government to work out the details of the process of implementation of the recommendations once they are accepted.